It's About Time

Jeff Porcaro
The Man and His Music

By Robyn Flans

HUDSON MUSIC

To Jeffrey
and his Family.

It's About Time

Jeff Porcaro
The Man and His Music

By Robyn Flans

Edited by Joe Bergamini
Executive Producer: Rob Wallis
Book Design and layout by Rick Gratton
Cover design by Mike Hoff
Cover photo by Rick Malkin

Jeff Porcaro Discography provided by the website Jeff Porcaro Session Tracks
Maintained by Mary Oxborrow
View the full discography with future updates at
http://www.frontiernet.net/~cybraria/

View an additional online photo gallery at:
hudsonmusic.com/porcaro
Password: toto99

HUDSON MUSIC

ISBN: 9781705112298

Table of Contents

THANK-YOUS

First, my thanks to my heart and soul, my twins Taylor and Jamie, whose love gets me through every day.

To Jeffrey's family, notably Joe, Eileen, Joleen and Steve, for trusting me, for allowing me to make them crazy for a few years, particularly towards the end when there were only questions they could answer. I know it was not always easy to relive memories, but they supported this project with love and grace.

I want to thank Jeffrey's Toto brothers: Steve Lukather, David Paich and David Hungate, who, in the process of writing this book, felt like brothers to me. I drove them crazy, too, trying to fill in historical blanks and they were there for me every step of the way.

Gary Katz, who always took my call out of his love for Jeff.

Then there was Dash Crofts, who didn't know me before this project and loved Jeffrey and championed his cause and cared.

Jeff Weber, who always tried to help connect me to someone I needed if he could.

Bob Glaub, who got me to a key person after I tried for two years!

Major thanks to Barney Hurley.

Thank you to my guardian angel, Karen Kent, whose continued help and belief in me has allowed me to work on this and actually keep a roof over my head many times. Thank you to Evan Kent for his guidance as well.

Thanks to Ed Eblen for being such a good cheerleader, and Rick Mattingly for his friendship and guidance.

Thank you to my awesome team Joe Bergamini and Rob Wallis; I couldn't have asked for better partners in working on this book.

And all of those who love Jeff, who have encouraged me along the way.

FOREWORD

L to R: Emil Richards, Jeff Porcaro, Joe Porcaro, Jim Keltner
(Photo by Jack White, courtesy of Rich Mangicaro)

I met Jeff when he was 17.

I was 29. That difference, in my mind, made him my little brother. But he was gone at 38 years and 4 months of age. I was 50 years and 3 months old when it happened.

My little brother had grown musically into a giant and was cut down just as he was beginning to add to his already many accomplishments: that of a badass producer. His mind worked that way.

He learned by being an absolutely essential part of so many well-produced records. His legacy is strong and will remain that way. People will talk forever about his incredibly inventive and beautifully constructed drum parts, like “Rosanna,” of course.

And rightfully so.

But the exquisite simplicity of his playing on Don Henley's "New York Minute" will always mess me up when I hear it. And especially because it was playing on the phone while I was on hold, calling the hospital where my mom had been taken, and had slipped into a coma. It was as if Jeff was trying to talk to me; calm me down.

I could go on and on about Jeffrey's drumming and his overall musical sensibility, or about the many albums he and all the great musicians who worked with him in the studios turned into big hit records. But as with all great artists, his work is so well documented, it speaks for itself. Jeff didn't get the chance to grow old, but he was definitely one of my favorite old souls.

He came from a big, loving family: tight knit, and all of them extraordinarily talented people. Dad Joe had a tremendous career in the studios, playing for the great film composers; brother Steve, an extraordinarily accomplished songwriter and keyboardist; brother Michael, a great bassist; sister Joleen, an actress and talented designer; and mom Eileen such an inspiration to my wife Cynthia and so many others.

Eventually he started his own family with Susan, his beautiful wife and their three sons: Chris, Miles and Nico. Jeff loved them all so much, and he was a good dad. He just seemed to have such a good heart. We had many deep conversations, and I loved how he was always helping somebody in some kind of way. He was a very giving type of person. I've thought for a very long time that a musician basically plays who he is inside. The way you play is a combination of your learning experiences and the influence of teachers and what you have picked up on your own. To me, Jeff played exactly like the person he was inside.

The very last time I saw Jeff was at a Paiste photo shoot with Joe and Emil and me. That was the morning of May 13, 1992. He was complaining a bit about his arms aching. He felt like it may have been a carpal thing related to holding the sticks too tight. I reminded him that his grip was that of a jazz player. He had an easy, loose, but firm hold on the stick. No one would have ever dreamed what the actual problem turned out to be.

As I write this from my home in Los Angeles, we are smack in the middle of the global Covid-19 virus pandemic of early summer 2020. We are in a 10:00 pm to 5:00 am curfew based upon massive protests on the city streets, globally, demonstrating a tremendous need for change in race relations and the way justice is administered, particularly for people of color. And as if that weren't quite enough, we just experienced a 5.5 earthquake.

My dear friend Robyn Flans, whom I've known since her early days as a writer for *Modern Drummer* magazine, has written this book about my amazing little brother Jeff Porcaro. I hope you will feel that you've gotten to know him, even a little, through Robyn's words.

Jim Keltner

June 3, 2020

PREFACE

The author with Jeff, 1982.

(Photo by Rick Malkin)

It's About Time–Jeff Porcaro's time was impeccable; every musician and producer with whom I spoke for this book said the same thing. But it wasn't just about the time. It was about how he *felt* the time; his groove, his deeper-than-an-ocean, golden groove and every piece of music he touched was infused with that time that he knew where to lay just right and that groove that was so much a part of his being.

It's About Time I get to share *Jeff Porcaro: The Man and His Music*. I was one of the lucky ones to exist in Jeff Porcaro's orbit. We spent countless hours interviewing, and I actually believe I conducted more interviews with him than any other journalist on the planet. There wasn't one phone call of mine he didn't take and if he was busy, I always got a call back. I think we became friends at the very first interview. It certainly wasn't difficult to like this charismatic, warm, dynamic individual who, when he was speaking with you, gave you his undivided attention. His enthusiasm and energy were contagious and as most people will tell you, Jeffrey was too cool for school: the way he walked—or strutted—into a room; the way he dressed and the way he spoke, prefacing something he was excited about with a common phrase he had heard his dad say, "So dig it..." or "Dig this," right before showing you something, or launching a compliment of another drummer's performance, or when he just had to point out something *amazing* that someone else did. And his eyes would get big and his hands would start waving with so much enthusiasm that it took up all the oxygen in the room. Then upon completion of the epic tale, he'd flash what many called that "shit-eating" grin and unleash that unique cannon of laughter. I always said if I could bottle his laughter I could make a million dollars. He was always full of life. I happened to be at his home one day when his friend and drum tech Paul Jamieson (Jamo) brought by some mixes of "Africa" sans vocals. We were dancing around the room.

I have been working on this book for many years. I stopped a few times when I felt I wasn't going to do a good enough job, like when Cher refused to talk to me. I just thought, "How could that be?" when Sonny & Cher was such a huge part of Jeffrey's story. When Mike Porcaro was too ill to contribute to the book, I felt I couldn't continue without his input. Brother Steve told me that Jeff and Mike were the closer two brothers than he and Jeff, which made sense, for they were closer in age as well. Mike's inability to participate felt so difficult for me to overcome.

But I picked myself back up for Jeffrey—which has been the motivating factor all along—to honor him and keep him remembered long after I am gone. My objective is that generations beyond our great grandchildren's children will recall that great drummer Jeff Porcaro like we talk about Chick Webb or Baby Dodds, and that this book will somehow be a reference. I hope there will still be books!

I have chosen to only focus on Jeff's childhood and musical life and the relationships that came with the music. Out of deference to his family, I decided not to touch on too much of his personal life or his death at length. I did include stories about the impact of his passing from certain people who I interviewed, but I really wanted this book to be about his wonderful life. The topic of Jeff's marriage is something I have decided to leave to his wife, Susan Goings, in case she would someday like to write a book about that portion of his life, including their children Christopher, Miles and Nico.

Not that the book is all Pollyanna. Jeff was Jeff. I can't change that, nor would I want to. He left a legacy of stories, including some he told me in detail, but I certainly am not interested in rumor or exploitation. He was a complex character, as many with whom I've spoken have attested, and he could at times have a somewhat odd or perhaps dark sense of humor. But the stories of kindness are all true, and you will read some here.

During the process of writing this, I also felt if I couldn't offer a book with more information than what had already been public knowledge, I would not pawn this off as something people should have. Hopefully, the voices I retained and the digging I've done have unearthed some treasures even the biggest fans didn't know, and that they will find it a rewarding read.

I'm hoping Jeff will forgive me for doing this. He didn't like anybody making too big of a deal out of him. But I do know for sure that if someone had to do it, he would approve of my doing it. We had an immense mutual respect and I hold that dear to my heart.

It's About Time...

PART ONE

Jeff receiving an engraved cymbal bag for Christmas, 1972, flanked by his grandmother and brother Mike.
(Photo courtesy of Joleen Porcaro-Duddy)

DESTINY

The sound of drums came through bassist **DAVID HUNGATE'S** headphones at Leon Russell's North Hollywood home studio that fateful night in January 1972.

Within two bars, Hungate thought, "He's a fucking genius."

The 22-year-old bass player, who had recently moved to Los Angeles from Texas, thought it was Jim Keltner on drums—or at least that's what he had been told. By then Keltner was already legendary, having recorded with the likes of Joe Cocker, John Lennon, Bob Dylan, and George Harrison (among others). That's why Hungate had shown up that night to play for the artist Sal Marquez, whom he knew from college in Texas. Sal Marquez was a trumpeter who, thus far, had played with Robby Krieger, Woody Herman and Buddy Rich, but would later go on to play with the likes of Frank Zappa and "The Tonight Show" Band.

Between takes, Hungate heard the drummer's voice on the headphones: "Who's the bass player?"

"I didn't know if he was bugged or digging me," Hungate recalls. "That's how insecure I was."

The sun was coming up as they finished tracking and Hungate went to meet Keltner. It wasn't whom he expected at all; some kid named Porcaro.

"There was this little kid with this deep voice," Hungate says.

No one could know at that moment that history would take a turn—for the two of them, and for generations of music listeners to come. After an exchange of smiles, Hungate left; a huge impression had been made: "Where his snare drum fell," Hungate simplifies. "It's like the difference between a picture that's out of focus and one that is sharp and has clarity."

The session's producer, percussionist **BOBBY TORRES**, entered the picture to produce the Sal Marquez session after a tour with the Beach Boys. By then Torres had toured with Joe Cocker and recorded with artists like Kenny Rogers and Spooky Tooth.

"(Drummer) Ricky Fataar had recommended me after he heard me play at a party," Torres recalls. "While we were on tour, other musicians were verbally hard on Sal to the point I felt bad for him. I know his personality was hard to accept, but not to the point where it went to. He had told me he had songs he had written that he wanted to record. I had been on the road prior with Joe Cocker's Grease Band, then Mad Dogs and Englishmen. When I got off the tour I moved to L.A. and lived in Leon Russell's house rent-free for about three-and-a-half months."

Torres had met Porcaro on Porcaro's very first session with Jack Daughtery and wound up playing with him and his group Rural Still Life.

"He was still in high school and I played at his high school events, I think his prom also," Torres says.

According to Torres, Keltner was never scheduled for that Marquez session; the budget quite simply could never have supported it. Everyone worked for free. Porcaro was always the intended drummer.

"So when I asked Leon if I could use his studio, he said yes again, no charge," Torres says. "I had also worked with and befriended Dean Parks, who was an exceptional guitar player, and I asked him to play on Sal's album. He brought in David Hungate. I asked Jeff and he was all for it."

DEAN PARKS had moved to California in 1970 to work with Sonny & Cher, after the duo hired a bunch of North Texas State students to play with them for an area concert. Hungate had been on that Texas Sonny & Cher date, too, but he had chosen to remain in school. He later joined Sonny &

Cher once he had graduated and moved to L.A., but that would come slightly after this episode. This Marquez session was the first time Parks had any musical contact with Porcaro as well, but somehow Parks had also heard Keltner was supposed to be at this Marquez session and was disappointed that he didn't show up.

To Parks' ears, Jeff was a little green at the time, describing his tempo as "a little on top of it," Parks remembers. "He played a little too much. He had this kind of fantastic technique that I really hadn't heard anyone else have. I'm kind of a closet drummer, so I would sit behind the drummer's drums, and Porcaro could subdivide all these beats and kind of play any combination of trading off what would be a right hand and left hand with the right foot bass drum and the left hand snare drum. He was as adept with that as most people were with their hands on it. So having all of that possibility, he used that a little too much, it seemed to me," adding that with all of that, "He wasn't rushing per se. He was very excited."

Parks says later on, after working on a few sessions together, he noticed that Jeff had figured it out.

"Jeff learned later to do the simple part of the beat as the part that would stand out front and let the other parts of the beat be softer and that helped him achieve that rolling feel that he admired from Keltner," Parks says. "It started happening within a year, but he didn't come on the scene like the Jeff Porcaro we came to know."

"Because I got to play with Jeff so much and so early on in my career, I had to relearn how to play with other drummers," Hungate admits. "With Jeff, there was no doubt where it was. I knew if I pulled a little bit or laid back a little bit, he'd make it feel good. It was always a challenge to not suck and be up to his level, but at the same time, musically it was effortless."

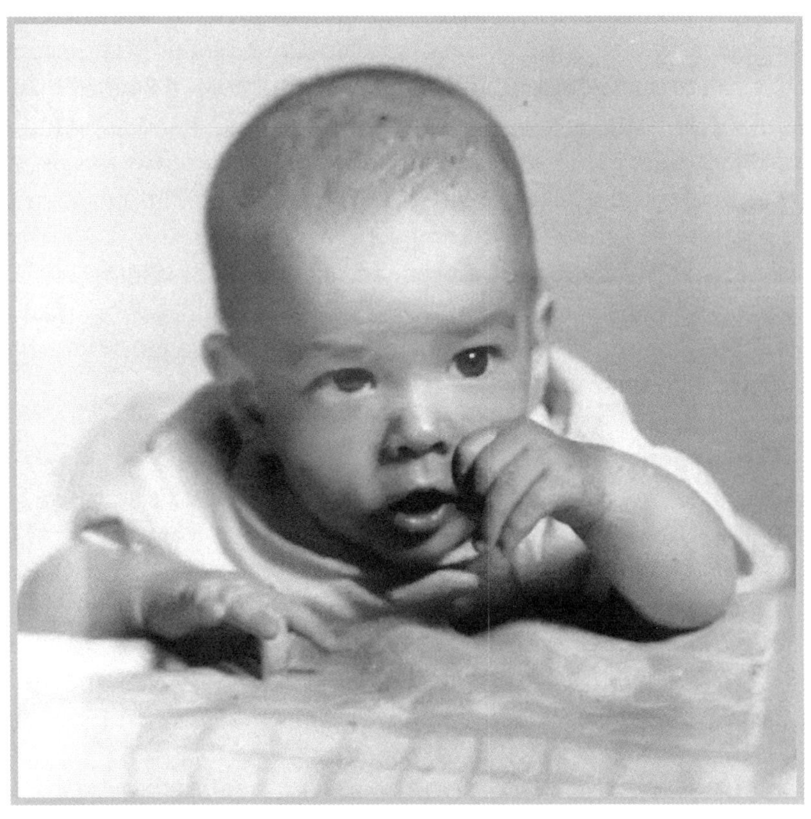

Jeff's newborn portrait.
(Photo courtesy of Joleen Porcaro-Duddy)

BEGINNINGS

Baby Jeffrey was meant to be a drummer. And his parents, Joe and Eileen Porcaro, knew that when he was a year and a half old. Jeff would be in his crib at night and his father would play Miles Davis' "Bags' Groove" on their little Victrola. "We'd go to bed and it got to the point where we'd hear Jeffrey actually sing the melody and he would sing Miles' solo," **JOE PORCARO** recalls. "Jeffrey would also sit on the linoleum floor tapping on it with his drumsticks. The landlord downstairs used to hit the broomstick on the ceiling like, 'Shut up!'"

Well, they were dad's drumsticks. Joe had been a drummer since the age of five, paying for his own lessons from money he made shining shoes with a shoebox he made for the Boy Scout Club. Joe, whose father was a drummer, was still living in a four-room apartment on Front St. in the east side of Hartford, Connecticut, above a grocery store with his parents, two brothers and two sisters when he met Eileen. There was a toilet, but they had to take baths in the public bathhouse up on Connecticut Blvd.

When Joe was 21 years old, he worked for Harry Gross at Budget Dress Shop. Among his duties were taking care of the fur coats women would bring into store for the summer and then fetching the fur coats for them from the refrigerated vault downstairs, "brushing them with a special brush like a dog brush," he recalls, and writing them up for the ladies when they came back for them. He swept the floors and even shopped for Gross' wife sometimes. One of his jobs was to deliver merchandise between the two shops Gross owned, and one of the stores was across town on Farmington

Avenue near the Julius Hartt School of Music.

"Going between the two shops, they didn't time me, so I'd pick up some coffee and take it to my teacher, Al Lepak, who taught at the Hartt School of Music, and I'd go hang with him for a while and sit in his studio while he would give a lesson," Joe recalls. "One day we went to lunch and we were walking down the hallway and Eileen was going to school there. She was a flute player and she was taking a music education course. She was taking a clarinet lesson and was just getting ready to take the lesson and I said, 'See that little chick over there, I'm going to marry her.'"

One day, Joe was there when Eileen was hanging out in the school lounge with Sadie, a friend of hers who lived in Joe's neighborhood and played cello and piano. Sadie introduced Eileen to him. That was it. He asked her out and took her to a Stan Kenton concert.

Eileen says lightning didn't strike quite as fast for her, but Joe proposed on their second date, when they went to see Joe's childhood buddy, percussionist Emil Richards, play.

"I said I'd think about it," **EILEEN PORCARO** says with a laugh.

In addition to his job at the shop, Joe had started playing in the then-brand-new Hartford Symphony when he was 20 years old. There was no pay for the first couple of years. When he went to meet Eileen's family in Maine at Thanksgiving, he borrowed a car to take her there. The next time they went, she told her father she no longer wanted to be a music teacher; she wanted to get married.

"I was 18. A year later we got married," Eileen says.

They married in 1953 with 75 cents to their name, Joe says. They found a walk-up apartment on the top floor of a four-story apartment house on Charles Street for $13.60 a month and "lucked out" with their own toilet.

"No shower or bath; we still had to go to the Connecticut bathhouses," Joe recalls. "For ten cents you got a bar of Lifebuoy soap and a towel, and you had to be very careful of people preying on young people."

The apartment had three rooms with no heat and a kerosene stove. That's where Jeffrey Thomas was born on April 1, 1954, fifteen months after

Joe and Eileen were wed. Joe and percussionist **EMIL RICHARDS** had been friends since they met in the schoolyard as young boys of about seven years old. A Catholic as well, Richards was asked to be Jeffrey's godfather. Richards recalls holding Jeff's head at the baptism.

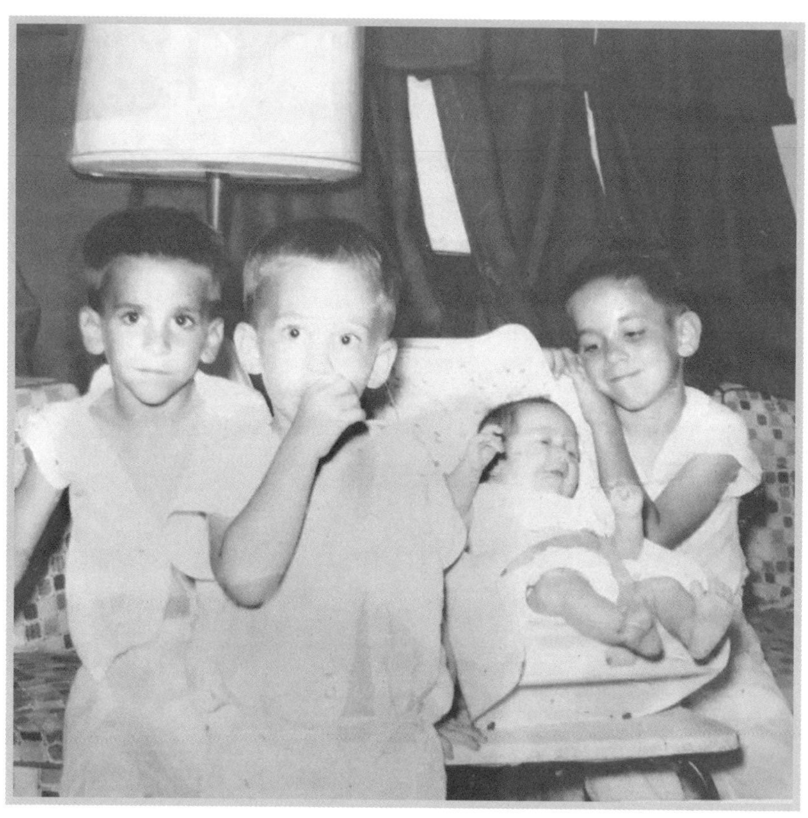

L to R: Mike, Steve (sucking thumb), and Jeff ogling his new baby sister Joleen.

(Photo courtesy of Joleen Porcaro-Duddy)

MOVING ON UP

Joe was already working as a chauffeur for the CEO of an insurance company and still playing with the symphony by the time Jeff was born. A year after Jeff came into the world, Mike was born.

"My job was to take the CEO to the bus station and railroad station, take his wife shopping and again, I would go to the school and hang out," Joe recalls. "Right around that time, there was a bandleader, a sax player named Tiny Quinn, who hired me to play down at the beach during the summertime, Saturday and Sunday, and we were sitting in the booth having a beer and he called me Skinny," Joe recalls of the nickname he had back in Connecticut. "He said, 'Where you living, Skinny?' I said, 'Charles Street.' He said, 'What you got?' I said, 'My wife and kids, we got a three room apartment.' He said, 'How'd you like to live in the housing project, Bowles Park off of Bloomfield Avenue? Up and downstairs, has a bath and shower.' I said, 'Bath and shower? Please!'"

A month later the Porcaros moved in. Each building had four apartments surrounding an open field so the kids could play in it. There was a Black family, a Jewish family, a Protestant family and a Catholic family, which is how it was intentionally set up. There was a school nearby. Steve was born in that apartment in 1957, and it was here that Joe bought a Remo practice kit with something to wrap around the cymbal and hi-hats for muting. That became Jeff's first drum set.

"Being in the projects, you couldn't play on drums because the neighbors would freak out, and I had an opportunity to play at the drum shop. There was a point where I was minding the shop because Al Lepak was teaching at the college," Joe says, adding that Jeff was on the practice kit all the time.

In 1960, Joleen was born in the same apartment, and they remained there until she was about a year old, at which time they got a three-bedroom apartment across the field. Once they moved to the new apartment, Joe set up a drum set.

"The original apartment was on the first floor, but in the second apartment we were all on one side with a big cellar. The Black family was into jazz, so when they found out I was a musician, we used to sit out back and listen to jazz and cook out," Joe recalls. "At the time, Chubby Checker was popular and their kids would come over and dance with our kids in the cellar. Jeff was a pretty good dancer."

Joe's brother Dominic (nicknamed Hick) lived next door and was part of the cookout contingency. His son **MARK PORCARO**, four years younger than Jeff, remembers a story that his Aunt Eileen told him about why Jeff may have established his meticulous rhythm early on: "She said when he was an infant, when she would burp him, she would tap out the be-bop jazz pattern lightly on his back and maybe that's how he got the unbelievable feel he got," Mark explains.

Between Joe and Jeff, the two influenced cousin Mark's career choice to become a drummer. Mark says initially it was seeing Joe with the Hartford Symphony and finally seeing Jeff when their grandfather took him out to California when he was 13 and Jeff was 17. That cinched the deal for him.

Eileen recalls Jeff's natural ability yielded him a "D" in music in kindergarten: "They would walk around to music and clap and he would clap on 2 and 4 and the other kids would clap on 1 and 3," Eileen says. "Wouldn't you love to send all his gold records to that teacher?"

But art was always the competition for Jeffrey's heart. At around six years of age, he was doing watercolor paintings and drawing intricate Civil War battles.

"One summer I was working with the son of an art teacher," Joe recalls. "I got to talking with her and said, 'Maybe it's just because it's my son, but one of my sons, I really think his drawings are good. Can I show you?' She said, 'Yeah.' So I brought them in and she said, 'Get this kid to a teacher right away.' He was good at decorating, too. When he had an apartment, everything was shiny."

The Civil War became a lifelong fascination for Jeff. Joe recalls taking him shopping for Christmas when he was about five years old, and he picked out a Civil War play-set.

"In those days they sold elaborate play-sets for plastic Army men," **STEVE PORCARO** recalls. "They had a great one for the Civil War called 'The Battle of the Blue and Gray.' Jeff played with it quite a lot."

"He used to set them up right in the middle of the living room floor, all over the place. He would get adamant if someone knocked over his display. He was into that for quite a while," Joe says, adding as an adult, Jeff painted molds of small Civil War soldiers from the North and the South and displayed them in a curio cabinet in his Hidden Hills home. "It was a very deep hobby. You had to have a really steady hand to paint these and he did such a beautiful job," Joe explains. "It wasn't a battle. On various shelves there would be a cavalry of the South and on another shelf there would be a cavalry of the North. This was the real shit—how the uniform of the general was different from the soldiers. He was really into it."

When Jeff was a child, Joe and Eileen fostered his interests in both art and music. At around age eight, Joe would take Jeff to the symphony when he played and let his son help him lug in the instruments. Not long after that, Joe began taking Jeff to Al Lepak's drum shop, where Joe taught on Saturdays.

"Especially in the summertime," Joe recalls. "Sometimes a teacher would have a cancellation and he'd say, 'Come on Jeff, I'll give you a lesson,' or if I had nothing to do, or even my teacher, Al Lepak would give him a lesson, so he got some great teachers like Artie Paretta, a great drummer who used to be with Tony Pastor. There were drum sets in there, too, so he would also get lessons on drum set."

Joe was on the road with the Tommy Dorsey Band when Jeff and Mike entered a talent contest at school. It had to be around 1958 or 1959.

"They played 'Tea for Two,' cha-cha. I think Jeff played congas and Mike played bongos, but it may have been the other way around," Eileen says. "They took first place and won $3.00."

While all the boys had an interest in drums in the beginning, they began to find their own instruments. Actually Jeff once told me that Mike was "way better" than he was on drums, as far as his time and groove, before first taking up the guitar and then the bass. Steve started piano at an early age and Eileen, having been to music school, would help the kids.

"I would go in the bedroom and Jeff would have the drum pad and I knew enough about music to know if he was doing it right," Eileen says. "He would practice from the Buddy Rich book. Then I would go help Mike on bass and Steve on piano."

By 1962, Joe was earning money strictly as a musician. He was playing clubs or casuals four or five nights a week, and was now getting paid by the Hartford Symphony. They saved enough money to buy a house close by Bowles Park in Bloomfield for $11,500. They got a Collie/German Shepherd mix they named Toby, and it was there that Jeffrey started to sit down and play on Joe's drum sets.

Steve Porcaro remembers how Jeff was still inspired by Miles Davis' "Bags' Groove": "He was in first grade and he would play 'Bags' Groove,' the Miles Davis song. Jeff would play along with the record and you could tell by the way he locked in with the record that he was way beyond his years."

Joe remembers one Memorial Day when Jeff was about ten years old. He was a Boy Scout at the time and the Scout leader, knowing he was a drummer, asked if he could get a field drum: "Jeff borrowed my father's Ludwig field drum and they had him march in the Memorial Day parade in front of about 30 or 40 Boy Scouts, and the beat he was playing was the Bo Diddley beat," Joe recalls.

A boy of many talents, Jeff was also about ten when he landed the lead in the school musical at Metacomet Grammar School in Bloomfield. While Eileen doesn't remember the name of the play, she recalls he was in a Robin Hood costume when he got really angry with her when he spotted her sneaking into a rehearsal, standing way in the back.

"He was the lead in the play and had to sing," she says. "He didn't want me to see it beforehand."

Did Jeff have a great singing voice? "Ya know, he was the only one who could get near the pitch," Joe says. "He had good rhythm, too."

February 9, 1964 was a big night in the Porcaro home, like in many homes across America. It was the Beatles' first appearance on "The Ed Sullivan Show" and it hit the Porcaro boys hard. They played a school assembly a week later, playing a Beatles song while wearing wigs Eileen got them. Mike played on Joe's Remo practice set and Steve and Jeff played on fake guitars.

Steve remembers well: "Within a week of seeing the Beatles on 'The Ed Sullivan Show,' we had cut-out guitars. Some dad in the neighborhood had cut out guitars for us out of very thin plywood, and with our Beatles wigs and our next-door neighbor, Mike, Jeff and myself were the Bloomfield Beatles," Steve says. "And it was within a week of 'The Ed Sullivan Show.' That's the kind of effect it had on us; that's how much we all kind of mentally pointed at the screen and said, 'I want to do this.' And then probably within a week after that, Mike and Jeff started taking guitar lessons from a friend of my dad's. That fell away with Jeff real quick, but Mike stuck with it for a while and that's what I think led him to playing bass."

Although musical buddies for a bit, Steve describes his sibling relationship with Jeff as complex.

"Mike and Jeff were just a year apart and when you're a little kid, three years apart can seem like 20," Steve recalls. "There were two years between me and Mike. Growing up I would see tons of pictures like Jeff and Mike would get the same Christmas present, they would get matching cowboy hats and matching this and that, because they were so close and I was kind of like the baby.

"There was a lot of typical brother shit," Steve admits. "Jeff and I were at each other a lot. Mike was kind of the peacemaker in the middle. There was that dynamic going on. I remember later on I was not allowed in Jeff's room. I was not allowed to touch his records. And I did it constantly, constantly. He had this great stereo in his room and this great record collection. I'd go in there and listen to Chicago's first two albums all the time."

Steve chocks their difficult dynamic up to the fact that they were different personality types, but he stresses that as they got older, there was never a doubt that the love and support was always at the core: "Jeff and I are very different. I'm different from both my brothers. Jeff and I had a strange relationship. We always loved each other very much, but when we were in close quarters, it was difficult," Steve reveals. "For instance, when we were at home, we were at each other's throats. The second he moved out, in the middle of high school when he got the gig with Sonny & Cher and he got his own apartment, he was the coolest older brother in the world and we got along amazingly well. The second we were in a band together—especially me with all my synths and sequencers and drum machines and trying to incorporate this stuff and clicks into the Toto music, he hated that stuff, he hated how much time I was spending on that stuff. It wasn't just playing and music to him. He hated seeing me spend so much time. But I knew there was a part of him that was proud of me too. He would brag about me and recommend me to people, though. It was a strange dynamic. And I understood. When it was a healthy balance was when you got a *Toto IV* album. Like with all bands, when it was the right combination and the chemistry is just right, it's good and when it goes out of balance, you lose that magic."

JOLEEN PORCARO and her brother Jeff had quite a different relationship. She has memories of Jeff from around the age of two. To her, he was absolutely the best big brother in the whole world. Not that her other brothers weren't great; it was just that Jeff was ultra-special. He was really excited about the fact that a little girl had come into the family and he was very hands-on.

As toddlers they all ended up with nicknames, sometimes just because names were hard to pronounce. Jeff was Jesse because the "f" was difficult for the others to articulate. Somehow Mike because "Meme," Steve was "TT" and Joleen was "Dodo"—and sometimes they called her "Goops." Joleen can't tell you how that one came to be, but even as an adult, she says Jeff continued to call her either "Jo," "Goops," or "Babe."

"As kids we were like homies. He was the brother who did everything for me," Joleen recalls. "I don't know if it's because I see so many pictures of it or if I actually remember it, but he was the older brother who did everything. Steve tortured me, Mike was sweet and was just 'whatever,' but Jeff was the big brother, the protector. He was the one who would get me out of bed like when my mom and dad slept in on the weekends, get me dressed, make me cereal and watch cartoons with me. He totally played with me. I remember Christmas morning him getting me dressed in my Christmas thing and the other kids were all still in their P.J.'s, and that never went away."

Wagon ride during a stop in Utah, on the way out to California. Joleen and Jeff are on the far right. Steve is far left and Mike is third from left. The other kids are from the family that owned the wagon.

(Photo courtesy of Joleen Porcaro-Duddy)

CALIFORNIA, HERE WE COME

In 1965 Joe decided to take an exploratory trip out to California to visit his friend, percussionist Emil Richards, who had moved to Los Angeles in 1959 to work in the studios. Richards had already recorded with such artists as Julie London, Peggy Lee, Nat King Cole, Nancy Wilson, Ella Fitzgerald, Bobby Darin, Dizzy Gillespie and many others, and had made quite a name for himself. Porcaro stayed with Richards and shadowed his friend in the studios. When he returned to Connecticut, he decided to hone his reading a little bit more before moving the clan to L.A. a year later.

In August of 1966, the family drove across the country, staying in Holiday Inns along the way. When they reached Los Angeles, Joe, Jeff and Eileen stayed in a hotel while the other kids stayed with family friends who had kids their age while they looked for a place to rent. Joleen says she thinks her brothers were excited to move because they were getting into music at the time and L.A. was the place to be, but it was a huge uprooting for the Italian family. While she was only six, she admits leaving Connecticut was somewhat traumatic.

"All the cousins were younger than I was. One was my age and one was older, but at that age, they're like your best friends because in an Italian family you see your relatives like twice a week," Joleen recalls. "We had Thursday night pasta and Sunday pasta at my grandma's, so these were like my besties. My brothers were my brothers, but they were a little older and they would be doing Army games and right before we moved they started doing music, but when we went to family dinners, I'd play with the kids and even my aunties and uncles, so to move where we didn't know anybody..."

Joleen still has vivid memories of that last house in Connecticut and how the upper floor was like a giant bonus room that just belonged to her three brothers. And there were three twin beds all in a row.

Joe wanted to find a house in California for the family.

"Between Jeff and me and the boys, we would never survive in an apartment," Joe says. "So we got a newspaper and my friend Freddie took us out in Burbank looking and we'd go into a place and he'd say, 'No, this isn't good enough,' or 'This is too much,' and finally after two hours I saw a sign on Olive in Burbank for a realtor company and told him to pull over."

Joe told the first realtor he wanted a rental house with a garage he could soundproof. She asked if he could afford a three-bedroom house for $135 a month, and they went to see a house on Cordova Street, one block over from Hollywood Way.

"We drove over and saw this house with a cute little yard with lemon trees and it was clean as a whistle," Joe remembers. "It was right across from Columbia Pictures and down the street was Riverside Drive where NBC Studios was on Alameda. She said, 'Who knows, maybe you can get work at NBC.' And I did, I got a couple of gigs there, subbing for Jack Sperling. There was a public swimming pool on the next street."

Joleen recalls one of the first things they did in California was Jeff's idea to organize a parade: "I was dressed up and we got the wagons and bicycles and did this parade," she recalls. "He did things like that. He was such an organizer, such a leader, such a motivator, with such an imagination."

They bought some old rugs that they nailed on the garage door to soundproof it. Joe had his marimba and timpani set up in the garage and Jeff met some musicians quickly. One of them happened to be young actor Ron Howard, who lived on the same block. Jeff never mentioned it to me, but Joe recalled that he came by to play. At the time, Howard starred as Opie Taylor on "The Andy Griffith Show" and later he would become a great director of films such as *Backdraft* and *The DaVinci Code*, even winning the Oscar for Best Director of *A Beautiful Mind* in 2002.

RON HOWARD says they only jammed once, but it was monumental in his life. He lived on Cordova Street also and says he didn't know the Porcaros very well, but he was in the same grade as Jeff at David Starr Jordan Junior High in Burbank. Because his parents wanted him to have as normal of a childhood as possible, Howard attended public school when he wasn't filming the iconic TV show. (During shooting, he was taught in the studio school.) When he was at the junior high, he would see Jeff in the hallways, he recalls. His best friend throughout elementary school, junior high and high school (and still a close friend), Noel Salvatore, who lived on the same block, took him over to the Porcaro's one day.

"I was trying to learn to play the guitar because Andy Griffith wanted me to be able to play the guitar on the show," Howard recalls. "I can read music just a little bit and play notes, but I can't play; I can't chord properly and don't really know what's going on. But my friend Noel is a pretty outgoing guy and he said he wanted to join up with these Porcaro kids and have a band and said, 'Do you want to play in a band? We can play weddings and things.' I said, 'Ok,' but I was reluctant because I knew I wasn't very good."

Salvatore with his accordion and Howard, 11 or 12, he says, with his undersized Gibson guitar, trekked down to the Porcaro garage and rehearsed. Jeff was on drums and he believes Mike was playing electric guitar.

"We had some sheet music and we were trying to play some Beatle songs. I couldn't chord. I couldn't really do anything to help anybody," Howard admits with a laugh. "Jeff Porcaro was awesome."

Because Howard had been around Griffith, who was a notable guitar player, as well as the guest band known on the show as the Darlings—who were actually the amazing band the Dillards—Howard knew musicianship when he saw it.

"That's why when I played with these guys, I knew the difference. I had been around musicians who could really play," Howard says. "I realized this was not the equivalent of us playing kickball over on the playground. They were already where I was as a kid actor. I could see just like I shouldn't be in the school play, they didn't need me playing in their band."

Howard admits he was entirely intimidated: "I said to Noel, 'Oh my God, these guys can play! They're not kidding around.' They would get going on these things and Jeff was rocking. They could actually play these songs and

I just felt like a complete doofus. They didn't make fun of me. Nobody smirked. There was no humiliation, but I put my guitar in my little cloth carry bag and tucked my tail between my legs, vowing never to try to publicly play again. It was the beginning and the end of my career in rock 'n' roll."

He says they were really nice to him and they didn't tease him about his role on the TV show.

"They didn't care. There was no joking around, like some kids at that point in my life would hit me with all that 'Dopie Opie' stuff. I had a lot of that sort of stuff at school," Howard says.

Howard never went back to the Porcaro garage, but years later he realized they had become Toto, and flashed back: "It was really vivid and cemented the memory. It was always sort of pivotal for me because I now play the guitar therapeutically. I never got to be any good and I can't play with other people," Howard says, humbly. "But it's become a lifelong companion."

Jeff wasn't always so humble. Sometimes he was a bit of a "wise-acre," recalls Emil Richards, who was hanging out at the Porcaro house one day. Joe was doing some teaching to make some extra money and a student had just left.

"Jeffrey came in and reprimanded Joe by saying, 'Do you have to show all your students everything I show you?'" Richards recalls. "I reprimanded the hell out of him: 'How dare you talk to your dad that way? Everything you are is because of him.'"

Richards concedes Jeff was a little full of himself as a youngster, but maybe "rightly so," he says. "He was playing so well even back then."

Richards says he and Jeff had a lot of musical conversations through the years, and Richards would bug him a lot about improvising. He says Jeff wasn't interested in being a soloist or the star in the band; he only wanted to enhance the music. When Richards would bother him about it, Jeff's response would be, "I only want to keep time; I want to be the timekeeper."

"And he became the best at that," Richards says.

In 1983, Porcaro told me how he came home from junior high and practiced every day: "I'd go into the den, put on headphones and play to 'Boogaloo Down Broadway.' The drums were cool on that and I used to dig that feel," he said. "I used to play with all the Beatle records, all the Hendrix records, and that's where I think I got a lot of the versatility as far as being able to play authentically one kind of music as opposed to the complete opposite. It's copying what every other drummer did on records. If a drummer takes something Bernard Purdie played on and sits for two weeks with the phones so he can still hear Bernard, but he's also playing along where he doesn't hear himself flamming with him or rushing—just grooving with the tune—the next time he goes to play a tune that's similar, he might start playing that feel. I can't tell you how many tunes I've played where I've ripped off the same thing Jim Gordon used on 'Charlie Freak' on *Pretzel Logic*. The beat I used on 'Lido Shuffle' is the same thing Gordon did, except at twice the tempo. There's no originality there. I think it's bad to clone yourself after someone, although I actually cloned myself after Jim Keltner when I was 17 and 18. I even thought it was cool to wear a vest and I copied his style. A drummer's own style comes from eventually being on his own, but I copied Gordon and Keltner and all these guys I dug. I remember realizing this, but after a while, the accumulation of all the guys you copy becomes your own thing, hopefully."

Aside from playing, Jeff got a job delivering newspapers after school and Joe followed behind him.

"He'd be on one side of the street and I was on the other," Joe says. "I would watch him cross the street further down. I was worried about him."

Jeff and **KERRY MORRIS** became instant friends the minute they met at David Starr Jordan Middle School. While Kerry was a year older, they were in orchestra and band classes together in the fall of '66, and music became the bond that would glue them together throughout Jeff's life. Kerry, an eighth grader, says his first impression of the seventh grader who played snare in the orchestra was that he had an East Coast sensibility.

"I remember he seemed to be very self-aware," Kerry says. "He came off as very confident."

They lived a block apart and Jeff would walk to Kerry's house in the morning so they could walk to school together. While Kerry would become a bass player later, at the time he played baritone sax, a very large instrument to lug back and forth to and from school, two miles each day.

"Jeff was slight, short and thin," Kerry remembers. "I was the bigger guy, so they said, 'Why don't you play baritone.' I would take the baritone home to practice on it. I'll never forget this one time I was sick and I had the baritone, which had to go back to school. Jeff carried it all the way back to school for me."

In fact, Kerry describes Jeff in those days as somewhat "nerdy," with glasses he had recently gotten at around the age of 12 because he was having trouble reading: "He had those Ray-Ban style glasses, big thick black frames. No tape, though," he adds with a laugh.

Right after school Kerry and Jeff would go straight to the Porcaro garage and rehearse with their very first band, Method Plus. The band consisted of Page Porrazzo, Stuart Levin, Larry Rosenthal and Mike Porcaro on rhythm guitar. Kerry and Jeff went to all the concerts they could and pushed their way to the front, where they could put their chins on the stage and watch the musicians play, Kerry recalls. A couple of shows he remembers attending were Leon Russell and the Buddy Miles Express, which made a huge impression on them, musically. They saw the Vanilla Fudge and Jimi Hendrix a few times. For a while they went through a fusion period and saw Return to Forever and Weather Report.

"Some types of music take so much dedication, like fusion and be-bop. You have to go to school ten hours a day to get those chops," Kerry remarks. "It's all about the chops. As well as being R&B and funk influenced, we were going through a progressive thing. So we were going to all these concerts like Herbie Hancock, Return to Forever and Weather Report at the time, and then we went to see Buddy Miles Express at the Whiskey. It had a tall stage and you could put your forearms and chin on the stage and be just right there, and that's what we did there. And after hearing all the chops in the world at those other concerts, we heard Buddy Miles Express just hitting a hard pulse and we looked at each other and said, 'This is the shit!' At that point we both just started to understand and appreciate pop music."

Kerry remembers Jeff the artist/fashionista, too: "I was the first among our friends to get Beatle boots and he was with me when I got them at Hardy's Boots on Hollywood Blvd. I was like 13," Morris recalls. "He said, 'Let's do a sleepover at my house,' so we did a sleepover and we were ready for bed—the sleeping bags were all laid out on the floor, and he said, 'Man, I gotta draw your boots. They're so cool, I gotta draw them.' So he took the boots and put them up on the windowsill and sketched the boots."

Kerry says Jeff was always drawing something. Joleen says he was extremely artistic in junior high and high school and they dedicated a wall in the house to his one particular craft project that derived from a piece of wood. Jeff would stain it, then he would find a picture from a magazine or somewhere—one was a flute player, especially for his mother who played the instrument—and he would burn the edges and then shellac it to the wood.

And Jeff was still helping Joleen out with her artistic school projects: "He was an artist, so he was the one who did school projects with me," Joleen recalls. "I don't remember my mom doing them with me. And when he got older and he was driving, he was the one who drove me to Kit Kraft and bought all the supplies with me. I can remember elaborate school projects like we had to do this whole Indian reservation in grammar school."

Joleen says at one point she asked her mother if Jeff had been prompted to help her with school projects. Eileen told her it was all Jeff's idea. It was also his idea to participate in Joleen's extra-curricular activities.

"He drove me to my dance lessons and also came to my dance recitals. He was the only one of my brothers who came to the games to watch me cheer, too," Joleen says.

In tenth grade Joleen was taking a tennis class at school for gym and Jeff custom-made her a racket cover with her name in cursive on it and a cartoon drawing of her face. She marvels how her brother would constantly do those kinds of time consuming projects—how it took time to buy the racket, the paint and design and execute the project.

Then there was Joleen's homecoming: "I was in the homecoming court and I had to be driven around in a convertible and he drove me in his Mercedes 450 SLC convertible," she remembers. "Can you imagine? Just stuff like that. I did some cheesy horror film when I was 18, and he showed up to the screening at a Studio City movie theater on Ventura Blvd. with some chick he had clearly been out with the night before."

In high school, Kerry and Jeff started a band called The Haze of Saturn that began as a five-piece with Ron Ravenscroft, Rick Labgold and Page Porrazzo. Most of their dads were in the entertainment business like Jeff's dad: Kerry's father was a make-up artist for films, Jim's father was a touring guitarist and Ron's dad was the voice of "Tony the Tiger."

In March 1968, the band was even written up in a local Van Nuys newspaper, having just played at a meeting of the North Hollywood Zonta Club, and just about to perform at the Lankershim Auto Show at the Lankershim-Oxnard Shopping Center. Later, Rick Zunigar (who went on to play with Stevie Wonder) joined, and the group became a trio that played only Hendrix and Cream material.

"We played private parties all over the place," Kerry says. "Rick Zunigar was a great singer and guitarist. Those were fun days. That lasted about a year or two."

The Porcaro family stayed in the Cordova rental house for a year, and then bought their first home on Milbank Street in Studio City off Coldwater Canyon. Jeff attended Millikan Junior High through the eighth and ninth grade and then went to North Hollywood High School. After living on Milbank for two years, in 1970 Joe decided to sell that home and buy a new one on Valleyheart Drive in Sherman Oaks. While they were on Milbank, Eileen's mom had started living with them half of the year. After Eileen's dad passed away, her mom began visiting them every winter and eventually stayed for the cold months and then returned to Eileen's sister in Maine for spring and summer.

"We fixed up the extra bedroom," Joe says. "Eileen's mother was a chain smoker. She would get up in the morning, make her coffee, sit down in front of the TV, like clockwork every morning, and I'm in bed and I can see down the hallway to the den and it was funny—well, it really wasn't funny—because you would look down and the sun was shining in and you could see the whole room filled with smoke. She would have one cigarette after another. She would have about three cigarettes in a row watching the morning shows."

Joe finally put a stop to it and put a TV set in her room, so she would do her smoking in her room. But when the boys would come home from school, they would go straight to grandma's room.

"They were really close to her," Joe says. "And all three boys—Jeff, Mike and Steve—were smoking. And between all three boys and her, the door was closed because they knew the smoke bothered my asthma, but you could see the smoke coming from under the door."

Grandma adored them, although Joe does recall sometimes she would get upset with the boys. As a product of the Great Depression, she couldn't understand how Steve, Mike and Jeff would just open up the refrigerator at a rehearsal to all the musicians at their home and say, "Help yourselves. Make yourself at home."

"But I don't think she ever said a bad thing to Joleen or the boys," Joe says.

Jeff met Kelly Shanahan and Merrell Brown at North Hollywood High School and they became lifelong friends. Like Jeff, Kelly was a drummer in the marching band and Merrell Brown was on the drill team. Kelly and Merrell were two years Jeff's senior, already boyfriend and girlfriend. Merrell already knew Steve Lukather because Lukather and Merrell's younger brother Bobby were best friends growing up. They had a band and shared an odd sense of humor..

"They used to light their farts on fire, until my brother's pants caught on fire," she recalls with a laugh.

Kelly and Merrell graduated the next year and Jeff encountered a rough time with a bully at North Hollywood High.

"He wanted to get out of there," Joe says. "Some guy was giving him a hard time and Eileen got him out of there."

They transferred him to Grant High, but Kelly and Merrell stayed in touch with Jeff, and when they got married in April 1970 and had their first apartment, Merrell says Jeff came over all the time. And Jeff and Kelly played drums together all the time.

"At 16, 17, and 18 years old, that's all they did," Merrell says. "It was just wonderful to watch, magical to sit in that studio and watch those two animals play. They were so fantastic."

Grant High was right across the street from Valley Junior College and sometimes Jeff would cut school and hang out in their band room while they were sight-reading charts. He indicated that he could hold his own even though he didn't consider himself an ace reader: "When you're dealing with eighth notes and reading figures that you would do just hand-to-hand on a practice pad, it's pretty much the same as reading a chart," he told me. "The figures are there; you know what they are and it's just applying the fact that you're playing time and then you want to kick a figure or play a figure. I'm really not an incredible, incredible reader, but I can read well enough to do what I've done so far. But you just get to know it. It's like reading words. You'll see two bars playing a groove, and eight bars ahead on the paper you see this figure coming up and you don't even have to read it. All of a sudden the figures look like a word; you know what it says just by the way it looks."

In 1969 Jeff competed in his first Battle of the Bands. That same year, drummer **TOM DRAKE** was going to Birmingham High School in Van Nuys and also decided to enter the competition with their stage band (which he says was not particularly good). The previous year Drake had become very enamored of Don Ellis and had noticed Joe Porcaro's name on one of his records.

At the preliminary Battle of the Bands competition, Drake recalls: "When we were done, I went in the back and there was this kid packing up his drums into cases that said 'Joe Porcaro' on them and I thought, 'Ooh, that's the name from the Don Ellis album,' so I said, 'Who's Joe Porcaro?' And he said, 'Well, he's my dad,' and that was the first time I met Jeff."

Drake says Porcaro was in a small group that he believes was called the Jazz Youth Workshop that made it to the finals that year. Drake's trombone buddy was playing in the production band—the house big band that organizers put together to play for all the competing vocalists, dancers, etc. made up of the best musicians from the competing bands. You were eligible to try out if you had already competed in the Battle of the Bands, so Drake decided he would audition for the production band the next year, 1970. Drake and Porcaro both tried out for the production band that year. Drake didn't get in, but Jeff did. Mike was chosen to play bass in the band as well, and Joe spoke to the band director and told him he would take the drum chart home and work with Jeff. Even though he didn't get in, Drake would accompany his trombonist friend, who made it in again, down to rehearsals at L.A. City College.

"That's when Jeff started blowing everyone's minds with what he was doing," Drake recalls, adding that that year they did a medley of music from the show *Hair* and lots of Motown songs, and Jeff killed it. "He opened a lot of eyes. There were actually two drummers that year and they switched off," Drake says, explaining that Jeff played the grand finale and everyone was shaking his head, asking, "Who is this guy?"

It was the next year, in 1971, that Jeff was the solo drummer in the production band for the Battle of the Bands. Drake and his trombonist friend were competing in an independent stage band that made it to the finals. Henry Mancini was the guest conductor and Jeff was acknowledged that year.

"At the end of the gig at the Hollywood Bowl, they were presenting trophies," Joe Porcaro recalls. "People on the committee were people like Henry Mancini, Clare Fischer and Lalo Schifrin and the announcer said, 'And for the first time, we're going to give a trophy to the most outstanding musician: Jeff Porcaro on drums.' We could feel something was going on with Jeffrey."

Not long after that, the band Jeff was playing with began to look for a new keyboard player.

Dec. 1, 1984: Jeff was best man at David and Lorraine's wedding.

(Photo courtesy Paich Family Archives)

THE FRIENDSHIP THAT CHANGED MUSIC

Joe's first TV gig was playing for "The Glen Campbell Goodtime Hour" on CBS. The composer/bandleader was Marty Paich.

"My father was looking for a great tambourine player," **DAVID PAICH** recalls. "My father loved gospel tambourine because he only worked with Black artists like Ray Charles, Mahalia Jackson, Ella Fitzgerald, Lena Horne, and Sammy Davis. I thought I was Black until I was 16. It was a real coup for 'The Glen Campbell Show' to get my dad because he was a recording star and recording arrangers didn't used to do TV. So my dad was going through the regular players and Joe Porcaro gets recommended. Joe Porcaro came in and was playing the tambourine like gospel singer Clara Ward. My dad was like, 'You're hired.'"

Fourteen-year-old David would hang out at the television studio rehearsals and on the breaks, his father would get jams going and let him sit in sometimes.

"A couple of times my dad would let me do a little piano solo," Paich recalls. "My dad would just point to people to take a solo. Joe Porcaro sees this and comes over to me and he says, 'My son just won the Battle of the Bands in the San Fernando Valley and he just lost his keyboard player. I should hook you guys up.' I said, 'Absolutely.' I had been very disappointed with guys who had tried to hook me up with their sons."

Joe Porcaro took David's phone number and he had Steve Leeds, the saxophone player in Jeff's band, call him, since Leeds was running the rehearsals. Leeds told Paich they wanted to audition him, and one day in 1969, David Paich showed up at Leeds' house off of Coldwater Canyon in the San Fernando Valley.

"My parents had horses, so I used to be a stable boy—so I show up in cowboy boots, jeans, and t-shirt. I knocked my front tooth out, so I was missing a tooth for a short time, and I had short hair," Paich remembers with a laugh. "I was going to an all-boys Catholic preparatory school. These guys were like hippies going to Grant High School. I open the door and here's this kid like John Boy in 'Little House on the Prairie.' Steve brings me in and says, 'We want to hear you play.' And there's a drummer in Steve's room and a bass player, guitar player and a little piano. And the drummer is incredible and I think it's Jeff Porcaro, but it's not Jeff Porcaro. These guys were unbelievable. They're playing like pros. They were doing songs like Blood, Sweat and Tears and I'm thinking, 'This is really cool.' I'm sitting there and they say, 'We're starting a band and we want you to be in our band.' And I say, 'Which band is this?' and they say, 'This is another band, this isn't the band that you're going to be doing. This is a side band with Dan Sawyer,' and Dan Sawyer, this guitar player who is an amazing guitar player, picks up a tenor saxophone and he's like Dean Parks. Dean Parks played lead alto at North Texas State before he played guitar. Dan Sawyer is a tenor player and guitar player and I'm going, 'Wow, these guys are really talented guys, I think I found my niche,' and then I find out these aren't the guys I'm going to be playing with. They're just having a rehearsal. I knew it was too good to be true."

Paich turned to the drummer and said, "You're Jeff, right?" And he answered back, "No," and he pointed to the door.

"All these guys are dressed like normal guys in golf shirts, and there's this little skinny guy in the doorway with a headband, long hair and glasses, faded blue jeans and an American flag sewn in his crotch." Paich laughs. "And I knew I wasn't getting in the good band. I thought, 'I gotta deal with that? That's the drummer.' Then Jeff grabs the sticks and sits down at the drums and absolutely annihilates them. I was a huge Three Dog Night fan with Floyd Sneed, and no one played like this drummer. Jeff sat down like I never heard anybody play drums. The closest thing was a cross of Bobby Colomby with Blood, Sweat and Tears and David Garibaldi with Tower of Power, but more powerful. The bass drum and all these chops—and he's 14. They go, 'You know, 'Feeling Alright' by Joe Cocker?' 'Yeah, I think I've got that down,' and I play it from top to bottom, piano solo and everything," Paich continues. "And they go, 'Wow, you're in the band.'"

The band was called Merciful Souls, and the musicians all wore purple Nehru jackets. Paich says that he suggested "losing those outfits."

"They were playing soul music: Chicago; Blood, Sweat and Tears; and Santana," Paich says. "I came in and brought in Rolling Stones, Creedence and Joe Cocker. Scotty Page played flute and trumpet."

SCOTTY PAGE says everything from then on set the tone for his life; he just didn't know it at the time. He was the oldest member of the band (at 17) when his friend Frank Szabo, who also played trumpet, brought him into the group. Page played second trumpet (like many of the other kids, his father Bill Page was a professional musician) and says he was the worst musician in the band.

"I wasn't even in the same league," Page admits. "But I was good enough to play second trumpet, and we got along good and we had great times."

Page wasn't actually planning on making music his career at that time. He was aspiring to be an architect—until he noticed the girls noticing. The band was so good that they played schools and began to win some battles of the bands and suddenly, while Page was sitting backstage drawing for his architecture studies, he realized there were lots of girls. Like many musicians, this element made music even more appealing and for Page, music became a real career contender. The fact that the level of musicianship he was playing with was so high also began to change his mind.

"Jeff was *really* the driving force," Page says.

In fact, Page remembers that they were so good that they were offered a record deal, but the collective dads put a kibosh on the idea. Page says Jeff was the first one—or at least among the first couple—of drummers to play drums at the famed Sound City Studios in Van Nuys. Scotty's dad Bill worked there. The place was initially called the Vox Sound Lab.

"We brought the band in to record a couple of cover songs," Page says. Pointing out the inaccuracy in Dave Grohl's documentary on Sound City, he continues, "In the movie, he called the early years a warehouse and that's not correct. It was a studio. I went to that place the day it was picked. My dad was working for Vox and they wanted a place to develop the amplified orchestra, and I remember coming home from school and my dad said, 'You want to go look at this building?' and we went to the building and we looked around and two days later they got it. About two years later it became Sound City."

Eventually Merciful Souls ditched the uniforms and named the band Rural Still Life, after a song keyboard player Mike Lang wrote for a Tom Scott album. Jeff did the art for the band and constructed the flyers, and Steve Porcaro printed them up.

"Still to this day some of my greatest musical memories were in that band out of all the stuff I've done. God bless Toto and everything, but that was the best band I've ever played in, in all my life," Paich declares. "We patterned ourselves after the Joe Cocker album *Mad Dogs and Englishmen*. We were auditioning girl singers and I was at an all-boys school. Girls were coming in and I was going, 'Yes, you're in the band, yes you're in the band, yes, you're in the band.' We had a singer named Cliff Gordon who sang like David Clayton Thomas, but we ended up not liking him because he was limited, so Steve Leeds says, 'Get in the car, we're going to get the new singer.' I go, 'Where are we going?' He says, 'Downtown L.A., Washington, down in the ghetto. A guy named Frank Hayes, he just got out of jail, he's 25 years old, he shot a policeman and he works at the House of Pancakes.' We're 16 years old and we're going to pick up this guy."

For a couple of years, Jeff had buddy Kelly Shanahan play double drums with him in the band because he was so deeply into the Buddy Miles Express. Paich explains: "So Jeff said, 'We're going to have two drummers and a percussionist," Paich recalls. "And we're going to learn Santana stuff and guitar and we had a full horn section. There were like 30 people in the band and we would do Sly Stone stuff and 'Gimme Shelter' with Frank Hayes, this Black guy singing and Black and White girls, and this was like '70 and '71."

They played at Grant High School and even the Brass Ring with fake IDs. And then there was the day they were on the way to play a prom at the Castaways Restaurant in Burbank that Paich recalls vividly. Paich had Porcaro in his old used Ford pick-up truck, which, as the stable boy at the Paich homestead, had a bunch of hay in it, covered with a tarp. Jeff was wearing his dad's white suit, which he loved because it reminded him of the one

John Lennon wore on the cover of the 1969 album *Abbey Road.* The cab of the truck was full of Paich's equipment, so Jeff threw the bag of cymbals that he borrowed from his father on top of the tarp covering the hay.

Paich tells the predictable ending to the story: "We're on our way, and on the freeway, in between Topanga and DeSoto, and we see these circular metal things rolling on the freeway. The cymbals had fallen off the truck and were rolling like hubcaps. We stopped the truck and Jeff and I—mainly Jeff—like the movie *Bowfinger*, where Eddie Murphy has to cross in front of the traffic back and forth, Jeff and I were trying to dodge the traffic trying to pick up his dad's cymbals on the freeway. We got the cymbals back and one of them was cracked and he was afraid to tell his dad. Jeff said, 'I'm in the shithouse now.'"

Then one day, after playing softball at the Studio City Park, which they did often, some of the college students found out they were a band and asked them to play for a Halloween dance at the park. Trumpeter/contractor Jules Chaikin happened to take his son to the event and was very impressed with young Porcaro.

Jeff and Jim Keltner.
(Photo courtesy of Cynthia Keltner)

THE FIRST SESSION AND HIS IDOL

Not long after, that same Jules Chaikin was the project contractor for an immense Jack Daugherty project. Daugherty had formerly been a trumpeter with Woody Herman and had basically retired. In 1971 he decided to come back for a series of three records called *Jack Daugherty and the Class of Nineteen Hundred and Seventy One*, intended to feature the super session players. When studio drummer Hal Blaine couldn't make the rehearsal, Chaikin called on 17-year-old Jeff. When Chaikin said he wanted to hear Jeff play to possibly sub for Blaine at some rehearsals, Joe said Jeff's first reaction was, "You should hear Kelly (Shanahan). He reads better than me, he does this better than me..." which Joe said he always did. Chaikin hired Jeff for the rehearsal band and Jeff told me about how he played with the band about five times, and then they stopped calling for a little bit.

"The band was everybody I would see as a kid: Max Bennett, Louie Shelton, Larry Carlton, Chuck Findley, all those cats," Jeff told me in our earliest interview. "I knew that they were going to do a record because I heard them talking about it. Then Daugherty called me and asked, 'Have you ever heard of a drummer named Keltner?' Well, at that time, my biggest heroes were Keltner and Gordon. I said, 'Yeah.' He said, 'Well, he just got off the road with Joe Cocker and you and he are going to do the rehearsal band for a couple of weeks.' "

Jeff was 17 and didn't have his driver's license yet. Joe says Jeff didn't want to learn to drive and didn't get his license until he was 18.

"My mother drove me to my first session with Keltner at the soundstage at A&M," Jeff told me. "I borrowed my dad's black diamond pearl Ludwig set, which was just like Keltner's, because I wanted to be just like him. I wore a vest just like Keltner, I tried to get the heaviest boots I could, because you want to emulate your heroes, and just before I got to the door, I was so nervous, I threw up everywhere. And thank God it was a samba because my hands were shaking. I remember Keltner sat down next to me and looks over at me and goes, 'Man, do you read, because I don't read that good. You do the fills, I'll just keep the time,'" Jeff recalled, laughing.

JIM KELTNER was present as Jeff told this story at the L.A. Studio Roundtable in 1990 for *Modern Drummer* magazine, and interjected: "Tell her what you did."

Jeff replied: "What did I do?"

"He was ridiculous. He was like Vinnie," Keltner said, referencing monster drummer Vinnie Colaiuta.

"Oh come on!" Jeff protested.

"He was playing some of the most inside-out shit I ever heard," Keltner said.

"That was nerves going up and down. I had chops I didn't even know existed that day," Jeff said.

Keltner says it was the same for him with his heroes. He got the same drums as Hal Blaine and wore the same jeans as Jim Gordon and got the same cymbal bag as Gordon's. Looking back now, Keltner realizes:

"That's what Jeffrey did with me," Keltner says. "I guess he had been listening to stuff that I had been doing prior to our meeting, although I don't know what that was exactly, so he was kinda knocked out to meet me. You're always pleasantly surprised when somebody's knocked out to meet you, so I remember paying extra attention to him because of that. He was very, very mature for his age. We all know the kind of confidence he exuded for his age. You wouldn't call him gregarious; he had a good strong confidence."

Keltner says he can't imagine Porcaro throwing up before walking into

Emil Richards, Jeff's godfather, with Eileen and baby Jeff at his baptism.
(Courtesy of Joleen Porcaro-Duddy)

Jeff age one.
(Courtesy of Joleen Porcaro-Duddy)

Jeff's five year portrait.
(Courtesy of Joleen Porcaro-Duddy)

From right to left: Jeff, Mike and Steve, circa 1960.
(Courtesy of Joleen Porcaro-Duddy)

Portrait of the boys, Nov.1960. Jeff in the middle, Steve on left and Mike on his right.
(Courtesy of Joleen Porcaro-Duddy)

From right to left: Mike, Jeff, Joe, baby Joleen and Steve in front, in the family kitchen circa 1960.
(Courtesy of Joleen Porcaro-Duddy)

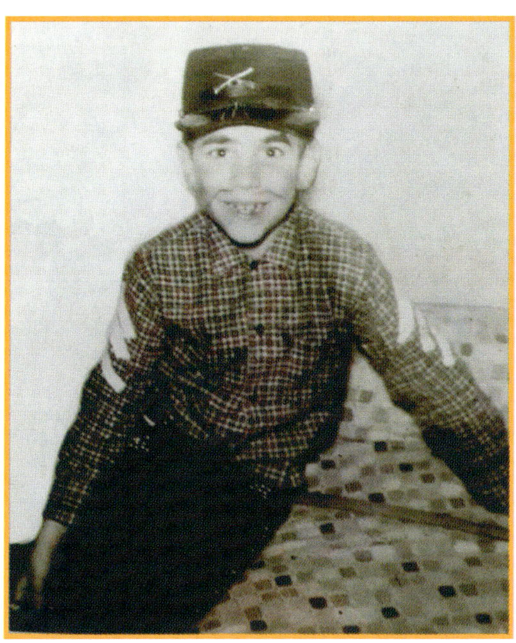

At around age 9, Jeff dressed up as a Civil War soldier for Halloween. It would be a lifelong fascination.
(Courtesy of Joleen Porcaro-Duddy)

Around age 11, Jeff led the Boy Scouts with his grandfather's field drum in Hartford's Memorial Day parade.

First Porcaro family portrait, 1967.

(Courtesy of Joleen Porcaro-Duddy)

First year in California, Jeff in front of the Cordova St., Burbank rental.
(Courtesy of Joleen Porcaro-Duddy)

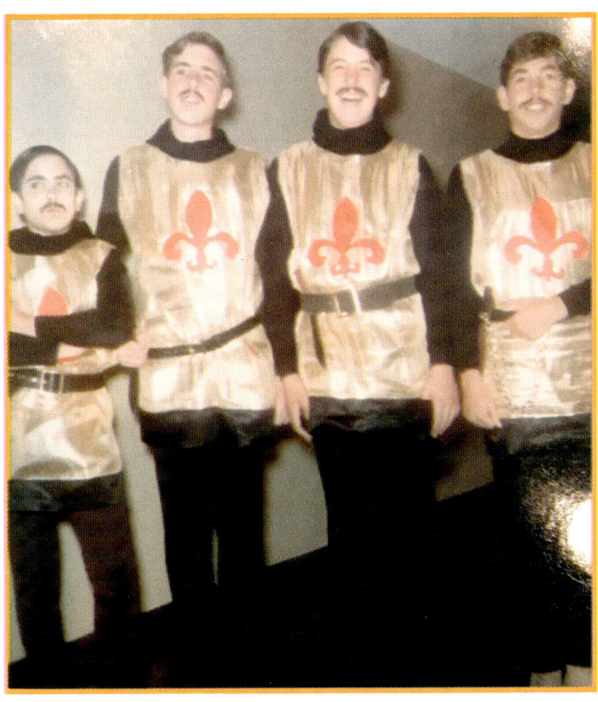

In Junior high, Jeff was a guard in a production of Sleeping Beauty with his friend Kerry Morris, the tall guard in the middle.
(Courtesy of Kerry Morris)

Jeff's second childhood band, The Haze of Saturn. Bottom right photo left to right: Ron Ravenscroft, Kerry Morris, Jeff, Page Porrazzo, Rick Labgold.
(Courtesy of Kerry Morris)

The 1970 Hollywood Battle of the Bands Production Band with Jeff as one of the two drummers.
(Courtesy of Tom Drake)

A photo of the production band from the 1971 Battle of the Bands program.
(Courtesy of Tom Drake)

Jeffrey is capable of doing better work than he is doing at present.

DECEMBER REPORT

Teacher's Comment He works too slowly.

Parent's Comment

Parent's Signature Mrs. Joseph Porcaro

MARCH REPORT

Teacher's Comment Jeffrey needs to improve in spelling, especially in language work. He has shown some improvement in arithmetic although he needs to learn the number facts.

Parent's Comment He needs to work for better self control.

Parent's Signature Mrs. Joseph Porcaro

JUNE REPORT

Teacher's Comment Jeffrey has a beautiful singing voice. He needs help in learning the basic number facts in arithmetic, especially 3 through 5 in multiplication and division.

Parent's Comment

Parent's Signature

In September your child will be in

Grade 4

Room 136 Miss Romanelli

Jeff fourth grade report card.

(Report card images courtesy of Joleen Porcaro-Duddy)

REPORT FOR SEPTEMBER – NOVEMBER

SUBJECT MATTER	MARK
READING	
Understanding of Material Read	G
Oral Reading	G
Application of Phonetic Skills	G
LANGUAGE	
Written	F
Oral	G
Spelling - as used in written work	G
ARITHMETIC	
Fundamentals	G
Problems	G
SOCIAL STUDIES	F
SCIENCE	F
WORK HABITS	
Finishes work in given time	S
Listens to instructions and follows them	S
Takes part in class discussions and activities	S

TEACHER'S COMMENTS

Jeffrey is a good conscientious student. He tends to talk before he has thought. He enjoys his art.

Signature Mabel Prescott

PARENT'S COMMENTS

Signature Mrs. Eileen Porcaro

Fifth grade report card.

Progress Report — Grades 1, 2, 3

The checks on this page indicate your child's progress in relation to his own individual ability and effort.

	Dec. Report			March Report			June Report		
	Very Good	Satisfactory	Unsatisfactory	Very Good	Satisfactory	Unsatisfactory	Very Good	Satisfactory	Unsatisfactory
ACADEMIC PROGRESS									
Reading		✓			✓			✓	
Language Arts		✓			✓			✓	
Arithmetic		✓			✓			✓	
CONDUCT									
Ability to work with others		✓			✓			✓	
Respect for authority		✓			✓			✓	
Courtesy		✓			✓			✓	
Self-control		✓				✓		✓	
Responsibility		✓			✓			✓	
Pride in personal appearance		✓			✓			✓	
WORK HABITS									
Effort		✓			✓			✓	
Attention		✓			✓			✓	
Response to direction		✓			✓			✓	
Completion of work		✓			✓			✓	
Neatness of work		✓			✓			✓	
Use of school materials		✓			✓		✓		
Initiative		✓			✓		✓		
OBSERVES HEALTH RULES		✓			✓		✓		
OBSERVES SAFETY RULES					✓		✓		

	1st Report	2nd Report	3rd Report
DAYS ABSENT	9	4	2
TIMES TARDY	0	0	0

The marks on this page indicate your child's progress in relation to what is usually expected of a child in this grade.

	Dec. Report	March Report	June Report
READING			
Word mastery	C	C	C
Reading for meaning	C	C	C
Oral reading	C	B	B
LANGUAGE ARTS			
Oral expression	B	B	B
Written expression	C	C	B
Handwriting	C	C	C
*Spelling	C	C	C
ARITHMETIC			
Understanding number meanings			
Knowledge of number facts			
Reading numbers			
Writing numbers			
Schott Arithmetic	C	B	C
*SOCIAL STUDIES	C	C	C
*SCIENCE	C	B	B
PHYSICAL EDUCATION	B	B	B
MUSIC	D	C	B
ART	A	A	A

*Not every subject will be marked in first grade.

A — excellent
B — good (above average)
C — fair (average)
D — poor (below average)

No plus or minus signs will be used

If a child is failing and may have to repeat the grade it will be noted under Teacher's Comments on the back of the card.

Jeff third grade report card. Note the "D" in music.

When The Haze of Saturn became a trio. In the Porcaro Milbank home family/rehearsal room. L-R: Jeff, Kerry Morris, Ron Ravenscroft.

(Courtesy of Joleen Porcaro-Duddy)

the rehearsal studio: "When he talked, you found yourself listening," Keltner says. "He didn't say dumb stuff. Jeffrey never appeared awkward to me. I remember feeling awkward when I was around Hal (Blaine) and Earl (Palmer) when I was younger, although I don't think I was when I was around them. But Jeffrey was really, really cool. He didn't say stuff that sounded young and kinda dumb. He was really focused.

"I had my back to him and I was messing with my drum stuff and I heard him play something and it was like a lick, but it was a combination lick and groove and I heard it and I immediately recognized this was some heavy shit and not your normal stuff. Drumming is like language," Keltner remembers of that first meeting. "You play it and you can know the language a drummer is speaking by how they play. You know them by what they play. He played this thing and I thought, 'This is a very serious cat.' He had just played something that blew my mind and got my attention, big time. I turned around and said, 'Where'd you learn to do that kind of stuff?' I asked him if he could play it again and he did, exactly the same way. At that point in time, he was already playing some very sophisticated drums. I told him it was amazing he could play that kind of drums—sort of inside out kind of stuff. And he said, 'Well, you know, my dad and all the studio guys tell me I'm playing fast and I should slow down a little bit and not play so fast and so busy.' I just remember saying to him—which I think is the reason we became such good friends—'Tell those guys to mess off, man. You're only 16 one time. You've got plenty of time to slow down.' "

It was instant friendship, or something like that. Maybe at first it was Jeff in idolizing mode, then a kind of brotherhood. But Jim remembers some early times together and one in particular around 1970 that was probably life-changing for Jeff: "I can even see us in the car that day. I said to him, 'I just heard the baddest shit I ever heard in my life, check this out,'" Keltner recalls. "And I played him the Platters' 'With This Ring,' He flipped out just like I flipped out, and it was (drummer Bernard) Purdie playing his version of a pop song and it changed his whole life. I said, 'Check this out,' and we laughed so hard and I loved him because he laughed because he knew the shit that was bad. From there he wanted to know everything Purdie played on."

Keltner wasn't just an influence; he used his influence to turn Jeff on to others.

"He would play me shit and he'd have that look on his face like, 'Right?!'

The first thing I said was, 'Don't listen to me; listen to Jim Gordon. If you listen to me, you're never going to be able to make records the way you're supposed to make records. I do that shit on purpose; that's my thing. You can't do that. You're going to be the baddest guy on the planet. You gotta listen to Jim Gordon. You gotta listen to John Guerin and Paul Humphrey and these guys who are playing on records and killing everybody.' And he did. He started studying that. He would go listen to John Guerin at Donte's all the time. Every time I would go to listen to John Guerin, Jeff would be there."

When Jim thinks about their relationship he reminisces, "I would do some dumb-ass thing and I would look down and he would be looking up at me and I took all that for granted and now when I look back, he just wanted to be around me so much and there are times I thought, 'I didn't deserve that.' It truly was like a big brother thing. I always called him my little brother. But I absolutely love being able to say that during the last years we would have talks and I would tell him, 'Jeffrey, you are the baddest motherfucker on the planet. There's nobody who thrills me with the time and the whole thing; you've got it now; you're the cat, ya know? Nobody can do that.' I would tell him as forcefully as I could, because people would still say, 'Ya know Jimmy, you're his biggest influence,' and I would say, 'Man, are you kidding me? This guy is everybody's biggest influence now and it's even going to get more so.' And that's exactly what happened. And I was so glad to be able to tell Jeffrey that. I said, 'Jeffrey, everything is upside down now. All that shit about me being your influence.'"

It wasn't long after that very first session with Keltner that Porcaro blew Hungate away at Leon Russell's place. About eight months later he got the call to audition for Sonny & Cher.

Walking through an airport with Sonny & Cher, 1972.

THEY'VE GOT HIM, BABE

When drummer Willie Ornelas was out of the Sonny & Cher band, Hungate says he immediately thought of Jeff: "I always just wanted to play with the best musicians I could play with. I always wanted to be the worst guy in the band. Who cared that he was 16 years old? I probably told Denis Pregnolato, who was Sonny's manager who was on the road with us, about him and I didn't have a terrible time convincing him that Jeff would be wonderful."

The first time I interviewed Porcaro he looked back at that moment at Leon Russell's house as the key to his career: "If I wasn't tripping off into the hills to Leon Russell's house one night with some people, I would never ever, ever have met Dave Hungate for him to go to Sonny Bono, 'I remember this 17-year-old kid. Why don't you call him up to audition?'"

Porcaro told me it was about eight months after the Russell house session that he auditioned along with 40 other drummers for the Sonny & Cher gig, not quite taking it seriously until he heard how much money was involved. No surprise there; since the married couple's first No. 1 smash, "I Got You Babe" in 1965, they were turning out hits and setting trends, even beginning a summer replacement TV variety show.

"In my senior year in high school, I had three studio art classes, which was three periods a day and I could do what I wanted in art because I had taken every course I could take," he told me. "I remember this friend of mine was going to Israel or something to go to art school and I really wanted to go to art school and then I got an audition with Sonny & Cher to go on the road with them."

When Jeff got the audition for Sonny & Cher, Joe drove him to the duo's house in Beverly Hills. He says his son was excited, but he could tell he was "a little uptight." Joe assumes that Sonny & Cher had a music room where they auditioned musicians. "I dropped Jeff off and just waited in the car in the back parking area of their house," Joe recalls. "He came out and I think he said he got the gig or, 'I think I got it.' It was no big deal, he wasn't freaking out; he was very casual about it. I said, 'Ok, great, the only thing we have to do is talk to your mother about school.'"

The dinner table temperature was another story. Joe wasn't quite as nonchalant when he asked Jeff when the tour started and his son answered that it would be beginning right away.

Joe said, "No, no, you're going to finish school."

Jeff replied, "No, I want to be a drummer, I'm going with Sonny & Cher."

"I said, 'Jeffrey, come on. None of my brothers or I graduated high school. You gotta do this for me. I gotta have somebody in the family graduate high school and set an example.' It got into a little bit of a heated conversation," Joe recalls. "Eileen butted in and said, 'Look, let's go talk to the principal and see where he stands.'"

Joe and Eileen met with the principal at Grant High School. They explained the situation and the principal asked: "What does Jeff want to do with his life?"

"We both said he wants to be a drummer and he has this great opportunity to play with Sonny & Cher," Joe recalls.

The principal checked Jeff's records and saw that he had more than enough credits to graduate. To his advantage also, Jeff had played in all the school musicals and with the woodwind and percussion ensembles.

"The principal said, 'As far as I'm concerned, we can let him go and the only thing I ask is that, come June, if they're not on the road, that he sit in with graduation,' but as far as I'm concerned he can get his diploma,'" Joe recalls of the conversation.

Joe doesn't remember ever meeting with either Sonny or Cher about Jeff going on the road with them, but he knew them from having recorded with them prior to Jeff's audition, and he knew their manager Denis Pregnolato.

In the spring of 1972 Porcaro joined the band. Hungate reminisces about their first stop on tour in Vancouver: "We were staying in that motel that's out on the waterfront where you can rent a fishing pole and fish out your window," Hungate recalls. "It's a rock 'n' roll hotel. We fly up there and I'm the older guy and got him on the gig. Eileen was worried about him and I reassured her I'd keep an eye on the kid. We check into the hotel and it's probably 2:00 in the afternoon and I go into my room and unpack my bags and watch a little TV. It's been about an hour and I decided, 'I'd better go check to make sure Jeff is okay.' I go down and find his room and knock on the door and here's Jeff standing with a girl already with that idiotic grin on his face; 17 years old."

Conductor/keyboardist Michel Rubini left some months later. Paich says that was when Porcaro began to talk him up to Sonny Bono: "I was waiting to graduate high school," Paich recalls. "And in the meanwhile, my father was asked to arrange a song for Cher's solo album or a Sonny & Cher album. I was 17 at the time and I played on it. Sonny had heard me play with (drummer) Hal Blaine and (bassist) Joe Osborn on my dad's tracks over at Larabee, so Sonny asked me if I'd be interested in going on the road. I was like, 'Wow, yeah.' It sounded exciting."

The next week, Porcaro told Paich that Bono wanted to meet him, but at the last minute, Bono told Porcaro not to hire his friend because he had already found someone. Paich recalls the scene with a laugh: "When we got to rehearsal, Sonny walks in and says, 'Hey, that's the guy I told you about, Jeff.' And Jeff says to him, 'Well, that's the guy I told you about.' I was both guys."

Paich took over organ duties with Sonny & Cher and got to go on the road with his best buddy.

"We had a private jet; at one time we had the Hugh Hefner jet. They had like six Playboy bunny stewardesses there and they would rotate. And we were just out of high school. Need I say more?" Paich says, adding that musically it was incredible playing for sold-out crowds. "They were the hottest things on the planet, getting $100,000 a night," Paich says. "Jeff had wanted me to meet David Hungate because he thought he was a great bass player and it was a great band. We became their rock 'n' roll band and we were their guys. We would be jamming all the time for the people at soundcheck."

Paich says that's where they got their road chops up—jamming for the audience waiting for Sonny & Cher to make their entrance—and already talking about forming a band one day. He also remembers the insanity of the backstage celebrity quotient of people like iconic singer-songwriter Bob Dylan and filmmaker Woody Allen. And sometimes family would show up. Cousin Mark Porcaro says in September 1972, the duo played in Connecticut, and his Aunt Josie and Uncle Vin—Joe's youngest sister and her husband—brought their father (Jeff's grandfather) to see the show.

"Jeffrey got our grandfather right on the stage to watch him play," Mark says. "Jeffrey was very proud of his family. All those guys out there in California. They're all very proud of us back here. They're proud of us? We're the ones proud of them!"

When Sonny & Cher were in Vegas for weeks at a time, Paich says sometimes after the gig at the Sahara, they would go play poker or craps with the opening act. Sometimes they'd go out clubbing and even Cher would go with them. Paich says Porcaro was a great dancer.

"Dancing went back as far as high school," Paich says. "Jeff would dance with my sister. We would have soul lines. Jeff loved guitar players and musicians who danced when they played, like Verdine White (Earth, Wind & Fire) and James Brown. Jeff liked to play air guitar. On lots of gigs we played, he would find a drummer to play the last song of the set so he could go out front and play air guitar and dance like Verdine. Jeff and I would dance down these soul lines at Grant High School. Another great drummer-dancer is Steve Jordan. I don't trust a drummer who doesn't dance."

After a gig, the two would mostly listen to music, Paich says, describing: "We would go to Jeff's room and he would have new cassettes from people like Steely Dan and there was another band called S.S. Fools that we had played some tracks with. Whoever we had been playing with in town, Jeff would have a cassette of. We'd go to his room and have a drink, maybe a smoke and listen to tapes all night. It was a time when people were into music and bands. We were listening to Seals & Crofts, too."

Reflecting on their growing friendship, Paich says it was the music that first bonded them. At the beginning they had gone to different high schools so they really weren't able to hang out together, but the playing bound them. Once they began to tour with Sonny & Cher with rooms across the hall from one another, the friendship blossomed.

Porcaro said traveling was an education, "Especially in music. You get to meet lots of different people and in the music field you run into lots of different people with different ideas and you get the chance to play with lots of different people."

Sometimes it was a chance for Porcaro to spend some time contemplating the future. He explained: "When you're 18 and you're away from home as I was on the road with Sonny & Cher, you're sitting there going, 'Well, what am I going to do with my life? Is it going to be a party like this, or what?' And I dug art, but the reality of getting into art is real ugly, so it was the kind of thing where I said, like with Sonny & Cher, if I played my cards right, it was a steady gig, plus they did a TV show. So I did their last two seasons of their TV show and I figured if I stayed legitimate here, at least I knew there would be some security if I kept my head together and did the gig right, and it was a pretty good gig. So if I played Mr. Straight for a while, I could make some money to put away. It was like, do your gig and do it right. So that's about as seriously as I took it."

Jeff had already been out of the house, on his own. Joe recalls while he was still living at home, having a heart-to-heart with him as soon as he was starting to make some money doing casuals and such even before the Sonny & Cher gig: "Eileen and I had talked about it and he was doing pretty well and we thought he should start having some responsibility," Joe recalls. "So I said, 'Look, you're working quite a bit and you gotta give your mother something. I don't care what it is, but you need to pitch in.' What we were going to do was start a savings account for him. He said, 'Okay, Dad,' and then the next day he says, 'I'm moving out, I'm getting a house off of Laurel Canyon.' And then Mike did the same thing."

Jeff lived there for a little while and then when he returned from the road with Sonny & Cher, he moved in to the apartment next door to the Shanahans. Their daughter Kristie had been born in 1970, and after seeing how loving Jeff was to his little sister Joleen, they made him Kristie's godfather. When he moved next door, she was three years old.

"In the morning he would call out on his balcony, 'Kris, Kris,'" Merrell recalls. "And she would leave the apartment at three years old and go over to his apartment. I would wake up in the morning and she would be gone. The first time it happened, I nearly had a heart attack. Then I would always hear him go, 'Kris, Kris.' I would go, 'You brat, Jeff, come over here if you want to see her.'"

When Kristie was about 11 years old and got a bad report card, she ran away to Jeff's house on Hesby Street. Merrell recalls how frightened they were when their daughter was missing, but Jeff called telling them that their daughter was with him and scared to tell her parents about her report card. They immediately went over to Jeff's house, and Jeff made a deal with Kristie that from then on, for every "A" on her report card, he would give her $100. She got "A's" from then on and Jeff never missed a payment until she graduated.

A great memory for Merrell is when Jeff took Kelly and her over to Cher's house once: "Just walking into that room with this lavish entrance with this huge chandelier hanging over us, I had to pinch myself," Merrell recalls. "I didn't believe I was really there. I met Cher and you know, everybody thinks she's really tall, but she's not really tall at all. She's got high heels on. She's 5'6", but with heels on, she's tall."

Merrell says when Kelly and she broke up and she went through tough times, Jeff helped her financially. By then there were two daughters and Jeff took both girls out and bought them winter coats.

Clowning around on tour with Seals & Crofts, 1975.
(Photo courtesy of Michel Rubini)

THE NEXT DUO

Louie Shelton, the guitar player on "The Glen Campbell Show" (the show on which David Paich's father was musical director) was producing a duo called Seals & Crofts. Their second Warner Brothers album *Summer Breeze* had gone to No. 7 on the *Billboard* charts and towards the end of 1973 Shelton, who had sometimes heard young David Paich jamming downstairs with the Campbell band, told Paich he might be looking to add another keyboard player for Seals & Crofts.

"'Diamond Girl' was my first hit record, and that's how you got work in this town: if your name was associated with a hit record," Paich explains. "My phone started ringing off the hook. So immediately I started trying to get Jeff into that circle. Louie knew about Jeff, but Louie was hiring drummers like Jim Gordon, John Guerin and Harvey Mason. He had his core guys and Jeff hadn't done a hit record yet."

Porcaro was hired to cut one track on Seals & Crofts' *Diamond Girl*. It wasn't one of the hits, but as Paich describes it, it was his "baptism."

DASH CROFTS says they fell in love with Porcaro's playing instantly: "We were working with David Paich and then we got to realizing what a great drummer Jeff was," Crofts says. "And David Hungate."

JIM SEALS says in the studio he would sit with his guitar, Paich would sit at the piano, and they would play the song. Occasionally Louie Shelton would write a chart. Mostly it was just guitar and piano, and Seals says:

"Paich would come up with a signature lick on most every song. We would talk over the different parts if there was anything special, but you didn't have to tell Jeff where to fill or anything. He would know what to do," Seals continues. "If there were any arrangement changes or feel, we would talk it over and he would try it and adapt it. Those guys were so good, one or two times through and they had it. They would anticipate where the song was going to go."

Jeff talked about the difficulty of recording at certain sessions. "Sometimes you go to dates and the producers or the artists have the tempo that they want the time to be cut at and they have a little click machine," he stated. "They take the time to set the tempo and they listen to four bars, or a demo, and say, 'Yeah, that's the tempo.' It is not the tempo and you know as a drummer, feel-wise, or groove-wise, what the tempo should be. You are playing along and you know the chorus has got to be way up here, you know the bridge has got to breathe more, you know that the feel sounds stiff and it's wrong. That's a fine line."

He said at that point you would try to say something, "But even if you ask anybody who writes songs, there are some songs, I don't care what tempo you pick, that just don't make it with real time all the way through," Jeff said.

Then he brought up recording with Seals & Crofts: "I remember Seals & Crofts—before any of these things like the Linn came out—used to record with the Roland Maestro," Porcaro recalled. "They used to edit, take the tape and record pieces of the Maestro at four different tempos. They would make all the verse sections one tempo and all the choruses were at a tempo slightly above. You knew that when the chorus came, you could go up a little bit because they knew vocally and lyrically you could, and then you'd come back down and you'd have the old tempo there. Sometimes that was easier."

Seals says that he was so happy with Paich and Porcaro in the studio that he wanted them on the road. "We asked David if he could get Jeff to come with us," Seals recalls.

Both Jeff and his brother Mike went on tour with Seals & Crofts, as did Paich and Hungate. Crofts says Porcaro's time was impeccable: "It was precise. It was unmistakably deliberate. You could depend on that. It was just there."

Live, that was sometimes at odds with the duo, Seals confides. Both Seals and Crofts recall one incident slightly differently. Seals remembers that it was Crofts who turned around and gave Porcaro "the glance" and Crofts recalls that it was Seals, but no matter. Seals, surmises the situation as both of them were confusing Porcaro to no end.

"Dash would turn around and tell him he was dragging and I would tell him he was rushing and he couldn't make up his mind on what to do and finally he walked off the stage and shouted, 'More money!'" Seals recounts.

Now Seals admits: "Of course he was probably playing it perfectly. You know when you get on stage there's a tendency to play everything faster, out of the groove, so to speak. And he was right on the money."

To that point, Seals says Porcaro was a perfectionist. Thinking back, Seals believes it was on the song "The King of Nothing" on the *Unborn Child* album (on which Porcaro played all the tracks) that Porcaro encountered his first shuffle—and quite a bit of aggravation.

"He kept getting a few bars into it and he'd quit," Seals recalls. "It happened several times and finally he slammed his sticks down and walked out of the studio. David Paich followed him and said, 'Hey man, you can't do that. You'll never work again in this town.' He went back and got mad and played it again perfectly."

Hungate recalls Porcaro's "King of Nothing" as a "tearing his hair out" moment: "He said, 'I can't play fucking shuffles,'" Hungate recalls. "When he got the first test pressing of (Boz Scaggs) *Silk Degrees* and he was living over on Lankershim Boulevard someplace, he called me over to hear it and it was just me and Jeff and it got to 'Lido Shuffle.' I smiled and he got that silly-ass evil grin on his face and I said, 'Man, you can play shuffles.'"

Seals says he didn't know what to think when Porcaro walked out of the studio. He laughs now when he thinks about it. One not so laughing matter was an outdoor concert in Denver that both Crofts and Seals recall in horror: "When I would play the fiddle songs to end the show, a kind of hoedown, Jeff started getting up from the drums, walking up to the front with us, marching," Seals says. "That night in Denver the scaffolding gave way. He had just gotten to the front of the stage and it came crashing down on the drums on the last song of the evening. It just destroyed the drum set. It was a miracle he escaped it because he had just started doing that a couple of nights before."

That wasn't the worst of it, though. Hungate mentioned a harrowing plane ride that Paich was on which I confirmed with him—it was just Dash Crofts and Paich on a one-engine Piper Cub in a storm. The plane was listing from left to right as lightning was striking. Paich continues to explain that the airplanes Seals & Crofts were using for a while scared Jeff and him to death and they talked about it. It was a huge contrast to the travel they had been accustomed to with Sonny & Cher, which Paich says was a BAC-111 flown by President LBJ's former personal pilot. That plane had a bedroom in the back for the couple in addition to a chef and they felt safe. Paich says when they joined Seals & Crofts all that changed.

"They rented a plane and the pilots were the mechanics, too," Paich said. "These pilots they got, I won't mention any names, but he was like a tour manager and he had an Alaskan husky and the husky would travel with him everywhere, and it was so cold on the plane that you could see the cold air coming out of the vents. The visibility got to be not very good and it came time to land this one time, and we came out of the fog and we were about 20 yards off the tarmac to the left of the runway. At the last minute before we touched down, the pilot turned it to the right really fast before we hit the runway and it was screeching tires. Everyone thought we had crashed. That stuff happened a lot in those days. Jeff and I were both scared shitless and told them we should fly commercial," Paich says, adding that eventually they did.

Jeff's cousin Mark saw Jeff perform for the first time ever with Seals & Crofts at the Hartford Civic Center in May 1975. Afterwards Jeff's relatives went backstage.

"We were very proud," Mark says. "The whole family back here in Connecticut was there: my two aunts, my two uncles, my brother, my sister, cousins; the whole tribe was there. The whole Italian tribe. It was wonderful."

Offstage, both Seals and Crofts remember that Porcaro was so much fun to be around.

"We would go fishing," Seals recalls. "We hiked up in the mountains in Dillon, Colorado. We would all eat together and had some great times."

Paich laughs when I ask him about the fishing and recalls one particular fishing trip. He didn't go on it and to his recollection it was just Jimmy Seals and Jeffrey. He doesn't remember if they caught any fish, but Jeff came back with a tale to tell. Apparently, Jimmy fell into the water and the cap he never was seen without fell off his head and went floating down the stream—and Jimmy went after it.

When they returned from the road, Porcaro cut *Unborn Child* with Seals & Crofts and around the same time, the gig of his dreams began to happen, so when Porcaro left Seals & Crofts, both Jimmy and Dash were very unhappy.

"He's so good, there's no way to replace him. We went through a lot of drummers after that," Seals says. "Playing a combination of acoustic and electric was always a problem. After Jeff we found a lot of hot recording drummers like Hal Blaine and Jim Gordon, but it sounded rigid. They could play certain songs, but other ones they had trouble with the feel, but Jeff always knew exactly what to play."

Bassist **BOB GLAUB** concurs that Jeff always knew what to play. He'll never forget meeting Jeff around 1973 on the popular live television show called "In Concert" while Jeff was performing with Seals & Crofts and Glaub was playing with the Mark-Almond Band.

"Jeff came right up to me after we played, introduced himself to me and exclaimed loudly, 'Man, that's a bass sound! How do you get that sound?'" Glaub remembers. "He was very complimentary."

Little did they know then that the two young musicians would end up on countless sessions together in the not-so-distant future."

Jeff signing autographs after Steely Dan concert at the Palace Theatre in Manchester, UK, 1974.

(Photo courtesy of Barney Hurley)

PORCARO'S DREAM CALL

Porcaro loved Steely Dan from the minute he heard them. Like Paich said, he and Jeff would listen to tapes of their music in hotel rooms while on tour with Sonny & Cher. They only had two albums out by 1973: *Can't Buy a Thrill* and *Countdown to Ecstasy*.

Paich and Porcaro had an unspoken deal: each would include the other on the project they were working on at the time. So when Porcaro got the big call—the call to make music with Steely Dan, the band he thought was making the hippest, greatest music at the time, who else was he going to take with him that night to the Robb's Ranch out in Chatsworth, but Paich and Hungate, where Gary Katz was producing "Night by Night."

It was Steely's guitar player **DENNY DIAS** who sought Porcaro out at a club in the San Fernando Valley called Donte's, at the recommendation of a friend. As Dias recalls it, it was a night of fusion jazz and Dias was knocked out.

"I thought he was one of the best drummers I ever heard," Dias recalls. "He was solid. He made the band sound great."

Dias introduced himself, got his number and within the year, Dias was recommending him to cut for the band. The band Paich and Porcaro had talked about starting together broke up before it even began.

"Without Jeff there was no Toto," Paich says. "Jeff's in Steely Dan and how could we beat that? Jeff's like, 'We start a band? Nah, I just joined Steely Dan. See ya when I see ya.' So we waited around."

Paich began working on a solo record called *That's the Way I Am* with engineer Tom Knox, and everyone went his own way. Porcaro cut the music that he always declared he was most proud to have recorded and played.

Producer **GARY KATZ** recalls meeting Porcaro the first time at the Chatsworth ranch studio owned by the band the Robbs, now known as Cherokee Ranch. It was the precursor to Cherokee Studios that the Robb brothers opened in Hollywood in '74, when they received an eviction notice for an illegal use of a studio on the premises. But this studio in the San Fernando Valley barn had been worked over by engineer Roger Nichols, and he had helped attract some of the artists who ventured there to make their music, including a December 1973 evening of tracking for *Pretzel Logic's* "Night by Night." Katz recalls before he put the call out to Porcaro, they couldn't quite get the song because the drum track wasn't steady.

"Denny (Dias), one of our two guitar players, said 'I know these guys who can play this,'" Katz recalls. "And at midnight or 11:00 or whatever it was, Jeffrey and David Paich showed up. The studio was built around an oak tree. Literally in the middle was this big oak tree and in the doorway of the studio the guys who owned it—the Robbs at the time—had placed a noose at the top part of the doorway. When Denny introduced me to Jeffrey and David, as Jeffrey walked in, he looked up and saw the noose and said, 'This is a tough room,'" Katz remembers with a laugh.

Dias recalls that late night phone conversation that Katz had with Porcaro. When Porcaro told Katz he wanted to bring Paich and Hungate, Dias says Katz was hesitant, and Porcaro said, "If we don't get a track for you tonight, you can hang me in Chatsworth."

"He didn't realize the studio was a converted barn and over the front door was that hangman's noose," Dias says. "When he got there and saw it, he said, 'Hey, I was only kidding.'"

Although Porcaro often told the story that it was the Steely Dan founders and core musicians Walter Becker and Donald Fagen who came into that club and discovered him playing that night, **DONALD FAGEN** confirmed Dias' recount of the details in a phone call in 2020. Nonetheless, Porcaro was stoked and had said to me: "Talk about being in the right place!"

Fagen says he and Becker were very comfortable with Dias' suggestion of calling this young drummer whom they had never met. "We were always desperate and didn't mind trying people out," Fagen says, adding that Dias mentioned Porcaro had a job on the Sonny & Cher show and Becker and he recalled that the band on the show sounded great. "We hit it off right away," Fagen says. "He was so funny and talented."

Katz says the cutting of "Night by Night" was fabulous. Paich and Porcaro cut the track and Porcaro became his "kid brother." It wasn't long before Katz gave Jeff a nickname, just like he gave all people he adored nicknames—having no rhyme or reason, just whatever came to him. In the Steely Dan camp, Jeff forever became known as "Paco."

On *Pretzel Logic*, Porcaro also cut "Parker's Band," playing live double drums with Jim Gordon. Gordon, known for having played with Delaney & Bonnie, Derek and the Dominos, George Harrison, the Beach Boys, Joe Cocker's Mad Dogs & Englishmen and many others, was one of Porcaro's main heroes. Fagen says Becker and he were interested in trying out a double drum situation because they were thinking about taking two drummers out on the road; both were fans of Frank Zappa, who was one of the earliest to explore the concept of two drummers in the Mothers of Invention. Fagen describes Porcaro and Gordon's live performance as "a locomotive."

In Denny Dias' opinion, Porcaro was the reason that track was so solid: "Gordon has a different style. He's good and all, but he doesn't have that solid feel that Jeffrey has," Dias asserts. "Jeffrey laid down a groove and there was no escaping it. Jim Gordon was more flexible in his timing and stuff. He didn't have the solid backbeat that Jeffrey had."

Speaking of Jim Gordon, Katz recalls the day he was hanging out with Porcaro at Jeff's Hesby Street home, tinkering in the back studio. They were out front for a cigarette break when Jim Keltner drove up: "Jim walked up the grass and he told us what happened with Jim (Gordon)," Katz says. "He said, 'So dig this, guys. Jimmy killed his mom.' Jeffrey and I looked at him, 'What?!' He said, 'Yup. He went to her house with a hammer. She opened the door and he gave her one good backbeat on the forehead.' I can feel myself standing next to Jeffrey when he said that. That was Jeffrey, Keltner and Gordon in a sentence. Keltner went back in his car and Jeffrey and I looked at each other."

Dias says he and Jeff became good friends.

"I'd hang out at his place, he'd hang out at my place. We used to play poker all the time. He wasn't that good of a card player, but he liked it a lot," says Dias, recalling that Porcaro was able to get him a deal on a poker table. "He was decorating his house and he had a decorator get a discount on furniture. I had him have her get me a poker table that we had for years—the top would turn over and become a dining room table. He spilled his beer the first week we had the table, so it has a stain, and I didn't have the heart to have it fixed."

After *Pretzel Logic*, Steely Dan went on the road and asked Porcaro to join the tour. They did a few U.S. dates and some dates in Europe.

"When we did our tour in Europe, we had two drummers, Jeffrey and Jimmy (Hodder)." Katz says. "Jeffrey was full of piss. It was good for Jimmy. He was a great drummer. They liked playing with each other, but Jimmy really had to work to keep up."

One memory stands out in Katz's mind: "We arrived in London and the band was in one hotel and we were in another; Walter, Donald and I and Dinky Dawson, our sound guy. It was 1:00 or 2:00 in the morning, we were all sitting in a room, no lights on, doing things we did when we were younger, and there was a knock at the door. There was Jeffrey with his suitcase and he said, 'Where are the bitches?' And we said, 'Ok, you can stay here with us.'"

Fagen recalls a more subdued Porcaro on the road. Of course the European dates were later on in the tour and it's possible Jeff was feeling more comfortable. Donald says they had a lot of fun on the road and shared a similar sense of humor, but earlier on, it's possible Jeff may have been trying to make a good impression on them. And he did, Fagen says. "I think later on Jeff might have become a party guy, but when he was with us, he wasn't into that. He was very conscientious. Walter and I were boring on the road for the most part. The thing that may have freaked Jeff out was our whole relationship with our manager at the time, who we were trying to get rid of. We used to tease this guy unmercifully. Jeff thought that was funny," Fagen says, conceding that maybe it was a little cruel. "Although he understood we were being abused and exploited."

After the tour, they cut *Katy Lied* and used Porcaro on all the tracks, except "Any World (That I'm Welcome To)," which was Hal Blaine, who Fagen says they decided to use because "he was legendary and we were then living in Los Angeles, and I think it was probably the last track we did. We thought, 'Let's see what Hal Blaine sounds like?' And that was really fun too." But they used Porcaro because they liked his style, Fagen says, explaining, "He sounded different from other drummers. It's usually difficult to pick out one rock 'n' roll drummer from another often, but he had a groove that he developed; a really popping groove, so we thought we'd use him."

Describing how they worked in the studio and would present their work to the musicians back in the *Katy Lied* days, Donald says: "We probably had little piano and bass cassette demos that Walter and I had done with me singing the lead just to demonstrate the song. We would play that for the players, and we also had lead sheets which I would write out. Sometimes there would be a piano part and a bass part, but generally speaking we wouldn't write out the drum parts. Jeff just came up with a groove for each tune. We didn't have to talk about it much; it just sounded good," Fagen says, further explaining some of the details on the songs, such as the half-time section on "Bad Sneakers": "That may have been Walter's idea, because he was going to play the solo over that." On "Doctor Wu," Fagen says the orchestration and build of the song was something he and Becker wrote into the song, which they played for Jeff. "He heard the lyrics and that track was probably three or four takes."

One track Porcaro and I talked about on *Katy Lied* was "Your Gold Teeth II" because it was complicated: "'Your Gold Teeth II' was a composition that was written in 6/8, 3/8 and 9/8; that is the way the bar phrases were written for us," Porcaro told me. "It was (bassist) Chuck Rainey, myself and (keyboardist) Michael Omartian for the basic tracking session. We ran it down at the beginning of one night once and all of us thought, 'Wow, this is going to be unbelievable,' especially for me because I was 21 and I wasn't the most experienced be-bop player (and I am of the same mind today). I remember when I heard 'Your Gold Teeth II,' my first reaction in my nervous little body playing for these guys was, 'I am the wrong guy; I should not be here,' knowing the kind of tune and knowing those guys real well. They weren't really aware of a lot of drummers back then, but they were aware of Gordon and I thought Jim could do a better job than I playing that. He was more experienced at getting a better feel. I was very nervous about that. Fortunately, the whole rhythm section had a bitch of a time. This was the first sight reading."

Porcaro explained it as "a big band, but not a big band" tune. He recalled that he lived near Fagen and when they hung out, they would listen to Charles Mingus together: "He gave me some Mingus album with Dannie Richmond on drums and basically most of it was 6/8 or 3/8, all fast ding-dinga-ding, ding-dinga-ding, and he said, 'Listen to this two days before coming to the studio,'" Jeff explained. Porcaro said between copying Richmond and things he had heard his father play, he got through "Your Gold Teeth II."

"There was this Mingus vibe to the rhythmical thing of the song," Porcaro said. "I remember it ended up everybody had such a hard time that we would record other Steely Dan songs and every night before we'd leave, we'd play 'Gold Teeth II' once. I think it was by the fifth or seventh night of a four-week tracking date that we got the track."

Katz says Porcaro was the consummate pro, always early on the gig, which is why he got very worried one day when Porcaro was late to a session called for noon at ABC Studios.

"Not only was he never late to our dates, but he was two hours early," Katz recalls. "I'm waiting and waiting, and this was pre-cell phones. I couldn't reach him. I had no idea he had partied the night before at Cher's, playing volleyball at 2:00 in the morning, and he broke his thumb. We were cutting 'Black Friday,' and Donald gives him a dirty look and we hassled him for being an hour late, and we started playing," Katz continues. "'Black Friday' is just a plain shuffle, which he always said to me he couldn't play. He played for about a half hour. It was an iso booth, which I could look into, all glass. He took the sticks and threw them against the wall and said, 'Fuck this! Get Purdie. He plays shuffles,' and he left. Donald said to me, 'Don't worry, let him walk around the block, he'll be back.' And he did. He walked around the block, came back 20 minutes later and played 'Black Friday' with a cast on his hand."

Porcaro didn't play on Steely Dan's next two albums, *The Royal Scam* or *Aja*. Katz assures there was no particular reason why he didn't. He says there was never a reason *not* to use a certain musician; there was only a reason to use someone. Apparently, though, Jeff was upset about not being hired for *The Royal Scam*. He told *Modern Drummer's* Rick Mattingly in 1992 that he had gotten very excited when Steely's Walter Becker called him to ask if he could borrow a set of Porcaro's drums to begin putting some ideas down for a new record. Porcaro assumed that meant he would be on the project.

After a few weeks a friend mentioned they were already in the studio working on an album with Bernard Purdie on drums. Admittedly Porcaro's feelings were hurt, but Porcaro conceded that he ended up learning a lot from what Purdie played on *The Royal Scam*.

Truth be known, Porcaro was busy with *Silk Degrees* and in talks about Toto at the time, but we'll get to that. Porcaro did record the title track to *Gaucho* (1980) two albums later, something Katz says Jeff was particularly proud of, which Porcaro corroborated.

"We were in New York. It was Rainey, Paul Griffith, and we were recording 'Gaucho' at A&R's A-1 studio. We played it for about two hours and Donald had this thing, used to drive me crazy," Katz says. "If we didn't get a track within a reasonable amount of time, he would say, 'Fuck this song, there's something wrong. We have the best musicians, if they can't play it, it's got to be the song.' Most of the time it was frustrating to me. And we lost, I would say, eight or ten songs over the years like that. 'Gaucho' was one of my three favorites (for the album). I was just nuts about that song. We played for two, three hours and Donald looked at Walter and said, 'Fuck this song, there's something wrong with this song. We're going.' I said, 'Oh no, not tonight. We're not losing this song.' He said, 'Okay. Walter and I are going home. If you get it, call me.' He and Walter left. It was like midnight and all night we played until 5:00 in the morning, two bars at a time. I had a chart and they would play. I would mark each bar, 'This is a good bar, this is a good bar, this is a good bar,' and they would play it again for about four or five hours until I felt we had (it). Each bar, I filled up with a track number. We did I think about 47 edits. We were on tape. And Roger (Nichols), who was the world's greatest technical engineer who ever lived, was outside inventing Wendell (earliest drum sampler), and Elliot (Scheiner) was recording, and when we got to a point we needed edits, Elliot would yell out the door and Roger would walk in the door and do the edit in 13 seconds and walk back out. It was 5:00 in the morning with all these tape edits when I called Fagen and told him to come back, and he did. He said, 'Good work,' and then left. I would say, notwithstanding at the end of the day, Jeffrey was more proud of that than anything else, and with good reason."

Porcaro told me the pressure was nerve wracking, but he loved it: "That kind of pressure with those guys is cool because the music is the most prestigious music that's ever existed from my point of view, and it's great to hear, no matter what," Jeff declared. "Some people can't stand the perfection. Nothing has been too ridiculous a demand, except for hours spent on mediocrity," he said. "*That's* ridiculous. When something is ass backwards, everybody knows it, and yet somebody keeps you there, working for endless hours, and it's not happening. There are times when you have to record six tunes in three hours and do it perfect, or there are times when you only have one tune to do and you have all day to do it and it's a big party. It depends on who the artist is. But the ultimate is that you've got to leave knowing you've done your best. There's not one record that I can listen to all the way through that I've done without getting bugged at how I played. That's going to be there forever. Sometimes I'm unhappy about time, feel—certain things bug me; just things I've let bug me. In all honesty, I would have to say the Steely Dan tracks I've done are the most challenging as far as perfection goes, so I would say they're my personal favorite performances."

When he recalled the "Gaucho" experience, his memory of it was a little harsher than how Katz recalled. He outlined the traditional Steely recording schedule: The session began at 2 p.m. They rehearsed until 6 p.m. Dinner break until 7 p.m. and then they'd record.

"This stuff is rehearsed so heavy that some of the spontaneity is maybe gone. They demand perfect time and while you're playing, things could be grooving, but if one little thing is off, they stop and then you get reprimanded in front of everybody," Porcaro told me, explaining that with "Gaucho," the object was to get all the musicians in the room, get it perfect, but only so they could keep the drums at the end of the night. "Most of the other musicians don't know that," Porcaro revealed at the time. "I just know it from experience. So their idea is we get everybody else in this band and put them through all the shit in the world to make sure they play perfect just to get the perfect drum track. And these guys are sweating, beads of sweat rolling down their forehead, nerves, shaking while they're playing—and they don't know what they're playing is never going to be used."

As Porcaro remembered this, at around 3 a.m., Fagen said something like, "Guys, does everybody know what this tune is supposed to sound like?"

"We're all looking at each other like, 'Yeah!' He was real sarcastic, like, 'Come on little boys,'" Jeff recalled. "He says, 'Good, you know what it sounds like, I know what it's supposed to sound like, then that's all that matters. We're done.' And he splits. So we did another track and we're all sitting there in the studio like, 'What?' And we all got pissed and said, 'Screw it, we're going to work on this track and get this track.' Just Katz was there and we continued to do five or six more takes and it's of those five to six takes that is the final product on that album. That's the kind of shit where most people would have packed up and split, but we just sat there feeling we had to get it, and we did."

When I mention "Gaucho" to Fagen, he says, "Now that's a story, actually. We had worked on it for a couple of hours and it was a difficult song with a lot of strange bars in it; strange time signatures. It wasn't happening and Walter and I were tired and we said, 'Oh well, we'll come in tomorrow.' We left and according to Gary, Jeff was really into it and really wanted to keep trying. The way I understand, they put it together in small pieces. I wasn't there for that, but I heard it was quite an elaborate business." When I counter with the word "ordeal," Fagen responds, "We used to sometimes have guys do a lot of takes, but I wouldn't have put him through that; it was voluntary on his part," he chuckles.

To Fagen, the quintessential track that Porcaro did for him was on his 1982 solo album *The Nightfly* on a track called "Green Flower Street." "It was very fast, but it had a great groove. I always really liked him on that one," Fagen says, adding that outside of Jeff's work for them, Fagen admired him on the Boz Scaggs tracks and says, "A lot of the Toto drum tracks were just fantastic. One of the tracks may have been inspired by one of the things Bernard Purdie played for us," Fagen says, referring to Toto's "Rosanna" and Purdie's shuffle on "Babylon Sisters." I remark that Jeff never thought he was very good at shuffles and Fagen says, "He didn't like them, but he was good at them," says Fagen, adding that Jeff and he kept in touch after they worked together. "I loved Jeff. He was a kid, so I saw him kind of grow up. It was really great to have him around."

Gary said he spoke to Jeff so often that his wife at the time would say all she would ever hear on the telephone was, "Yo," Jeffrey's signature salutation.

"I spoke to him pretty much every day," Katz says, adding they stayed in touch "until..." his voice trails off. "I wait for the phone to ring and for someone to say, 'Yo.'"

Jeff did lots of records with Katz. "Jeffrey played almost every other record I did," Katz says, explaining he always had a clear vision of him while he was recording and could communicate with him without words.

"He came to the studio every day to be great," Katz says. "He may have felt abused, but he loved every minute of it to be great. And he'd come in and listen back and say, 'Naw, not yet,' so he abused himself equally."

It was a mutual admiration society. Jeff appreciated Katz as much as Katz loved working with Jeff: "Gary is the kind of producer who knows his artist real well," Jeff told me. "Works for the artist. He also knows the musicians, he also knows the artist's music so well and he is such a fan of the artist's music. And in conjunction with his artist, he knows who is best suitable to make it an easy session, where you have the hand-picked rhythm section, or horns or singers that you need for the session. The fact that he knows the artist well, as a producer he has his set ways of doing records, but his set ways are many different ways. His set ways may be whatever works best and he'll know all the combinations of how to make it happen smoothly for whatever works best, whether you're cutting it quick, full rhythm section, any of that sort of stuff. Plus, he's the kind of producer that, as you're cutting any particular track, he has natural ears that may be able to tell you things aren't feeling as good as they should be, or somebody is playing something wrong and make those suggestions in a very non-threatening way."

From left to right, back: Jay Graydon, David Hungate, Jeff, Ray Parker, Jr., David Foster. Front: Neil Sedaka, Dara Sedaka.

(Photo courtesy of the Sedaka family)

THE PHONE STARTS RINGING

Around the time of Steely Dan, Jeff started getting calls for more sessions with people like Helen Reddy and Barbra Streisand, which he told me he found demanding. He worked on two Reddy albums in 1976 and 1977, and in the latter '70s Jeff played on Streisand's *Superman*, *Songbird* and *Wet*, in addition to countless other sessions.

"It's really a challenge to go in and play with somebody like that," he said. "If you talk about Streisand, I don't care what you're into or what you think is hip and all that, to be able to pull it off, to do the gig and be professional about it, was challenging. I was really into being a professional. You don't like people to think you're an idiot. You like to present yourself well and you like to impress people with good work done, whether it's digging ditches or whatever. That's just the way I am as a person. Musically, the more sessions you do, the more you learn, the more you learn about things to play, how to use brushes, how to play Latin shit, country and all that stuff. Because all that stuff can groove, you know."

And any music that grooved was what attracted Jeffrey. In fact, his father relayed a story of how one day Jeff got hired to record the music for a TV show. He thinks it was for the show "Ironsides." Joe was the percussionist on the gig and he remembers at one interval looking over at his son and Jeff shook his head and mouthed the words, "I can't do this."

"He could have made a great living doing that, but there just wasn't enough music to play. There would be a few bars and then nothing. And that was just not Jeff," Joe says.

By the mid '70s it seemed like practically every session Jeff was on, guitarist/songwriter and recording artist **RAY PARKER, JR.** was right there beside him on guitar. They were quick to become friends. Parker jokes that Porcaro took it upon himself to become his manager: "He single-handedly got me a deal on CBS," Parker says. "He made CBS pay attention to me. I ended up signing with Arista, but he did get me a deal with CBS."

Parker explains that once Jeff heard his song "Jack and Jill," he was like a dog with a bone. He insisted everyone listen to it at every session they were at together.

"He would personally take the cassette and stop the recording session no matter whose session it was—he did it even one time with George Harrison. He stopped and made everyone listen to 'Jack and Jill.' And that was before the first Toto album came out," Parker recalls. "We were in sessions together all the time and he would do it all the time, on every session, like crazy, obnoxiously. He would push my song like there was no tomorrow. You would have thought he wrote it and he was getting paid. Really? George Harrison of the Beatles? Stopped the session and made him listen to the song. It was, 'Check this out, you all have to hear this.'"

Porcaro obviously was right. "Jack and Jill," by Parker's group Raydio eventually became an international hit, reaching No. 8 on the *Billboard* Top 100.

Parker says he doesn't recall exactly when he met Porcaro or how they became friends, he just says, "Anybody you look across and they're jammin' and they look at you and you're jammin', y'all friends now. It's like you don't have to ask the other girl for her phone number, you're all in it now," he says with a laugh. "I remember when he was doing 'Rosanna' with that crazy drumbeat," Parker recalls. "He showed me how to play the drumbeat with the snare drum. I couldn't play the whole beat, but I actually learned it as he sat and showed it to me."

They did countless sessions together for artists such as Valerie Carter, Bill Champlin, Boz Scaggs, Airplay, Deniece Williams and Leo Sayer, and Porcaro worked on one of Parker's records.

"A lot of guys were excellent musicians and read the charts, but Jeff would always come up with something a little bit different than what the producer or anybody else wanted," Parker says. "And he knew he had the groove, because then he'd look at you and go, 'This is gonna feel good. What about this? Am I grooving yet?' The music was always spectacular. He was playing some crazy beat with all four limbs that just didn't make any sense and nobody else could do that."

They hung out as friends, too, Ray says. He'd go over to Jeff's house, but he says he can't remember exactly what they talked about.

"It could have been girls back then, you know," Ray says with a laugh.

During that time period one of Jeff's sessions was for a **JACKSON BROWNE** album, *The Pretender*, which was recorded late '75 to early '76 with producer Jon Landau. Browne's previous hits, "Doctor My Eyes" and "Rock Me on the Water" were only a small part of what had established him as a great songwriter and artist. Jeff was to record four tracks, including the title track. It was the first time Browne worked with Porcaro.

"I had heard about him though. I think I had heard about him before I had even made a record," Browne says. "By the time I made my first record I had met Russ Kunkel, and I started working with Russ and when I first heard about him, it was, 'You should find him and play with him because...' And in those days, I hadn't even played with a drummer. The guy who was telling me was a drummer and I had played with him in like a house with an electric guitar and drums in someone's den and it was a total mystery. I had done the same thing with Richie Hayward where we had gotten together in my house with a set of drums and a guitar and I thought, 'I don't know how this thing is supposed to work.' It wasn't as if Jeff had the reputation of playing with people acoustically, while Russ got that reputation, deservedly, because he could play with people who weren't used to playing with drummers and make a track and rhythm that made sense to them."

But as Jackson grew as a musician and did start understanding the drummer thing, he finally hired Porcaro for that very important album. At the session, Browne says most likely he presented the song "The Pretender" to the musicians in the studio by playing it on the piano: "Craig Doerge was playing piano and immediately invested it with these great inversions and this sort of gospel chording," Browne recalls. "It was also my first time in the studio with Fred Tackett (guitars) and in those days—especially in those days, I suppose it's the same now—you hoped that the people you called would bring something to it that you haven't been able to hear yet. The other thing to do is have it be really empty so you play it like when you play it by yourself. I do that too. There's this kind of an axiom that I hear more and more now that it's not a song unless you can sit down and play it by yourself. I made a lot of recordings where I couldn't do that; I had to learn how to play them later, but we made up a lot of stuff in the studio. Jeff with his hi-hat part on that song, he found the rhythm that could expand and could get big and also could be felt when everybody else came out," Browne recalls of Porcaro laying it down.

When asked about the dramatic stops and starts in the song, Browne laughs, "Well, they were written in, but they probably weren't in time when I played it. They *are* dramatic," he agrees, as he hums them. "The song is dramatic. And Jeff gave it a kind of grace and a surety, a confidence."

Browne says Porcaro was extremely creative and helped shape the song. At the lyrics of "Caught between the longing for love and the struggle for the legal tender," Browne says originally he had fewer words going forward, but something Jeff played was so inspiring, where Jeff ended up playing a tom part twice as long and Doerge instinctively went with him on it, so that it changed the form of the song.

"Jeff made it happen for two lines and Jon Landau said, 'It's great, right?' and I said, 'Yeah, but now there's too few lyrics,' and he said, 'Well, you're a writer, you can write something. Write another line.' To him there wasn't a question of whether or not you would disturb it."

Looking at the lyrics on Google while we spoke, Browne thinks because of what Jeff played, Browne probably added the words "and the church bells ring."

"It was that spark, that thing behind the drums of wanting something to happen," Browne says. "For somebody who writes, especially on that song—there are a lot of words—it was a great service that he did me and that song where he said, 'Let's do something,' and it made everything else have an expectation too, so that when it got big, it was really big."

Browne says he ran into Jeff years later in Santa Barbara and they talked about that session, and he told Jackson he really liked the way the song came out, but Jackson says, "Ya know, Jeff was kind of a joker. He would put you on and have you on for a long time. He would keep you going. There was something about him where he had a sort of hidden knowledge about things. He was an amused bystander in a lot of conversations and situations. It wasn't aloof; he didn't make you feel like he was above it, you just felt like he was a party to some sort of special information. He would say shit that was completely..."Jackson trails off trying to figure out how to say the rest. "One time he went on this long rant when nobody knew what he was talking about, because we were all high," Jackson admits. "He took out this handful of change and he looked at it and said, 'I mean *what*? Are we all fish?' And he started eating the change."

Jackson starts to laugh at the memory and I join in. "I know. I know," he says. "I mean, he wasn't swallowing it, but was pretending to gobble it, like he was gobbling the change – '*Are we all fish*?'" Jackson laughs. "I don't know."

I asked him if he hears Jeff when he hears "The Pretender," and he said of course, but more than that he hears the whole song because of the kind of drummer Jeff was. "He was one of those drummers who played the song. What I hear is the whole song, and he was the kind of drummer who made that song happen. He could play as flashy as anybody, but he made the song a success that it might not have been had it been another drummer, so yes, he helped shape it and I feel a debt of gratitude and a deep connection," says Jackson, who even attended his memorial. "I felt the loss everyone felt," Jackson says, adding that he tried to get Jeff to tour with him at one point, but Jeff was already in Toto at the time and told him, "I'm in a band and I work in the studio when I'm not on tour with them."

But we're not there yet...

Jeff with Boz Scaggs on the *Silk Degrees* tour, 1976.

(Photo courtesy Barney Hurley)

THE NEXT DEGREE—SUCH SILK

In 1976, Jeff worked on Helen Reddy's album *Music Music* with producer Joe Wissert. He recorded two tracks: the title track and another called "Music is my Life." Wissert introduced Jeff to Boz Scaggs and history was made. Scaggs had had limited success as an artist on Atlantic Records and three albums on Columbia, but no hits. At this juncture, he was producing (guitarist) Les Dudek, who had just left the Allman Brothers in 1975. Porcaro would be playing drums and they were looking for an organ player. Porcaro got David Paich on the gig, as was the usual deal.

"Jeff and I were jamming in between the Dudek stuff and Boz Scaggs started hearing that stuff and he said to Jeff, 'I'm looking for a guy to co-write an album with.' Jeff said, 'This guy would be perfect for you,'" recalls Paich of Jeff's recommendation of him. "'We could do this album and try David Paich,' because I had just started writing songs. I had written 'Miss Sun' already and Jeff had heard that song. Boz said, 'Okay, let's sit down and try it.' So Boz and I went up to my dad's ranch in San Ynez and cranked out most of the *Silk Degrees* album on my dad's piano, just he and I sitting there. It just came like butter. We were soul brothers.

"The riff of 'Lowdown' was the ending of a song I had written called 'Tale of a Man,'" Paich continues. "That was my answer to the song Steely Dan had written about Patty Hearst and the SLA, 'Don't Take Me Alive.' I wanted to write something like that, so I wrote something about the Manson family called 'Tale of a Man.'"

Scaggs had heard the tail end of that song during a break while on the Dudek project while Porcaro and Paich were just playing music they were working on.

"It had that little opening kind of riff that is now 'Lowdown.' We started with that riff and then I wrote some of that melody and chorus and Boz was the lyric guy, so he wrote most of the lyrics and most of the verse melodies," Paich says.

Hungate and Louie Shelton were brought in to record *Silk Degrees*. Paich recalls that Freddie Tackett played on some of the cuts. The album was cut live with Paich, Hungate, Porcaro, and Shelton. "Lowdown" was recorded in two takes, Paich says, and only because the first take wasn't recorded.

"We got the take the first time and we turned around and said, 'You got that, right?' And they said, 'No, we weren't rolling.' From then on, it was, 'When we're playing, roll tape.' So the next take was the take."

Porcaro talked about "Lowdown" and how he and Paich had demoed the earlier "Tale of a Man," thinking it would one day be a song for their own band: "When we got to the fade, we snapped into a completely different groove," Porcaro told me. "That groove was a quarter-note bass drum on one, the last sixteenth note of the second beat bass drum, the third beat a bass drum quarter note, sixteenth notes straight on the hi-hat and the backbeat on the snare drum on 2 and 4. When we cut 'Lowdown,' it was 1976 and there was an Earth, Wind & Fire album out that I had been playing over and over again," Jeff continued. "It might have been *I Am*, or the one before that. And instead of sixteenths, whether it was Freddie White or Maurice, the groove was quarter notes on the hi-hat and the same beat I just described. We wanted to get that kind of Earth, Wind & Fire medium dance groove, rhythm section-wise. But instead of doing quarter notes, I did eighth notes, so if you take the figure I described and add eighth notes on the hi-hat and every two bars or so, open the hi-hat on the last eighth note of the fourth beat, that's it. We cut it that way, with the hi-hat on the right and that was the groove, but the producer said, 'Gee, do you want to try adding sixteenth notes?' because disco was starting to come in around '76. I wasn't the keenest guy on disco and said, 'Naw naw, you don't want to do that, man. You don't want to ruin the groove.' He said, 'Just try it,' and Paich and Boz said so too, so I sat down and overdubbed the hi-hat that they put on the opposite side. While I was overdubbing the simple sixteenths, I started getting some accents and started answering the hi-hat stuff and it got to be a lot of fun."

Paich asserts he never thought it would be a hit, but it grooved so heavily, thanks to Porcaro.

"Lido Shuffle," Paich says, came from something Scaggs heard called "Magneto and Titanium Man" from Paul McCartney's *Venus and Mars* album.

"It was kind of a '50s doo-wop thing which he played on piano. I came from the Elton John school and immediately wanted to beef it up and make it more rock 'n' roll, so it got harder-edged," Paich says adding that, as he recalls, Freddie Tackett played guitar on the track, along with Porcaro, Hungate and himself, while Scaggs sang the lyrical riff: "Lido, oh whoa, whoa, whoa." "It was Jeff and Hungate on the first eight bars. Jeff has these signature intros," Paich comments. "Identifiable. You have 'Lowdown,' you have 'Lido,' you have 'Miss Sun,' you have 'Rosanna,' and you have 'Africa.' Those are all Jeff Porcaro intros. You know it's him."

About "Love Me Tomorrow," Porcaro told me: "The most reggae that I had heard in my life was probably Bob Marley. I hadn't heard Peter Tosh or any of those cats yet. Maybe the most up-to-date record that would tell you what I'm talking about would be 'Kid Charlemagne,' but if you listen to the groove on that and on 'Haitian Divorce' from *The Royal Scam* (Steely Dan), that's Bernard Purdie. You'll hear some of the same kind of groove on the Aretha and King Curtis *Live at the Fillmore West* albums, both of which Bernard Purdie played on. On King Curtis' *Live at the Fillmore West*, when they do 'Memphis Soul Stew,' you get a taste of this Bernard Purdie lope that I've heard a lot from Rick Marotta, too. My main influence for 'Love Me Tomorrow' was the Bernard Purdie kind of shuffling type lope, very reggae-ish, but it's a bad imitation of Purdie," Porcaro said, adding that he played the timbales that were set up by the drums, as well.

It's obvious *Silk Degrees* was a game-changer for the artist, as Scaggs was told it was the last album he was going to be allowed to make for the label. At a clinic Jeffrey gave at Musicians Institute in 1986, which I attended, he talked about how all the hired musicians on the project worked for scale and never charged extra on weekends and overtime. When the album was a mega hit, Scaggs gave them each a $30,000 bonus. Porcaro bought his first home on Hesby Street in Studio City with the money.

I was not able to get Scaggs to weigh in for this project, but he did speak with me about Jeffrey's contribution to *Silk Degrees* for the *MD* special tribute I did when Porcaro passed away:

"The real surprise and joy of working with those guys was that they shared my enthusiasm for contemporary urban Black music," **BOZ SCAGGS** told me in 1992. "We were trying to do something that not too many others were trying to do—the White boys listening to the other side of the radio. Jeff, David, and David had a feel for that stuff. 'Lowdown' was just a natural for them. David Paich and I wrote that one, knowing that there was someone there like Jeff to carry it. Jeff approached his role more like a songwriter, a singer, or an arranger would approach the song," Scaggs went on. "He did a lot more than just keep time. He actually moved me as a singer through the song. Everybody in the band would know what was coming up in the next few bars, because we could feel it in the way he anticipated, the way he moved us toward it, like a rider moves a horse.

"'Harbor Lights' was a song for which he was greatly responsible for setting the tone," Scaggs continued. "That was a songwriter presenting a song and getting back an interpretation from the musicians that wouldn't have been possible without his unique interpretation. I'd throw it out in the air, and this kindred spirit would collect it and transpose it back to me in a way that would give the song new meaning and new life. I could say that in general about the way Jeff absorbed things. I think a lot of drummers would say the groove he set up on a song like 'Lido Shuffle' was a classic shuffle. It's a very elusive little time that he plays. It sounds simple, but it's really not easy to execute. A lot of drummers recognize that Jeff had this shuffle that was unique. It's probably the hardest of all the grooves to keep, and Jeff was a master of that. 'JoJo' was another very elusive groove. It took a lot of innovation and creativity for a drummer to pull some of those grooves off.

"Any collaborative work reflects the soul of the person who is collaborating. Jeff was a collaborator, and any drummer trying to consider himself a part of a high creative process has to consider himself a collaborator and bring his personality and interpretation to it, not just a set of drums that sound like everyone else's, or what it's *supposed* to sound like," Scaggs explained. "It's not about what it's supposed to sound like; it's the individual's interpretation. After his energy, Jeff's interpretation was the important thing that all artists should aspire to."

Paich says none of the tracks on *Silk Degrees* took more than three takes to record. And all the time, the experience was cementing the knowledge that one day they had to be a band: "We had decided we were going to use other people to get experience making records," Paich says. "We wanted to learn how to produce records so when we made our first record it would sound like we came out with our eighth record."

In an interview I did with Toto for a *BAM* (Bay Area Music) magazine cover story in 1989 at Paich's house, Porcaro recalled with a smile: "While Paich and I were doing that album, the sparkle happened and Paich and I would just look at each other. I mean, here we were, we love Boz and stuff, and here was this producer, who was fine as producers go, but it was the first time in both David's and my experience where we weren't just sitting there reading charts. They let us have a lot of freedom and most of the tunes were co-written by Paich, so musically we were playing stuff that was very comfortable to us. That's really when we started thinking seriously about a band."

The *Silk Degrees* album was released in February 1976 and they went out on tour after that, through the summer. Joleen recalls that summer very well. It was the summer of her sixteenth birthday on August 2nd. Sometime around the date of Scaggs' Los Angeles Greek Theatre concert on August 15, 1976 (memorialized on a 2007-released Legacy album), the Porcaros were celebrating Joleen's birthday. They were sitting at their dinner table and Joleen had just opened up a pair of diamond earrings from Jeffrey, when the phone rang. Jeff picked up the phone and told Joleen it was for her.

"It was Boz inviting me to go on tour with them for the weekend for my sixteenth birthday," Joleen recalls. "So I went with the boys. We went to Minneapolis first and they played a festival concert I believe with Chicago and the Beach Boys. It was my first time ever flying first class. This was Boz's heyday. After the concert in Minneapolis we flew to Buffalo, New York, and I roomed with Mike. I always wondered if they flipped coins as to who had to share a room with me," she says with a laugh. "Then they opened for Elton John and Kiki Dee, who had that huge hit 'Don't Go Breaking My Heart.' It was at a baseball stadium and it was so much fun. Can you imagine brothers being that thoughtful and dragging your little sister on tour with you? I mean they were all good to me, but Jeff was just the big bro, just so thoughtful, so sweet."

When Scaggs played Connecticut, Jeff went to cousin Mark's house after the gig and upon seeing his drums, asked him for a knife.

"I brought him a knife and he cut into the front head of my bass drum," Mark Porcaro remembers. "And I'm freaking out because I love these drums. I said, 'Jeff, why are you doing that?' And he said, 'Oh don't worry Mark. Relax, don't worry. It's going to be okay.' He wanted to give me that thuddy sound. And I still have that head. I used it for years, and later on I got a head with the circle cut out, but I kept that one."

The *Silk Degrees* tour definitely added fuel to the band idea fire. Steve Porcaro was on the tour also, so that was almost the entire band. They were playing music that Paich had co-written which boosted his confidence and legitimized him as a writer.

"We already had a lot of experience from high school and we were like a rock band in back of him. Boz would leave the stage and we would come back and be jumping in the air getting 50,000 people out of their seats. It was like, 'Who are these guys? You should think about forming a band.' 'Yeah! Really? We hadn't thought of that,'" Paich says, sarcastically. "And record company execs were asking, 'Hey, you guys ever thought of forming a band?' We said, 'Wow, that's a really great idea,' and we'd wink at each other," Paich says with a laugh.

At about the same time they were cutting *Silk Degrees*, Porcaro worked on **LEO SAYER'S** 1976 album *Endless Flight*. The British singer-songwriter had reached great prominence in the UK with three previous releases, as well as having a couple of songs of his recorded by Roger Daltrey, the Who's lead singer, on his solo album, *Daltrey*. *Endless Flight* was Sayer's first album recorded in the U.S.

Released in February, 1977, the No. 1 hit "When I Need You" was the second single from the album, and is often mentioned as a favorite Jeff track. Porcaro's accompaniment, the way he plays for the song, his fills and deep soul creates a bed for Sayer's vocals and the mood and feel of the song.

"Jeff always played a 6/8 or 3/4 really well," Sayer says on a Skype call from Australia, where he has been living since 2005. "He had that swing time in him. He'd call it his shuffle. He'd do a 6/8 shuffle. It's there in Boz Scagg's 'Lido.' But if you kind of slow down Boz's track, you get 'When I Need You.' Most people do an on-beat on the hi-hat, but Jeff would do an offbeat on the hi-hat, which was really unusual. Wherever the snare wasn't, Jeff would introduce the hat and then he could swing off that. Jeff had a unique way of swinging off any drum."

Sayer says he sang live and Jeff and he had eyes on one another in the studio. Years later they talked about how they played off each other's timing.

"Richard (Perry, producer) used to cut up the tape, so he'd sit in the room with his engineers and I'd sit in the background going, 'What the hell?' while he was saying, 'I think I like the first two bars of 34 and the second bar of 1, but the cymbal of bar...' Sometimes we'd do 90 fucking takes and we didn't need to because the feel was there from take one and I had sung myself raw and Jeff would have played himself out," Sayer says.

Perry had been chosen by the record company, which Sayer was not too thrilled about. He had really wanted Jerry Wexler or Tom Dowd, but when he saw the group of musicians at Studio 55 that Perry assembled to cut the album, he acquiesced. That group included Porcaro, as well as Ray Parker, Jr.; Larry Carlton; Ralph McDonald; Leland Sklar and Lee Ritenour; they cut three tunes in three hours.

"I was introduced to everybody afterwards and I remember particularly getting on really well with this little guy, same height as me, with a huge personality and kinda pebble glasses. In the end, that was the guy I talked to the most and that was Jeffrey. And Jeffrey and I just hit it off. And when he said, 'Where do you live?' I said, 'Laurel Canyon.' I was just opposite the Canyon Country Store and he said, 'I'm on the street that's on your corner, Kirkwood,' so he said, 'Come out to my house.' So we went out to his place and had some wine together and some nachos that his then girlfriend made for us and talked into the night. We got on so well because Jeff was the biggest fan of British drummers and he loved British music. And I came from that, so he was quizzing me like mad. And in the meanwhile I was quizzing him on Boz Scaggs and all the wonderful characters he played with," Sayer recalls, adding that he knew from there they would be good friends.

Perry hadn't ingratiated himself to Sayer when he had told him he wasn't interested in cutting any of his penned songs. Overseas, Sayer had a stellar reputation as a songwriter and Perry wasn't honoring it. But when Perry heard the beginnings of "You Make Me Feel Like Dancing," he changed his mind and told him to finish it up with songwriter Vini Poncia. It turned out that Steve Gadd played drums on that track, which was the first No. 1 hit from the album, but what many might not know is that Jeff helped carve the tune during a jam session.

"Jeff and I had this crazy competition. There were no mobile phones in those days, so we couldn't call each other. We would set a challenge, 'Tell me what song you dig on the radio on the way in (to the studio).' This one morning I came in and said, 'Oh man, I just heard this song from Shirley & Company,'" recalls Sayer, singing a few lines from "Shame Shame Shame."

"Jeff said, 'I heard that as well. What a groove, it goes like this,' and he started drumming and I started singing," Sayer continues. "Pretty soon the whole studio was into it. I went into the vocal booth, because I had been standing by his drums, and I'm just jamming away and I think we were in between takes for another song that Richard was recording, and I didn't look through the porthole window where I would see Jeff on one side and Richard and the control room on the other. I don't think I even looked in because I was too busy into the headphones and listening to the guys. We had an amazing band that day: Ray Parker, Jr.; Lee Ritenour; John Barnes; Jeff; Willie Weeks."

Sayer explains how everybody was jamming and he was coming up with words that were bursting into his head: "Richard throws the reel—which was nearly finished—off the tape machine. He puts on a new reel and he's shouting and barking at the guys, 'Record now.' And that's how the jam got onto tape."

Then they got back to the work at hand. Sayer didn't think about that jam until about a week later when Perry called him into the office and played him the cassette on which he had transferred the jam and told him that was the hit. That's when Perry informed him he needed a chorus and had to write with Poncia. The two came up with the chorus in five minutes. He remembers it was only five minutes because Poncia told him that's all he had before needing to get to a doctor's appointment. They came up with it and sure enough, Poncia said, "See ya."

Jeff never ended up on the track because, as Bill Schnee recalls, while working on Steely Dan's *Aja*, at Producers Workshop with Steely's normal "revolving door" of drummers, they had booked Steve Gadd for two days. It was the first time Schnee had worked with Gadd. He was blown away and called Perry to rave about him. Perry immediately asked, "Do you think I could do a session with him?"

Schnee told him: "You'd have to come over here to Producers because I don't want to have to get the drum sound again. I'm happy with the drum sound. Let me ask Gary (Katz)." They gave him three hours to cut "You Make Me Feel Like Dancing" and they even managed to record "How Much Love" for Sayer's album.

"Steve just went out and played a groove that was close to '50 Ways to Leave Your Lover' and we recorded the track anew, so unfortunately the jam that Jeff and I recorded never got on record," Sayer explains.

Sayer says that while it was Perry who brought Porcaro into the original fold, it was he, himself, who brought him into the 1982 Arif Mardin-produced project *World Radio*.

"I insisted," Sayer recalls. "I was only going to do it if Jeff was aboard. By that time Jeff and I were such pals. We would go and jam."

Sayer describes Porcaro as always stepping up to the plate with no ego: "He'd always say to me, 'I hope that was good enough.' I'd say, 'Come on, man, you're Jeff.' He always would be, of course. I pleaded with him to come join my band, but by then, Toto had gotten going."

In January 1976, while Paich and Jeff were working on *Silk Degrees*, they had started cutting demos for their own band at Davlen Studios after the Boz sessions were over for the day. Then when *Silk Degrees* was finished, they continued to work on their own project while still working on sessions.

Jackson Browne doesn't recall who called Jeff for Warren Zevon's *Excitable Boy* album, which he co-produced with Waddy Wachtel in 1977. Porcaro played on one track, "Night Time in the Switching Yard," and at the mere mention of the work, Browne laughs with joy "because it came out so good." Browne says it could have been Wachtel, Zevon or he who hired Jeff, he's not sure—but he says they were all glad he was there.

Excitable Boy was Zevon's third album. The self-titled album prior to this one contained a few of his compositions ("Hasten Down the Wind," "Poor Poor Pitiful Me," and "Carmelita") that Linda Ronstadt recorded, but *Excitable Boy* established Zevon as an artist with "Werewolves of London," on which Mick Fleetwood played drums. Although "Night Time in the Switching Yard" was not a single, it was a work of art.

"Jeff really made that track happen," Jackson says. "Maybe some part of me slightly disapproved of Warren doing a song that was basically just an excuse to do kind of like a really powerful rhythm track. It wasn't as literate of a song as a lot of his songs are. Waddy didn't want it to be full of words. My job was... I don't know what I thought my job was, I sure wasn't playing anything. To say whether we should do another take? If there was a mistake somewhere? I don't know. Jeff was so excited about the track. He was so happy about the way it sounded when we played it back that he was dancing in the corner. He was in the corner, looking at everybody, dancing. He was looking at me like, 'That's it, that's the take,' but I was going, 'Let me see,' and he was pulling my fucking chain, like, 'Show me the mistake, you show me the mistake, play it again.'"

If you haven't heard the track, check it out. It is a magical connection between Porcaro and Glaub. Glaub agrees it has an amazing feel and recalls it was "a joy to cut."

"Anytime you were in the studio with Jeff, it was mostly in and out because Jeff was so fast and so competent," Glaub says. "Jeff was more competent than any musician I ever met in my life. He went right to the core of the song and performed brilliantly right from the first take. He kept everybody on his toes. He set the bar real high for all the players in the room. And he did not suffer fools at all. He expected the best from everybody too because he brought his A-game. Well he didn't have any other game, so to say that is almost condescending about Jeff because he only had one game and that was the A+++++."

The perfect example of Jeff not suffering fools—not to suggest that producer Kyle Lehning is a fool, only that he might have been guilty of a foolish direction—was while Lehning was producing an artist by the name of Marie Cain in 1977 with 22-year-old Jeff Porcaro on drums. Lehning, in his latter 20s, hired Jeff, along with Lee Sklar, Jai Winding and Richie Zito to work on the record in Studio C at the Record Plant in Los Angeles, his first time working with Porcaro. Marshall Morgan was engineering and the two were in the control room. As Lehning describes it, in order to get from the control room into the studio, they had to walk through a sound lock, which they were using as a vocal booth. They were recording a song and Lehning pushed the talkback button.

"I said, 'Hey Jeff, can you do one of those bloom da bloom da bloom kind of tom fills into the bridge?' And he says, 'Okay.' So the bridge is a good two minutes into the song, and we're playing the tune and we're about to get to the bridge. I look out there and Jeffrey's playing the tune and hooked around one of the lugs of his floor tom is his stick bag. He's playing and I realize he's playing the snare and the hi-hat just with his left hand and the track feels great, and he reaches down into his stick bag with his right hand and grabs a handful of sticks. There must have been eight sticks in his right hand and he very slowly raises them over his head as he approaches the bridge. I'm looking at him thinking, 'What's about to happen?' And just as we get to the bridge he just drops this handful of sticks over his toms, so it goes, 'blagablagablagablaga,' this horrible noise. Everybody cracks up and we stop the take. That was funny, let's cut it again. We start the take again. And as we get close to the bridge again, he starts reaching into his stick bag again and I think, 'No, he's not going to do it.' And he pulls the sticks out, holds them slowly over his head and drops them onto the toms, a second time, at which point I think, 'This is not funny.' And the guys crack up again. I tell Marshall to mute Marie's vocal mic and I get up and I walk into her booth, which is the way I have to go to walk into the studio, and I say, 'Marie, I have two options. I can fire him and we can cancel the session and get somebody else, or I can try to ask him not to do that. What do you want me to do?' She says, 'You're the producer. It has to be your call.' So I walked out there and as I'm walking out there, I'm thinking, 'This guy is one of the best drummers that's ever played,' and by this time I had worked with Larrie Londin and Kenny Malone and a lot of great drummers. So I got to him and said, 'Jeffrey, I'll make you a deal: I will never sing a tom-tom fill to you again if you promise me you won't do that again.' And he said, 'That's a deal.' And we went on to cut the rest of the album," says Lehning, who discloses they never had another issue making the record (which was never released) and he proceeded to hire him again for England Dan & John Ford Coley's 1978 record *Dr. Heckle & Mr. Jive*.

In 1981, Jeff went on to record with Zevon again for his record *The Envoy*, released the following year. Producers were Zevon, Greg Ladanyi and **WADDY WACHTEL**—composer, record producer and session guitarist. Wachtel says Jeff brought out the song every time he played: "He would play the song so great," Wachtel says. "He was very passionate and ready to play, always."

Wachtel doesn't recall the first time he met Porcaro, although I may have traced their first work together to the recording of "Daddy's Tune" on Jackson Browne's *The Pretender* album. Waddy does remember that on a break during one of the first sessions they did together they got a bite of food, went to Jeff's house and listened to some Steely Dan on "his crazy big speakers he had." And he remembers that Jeff was already on the scene when he got his start and began to do sessions, which makes the following story even funnier: "Jeff and I were doing a session for somebody and he and I went out for dinner," Wachtel recalls. "And he said to me, 'How do you know when you get double scale?' And I said, 'What? You're not getting double scale? Here's how you know. I'm telling you: from now on, you're getting double scale. Write it on your fucking form!'"

Glaub says he always had the feeling Jeff loved working with Zevon and found his lyrics inspiring, and bassist/songwriter Jorge Calderon says Zevon's intelligence, sense of humor and ability to think on his feet were qualities Porcaro appreciated.

"I was on sessions with him. If you're lucky enough to do what Jeff did and I still do, play with a lot of people and a large variety of songwriters, year in and year out, after a while you might get on a session where somebody is rolling his eyes," Glaub admits. "I saw him do that a few times and I can't name who they were because they were not memorable sessions, but he would play his ass off no matter what. But he might roll his eyes," Glaub adds with a laugh.

He continues on about Jeff: "The thing I miss about Jeff, besides, of course, his great playing and getting to play music with him, is every time I saw him, no matter what, he was from that old-school Italian upbringing, and the first thing he would do was give me a hug and kiss me on the neck. That warmth he exuded. And it was 'Yo, Glaub.' And sometimes we'd play in the Valley and on a lunch break he'd say, 'Hey let's go to my pad,' and we'd go over to his Hesby house and hang out, and he was so proud of that studio."

Glaub says he and Porcaro worked on some weeklong projects together such as Mike Finnigan and a John Fogerty record that Jeff didn't actually end up on, but he describes the time spent with him as always fantastic: "It was always beautiful. He was always up. On a break it was, 'Come to my car, listen to this.' He was always full of life. He was always into what we were doing and everything about him was infectious. In the year before he passed away he actually called me one night. After the John Fogerty week together where we were playing that kind of bluesy, swamp rock style, he called me up out of the blue and said, 'Yo, Glaub,' in that low voice of his, 'We should produce some blues records, man. You have a good feel for that kinda stuff, man. We should find some young acts—singers or bands—and produce some records, be their rhythm section or not.' We were going to do some stuff together and within six months he was gone. But the fact that he thought of that meant the world to me."

Bassist **LELAND SKLAR** and Jeff played a few tracks together on Zevon's *The Envoy*. Sklar can't recall where and when he first encountered Jeff; he just knows it was always a good day if Jeff was on a session. In fact, in his datebook, oftentimes he wouldn't even notate the artist; the only entry for the date would be "Jeff." That's all that mattered. He says if he knew Jeff was there, he could put up with anything else. Sklar brings up Porcaro's groove and says there are an abundance of wonderful drummers in Los Angeles, naming off a few like Keltner, Carlos Vega, etc., but Sklar says what was so amazing about Jeff was, "He embodied the best of everybody in one cat."

Sklar describes Porcaro as one of the bravest musicians he's ever known: "Most players always look for the thing that is going to most please the producer or the artist and Jeff really lived by his own playing ethics. I remember doing, I think it was a David Crosby record with him, and we did a song with him where almost any drummer in town would have hunkered down and just played a groove, but Jeff just sat there with his brushes, fluttering around the overheads and touching a few drums. It was the most minimalist approach and as soon as we went in to listen to the playback, we just looked at each other and said, 'That was perfect.' But it took a brave guy to do the most unorthodox thing you would have expected, where very few people would have had the courage to play, even if they had thought of the part."

Sklar can't help but bring up a time he and Jeff were in the studio to record a rendition of "Canon in D Major" with Marvin Hamlisch in 1980. The song, often heard at commencement ceremonies, was composed by Johann Pachelbel and is commonly known as "Pachelbel's Canon." The classical work was used prominently that year in the film *Ordinary People*, and actually accounted for a resurgence of the piece, so Hamlisch decided to record an electronic version with Richard Perry and Brooks Arthur producing. So there they were at Richard Perry's studio, just Sklar and Porcaro, in the studio to overdub on the orchestral track, looking into the control room at Richard Perry, Brooks Arthur and Marvin Hamlisch. As Sklar recounts with a laugh, he and Jeff looked at each other and said, "Obviously we were killed in a car crash on the way here and we've gone to hell." In the end, though, it turned out okay and Sklar says it wasn't as painful as originally thought.

One painful session he does recall, though, was at Capitol Records with Art Garfunkel and he believes it was Richard Perry producing. Sklar describes the session as "pulling teeth," and Sklar says Jeff threw his sticks across the floor and said, "Why don't you fucking call Marty Paich and get some arrangements." Sklar says, "These guys were just groping around, but Jeff was just an amazing cat because he spoke his mind. When he sat down behind the kit, he was joyous, but he was all business. He didn't take it lightly. He did what had to be done. But he was a gift to a bass player. You never had to accommodate for anything. Just as soon as we started playing, it was just there; it felt so symbiotic," Sklar says, recalling dates they did together for artists such as Richard Marx and Jude Cole. "He was so creative and so interesting and so smart. There might have been other players on the date who made it a little more difficult, but it would never have been Jeff. He always fit in. So much of that came from Joe and he understood what that seat required."

And, Sklar says he loved Jeff's artwork, which not only showed up on his drumheads, but depending on the session, Jeff would "noodle away on them." Sklar laughs as he says they not only connected musically, but in their dark humor: "He had such a dark side to his humor, that some of his cartoons were, oh my God, really grim, but beautiful. We always lamented that we never had a chance to be on the road together. We did so much together and we were kindred spirits. The loss of him was really quite staggering because it was one of those holes that was created that will never be filled."

In 1978, producer/engineer **BILL SCHNEE** was producing Colin Blunstone of the Zombies for Elton John's Rocket Records label and got very excited about the title track "Never Even Thought." Schnee assembled the band, which included Jeff, and had them over to his house a couple of nights prior to the sessions. He played the song for them and says when they began to work on it, they had a lot of trouble making it happen. "Maybe because I had too much of my own emotion invested in it," Schnee ponders. "It took much longer than it should have. Not days, but probably most of the day. On one of the early takes, in frustration—you know how guys will start goofing off at the end of a take—at the end of one of the takes, Jeff started goofing around with drum fills and stuff, just having fun. That was within the first hour or so. We get the take five hours or so later and something hit me and

I said, 'Jeff, I have an idea, I think you'll like it,' and I went and took those goof-offs that he played and cut them onto this track that we cut five hours later. The tempo hadn't drifted five hours later. I remember measuring it before I made the cut and I timed it and it was ridiculously close. I cut all that in and overdubbed everybody to it so it sounds like it was completely arranged that way, which it wasn't. We overdubbed everything on top of it and it's one of my favorite things I ever produced."

Schnee recalls the infancy of Toto, too...

PART TWO

First Toto press photo, 1976.

TOTO AND THE YELLOW BRICK ROAD…

"Jeff bounced into Sound Labs where I was mixing something and he threw a cassette at me and said, 'Dig it,'" Bill Schnee recalls. "They had gone into Davlen, just he and Paich and it was just grooves where Paich had played a synth bass and Jeff had played drums. It was phenomenal. It was like something I had never heard before."

Soon Steve Porcaro joined in and they had songs like "Miss Sun," "All Us Boys" and "Love is a Man's World." Paich says Jeff and he were deciding on who the guitar player in the band would be. It was between Steve Lukather and Mike Landau, both of whom had been in Steve Porcaro's high school band.

"Jeff saw Lukather on stage perform and he was just a bloody star from the beginning," Paich recalls. "He was running around and jumping through the air like Pete Townsend. That was the guy. And there we were."

Well, one more element: vocals. Paich says he was good for some of it, a "secondary singer," but Porcaro and he always admired groups with multiple singers like Fleetwood Mac and the Beatles.

"Luke sang pretty good, too, but we were missing *that* guy," Paich says. "That front man kind of guy, like bands that were hot at the time, like Foreigner or Boston."

Leo Sayer was recording his 1978 self-titled album *Sayer* in the larger studio at Studio 55 at the same time Toto was recording their first album in the smaller studio. Various Toto members were also working on Sayer's album at the time as well, and Sayer was checking in on them at times. Sayer recalls at some point that he was invited by Porcaro and Paich to be the lead singer of Toto. He couldn't do it due to a record company contractual situation, but he says he actually sang the original "Hold the Line" demo for them at Studio 55.

"I didn't know all the words, but we were hanging out all the time and I remember Jeff running out and saying, 'Hey we just came up with a new song, listen to this,' and Steve Lukather turned around and said, 'Get Leo to sing it, get Leo to sing it.'" Sayer recalls. "So I did a couple of choruses and jammed bits in the middle and the next time I said, 'Hey that song was really good, I should sing it with you,' and they said, 'Yeah, well, why don't you join us in the band? Come and be our singer.' Paichie said that. And I said, 'I'd love that, but I can't.' It was a watershed moment in a way because later on I thought, 'Fuck, I wished I had been the lead singer in Toto.'"

Paich says it couldn't hurt to try. Sayer already had an established career.

"In the middle of the session, Jeff mentioned Leo would be perfect," Paich recalls. "So I asked him to join. You never know unless you try. Wishful thinking on our part."

Bobby Kimball was fronting a band called S.S. Fools that Paich and Porcaro had been working with. Six months later, when S.S. Fools disbanded, they brought Kimball into the studio

"He could sing like Pavarotti, but he was like a gospel singer. Without a microphone he could break glass in a room, really loud and he had chops," Paich says.

So Paich, Porcaro, Hungate and Lukather tried him out at Studio 55, also on "Hold the Line," one of the first songs Paich had written in his new apartment. They taught him the verse.

"And when he opened up his mouth and sang 'Hold the Line' and Lukather played the guitar part, and Jeff and Hungate played, it sounded just like the record," Paich exclaims. "We looked at each other and said, 'Holy shit, we've got a band!'"

They demoed him on "Hold the Line" and then Kimball's "You Are the Flower." Paich says the album recording of "You are the Flower" is the demo recording.

"I thought that was such a great representation of our band that I played the cassette of that a hundred thousand times," Paich says. "Great guitar solo and Bobby sang the shit out of it."

Paich had accumulated an abundance of tunes through the years and while Lukather and Steve P. were certainly becoming great writers, they were only 18 at the time, and Jeff told me back then that they were probably intimidated by Paich's talent because they weren't bringing anything in to share with the band yet. Still, they ended up cutting 35 songs for the first album and having to choose 11.

The first time Hungate really knew Toto was a serious endeavor was when he heard the demos and they asked him to overdub bass. He recalls that's when he figured he was in the band: "I remember Paich said, 'We're gonna get a deal and then we're gonna have villas. We're gonna have a villa in Spain.' A villa? I wasn't sure what that was, but what the fuck! That stuck with me with crystal clarity all these years. Bobby Kimball and I were eight or ten years older than anybody else in the band. I was already married and settled down, so it was little awkward, but at the same time it was something I couldn't not do."

Porcaro told me many times that people questioned him on how he could think about committing to a band which would ultimately cut down on his session work. He always explained that being in a band was so worth it and the sessions worth doing would somehow continue to find their way to him.

"Nobody really took Paich and me seriously," Jeff asserted. "It was, 'You guys are going to give up doing studio work to form a band? You must be crazy. Why do you want to do that? You guys can't be serious and even if you think you are serious, you're going to be jerking us around.' Finally they realized we were serious when the actual deal was being made with the record company."

Jeff said even his father questioned his sanity. Joe had said to him, "People are still starving, waiting around for a phone call to do one record date."

"I remember being at my parents' house and telling my father we were going to do this thing and he couldn't believe it," Jeff continued. "He said, 'Man, you're crazy if you're a studio player and all of a sudden you split out of town for six months. It's so tight that usually somebody else will fill your spot.' So people were saying we were crazy. Everybody knows how hard it is to be a group and we talked about it a lot. We knew we had to take the chance and make a sacrifice and give up a lot of shit and starve. That's the way we had to look at it. Who knew what the album was going to do?"

Jeff thought that it was fun being in a band in high school, and still fun: "It was the same group of guys with that chemistry," he said. "Everybody has been together since we were 10, 11, 12 years old, except for Kimball. That makes it easy. And it's not whether the band has a record deal or is successful or whatever. Because of the innocence of childhood, you always remember the group who played in the garage. How long did you play in a back garage of an alley, man, seven days a week? Forever, man, five years straight and that's the kind of stuff you grooved on. You didn't make any money! Some people get in bands out of our necessity instead of out of love."

For all the members of Toto, it was purely love. Although Hungate remembers quitting once, really early on: "We were trying to figure out how to be a rock 'n' roll band—should we move around a lot on stage? I was into that when I was 17, but I was 28, 29 years old and it seemed a little fucking silly," Hungate says. "I was just trying to play as good as I can. So we did this big showcase at one of these big movie sound stages behind Sunset Sound and invited all these record company people and we had this discussion on how we should look on stage and I thought, 'Fuck, man, this is bullshit.' And it was mostly coming from Jeff and I felt he was bugged with me. So after the last tune, I took my bass and threw it up in the air and it fell down and I left. A real stupid rock 'n' roll exit," Hungate admits. "I called (our managers) Fitzgerald Hartley and told 'em I couldn't do this. We were getting ready to do our CBS show in New Orleans. Somehow I went over and talked to Jeff at his house on Hesby and we had a conversation. It had to do with how uncomfortable I was with that thing and he said it would be okay and let's do this. I remember saying to Jeff that I think we'll really be close friends one day when our personalities become unblocked or some stupid thing like that."

And then early in 1978 they got to perform at the big CBS show in New Orleans for all the record company bigwigs, where they were touted as the next big thing. They hadn't signed yet, so it was a really big deal and everything had to be just right.

"Jeff is really into the staging thing and he's decided the band would look really great in these Japanese looking tops and that's because Jim Keltner was Jeff's hero and Keltner always wore that kind of thing because it was comfortable to play in," Hungate recalls. "Jeff and his seamstress friend designed this silk outfit: loose pants with a tie and these tops like a kimono with sleeves that hung down below your arms, really far like two feet below your arms. So we go to New Orleans and we're making our big premier. We haven't signed yet. Everyone's there. Weather Report just got off stage. We get out and we've never put these things on before and we get on stage. We hadn't allowed for the fact that you can't play guitar, bass or keyboard with two feet of material hanging off the sleeves. It was a fiasco."

Despite the fiasco, they were signed and commenced to record their first album at Studio 55. **PAUL JAMIESON**, Jeff's drum tech and dear friend, says Jeff used his Gretsch drums. Jamo (as he is often called) and Jeff met in 1975 via an introduction through their then-girlfriends. The first session to which he accompanied Jeff was with Eric Carmen at Sound City with Gus Dungeon engineering. Jeff was also working on the *Silk Degrees* album at the time.

"Then he got me on with Boz as his tech," Paul recalls. "R&R was his cartage company and they would deliver and set up, and I would come in and change the heads and tune the drums. Jeff would come in and he would re-tweak the drums. I don't want to say I did all his tuning because that wouldn't be accurate. I got 'em in the ballpark. I got them so he could come in and sit down and play, though. And he was never late. He was always early."

As a sidebar, Jamieson shares a story that Jeff relayed to him during the Boz Scaggs days that he's never forgotten: Jeff was walking through JFK airport with Steely Dan on their way to their European tour when he ran into drummer Andy Newmark. "Fagen introduced Jeff to Andy. Jeff, of course, knew who he was, and he told me he was carrying his cymbal bag and his stick bag. He asked, 'Where you going?' And Newmark said, 'I'm going to England to do George Harrison's album,' and Jeff said right then and there to himself, 'That's me.' Everybody's got their moment of clarity. And that was his."

In the *BAM* interview, Paich explained the concept for the first Toto album: "We wanted to stretch out in a way that bands from England like Yes and ELO were stretching out and American bands weren't. But we didn't want to spend ten years doing that just to prove we were hip and then finally get a hit record. We thought we'd reverse that process and start out with getting a hit record, let everyone know who we were and then turn around and lay what we really felt was our 'hip' stuff, on them. The first album was also what we really felt, but it was really aimed to get a hit single off of it."

Mission accomplished. Toto's inaugural self-titled album was released on October 15, 1978 and its first single, "Hold the Line" reached No. 5 on the *Billboard* top 100. Explaining what he did on that song, Jeff said, "'Hold The Line,' was me trying to play like Sly Stone's original drummer Greg Errico, who played on 'Hot Fun in the Summertime.' The hi-hat is doing triplets, the snare drum is playing 2 and 4 backbeats, and the bass drum is on 1 and the 'and' of 2. That eighth note on the second beat on the bass drum is an eighth-note triplet feel, pushed. That's basically the groove. When we did the tune, I said, 'Gee, this is going to be a heavy four on the floor rocker, but we want a Sly groove.' That was David's writing, the triplet groove of the tune. It was taking the Sly groove and meshing it with a harder rock caveman approach."

Recalling the early days, Lukather says, "Jeff and Paich were definitely calling the shots as it was their baby. We benefitted from their gracious gift of making this a 100% equal split band and even in the production of it all, which we did all help, but the first couple of records some of us were kids, still teenagers, 19 years old. Jeff and Dave had more experience. Jeff was always the spiritual guru and tastemaker of the band in my opinion. A nod from Jeff meant I was doing the right thing."

"Georgy Porgy" was also released as a single, but did not fare as well. It only reached No.48 on the charts, but for Porcaro fans, the groove was deep and admired. Lukather says Paich came in with "Georgy Porgy" completely finished, even with that middle break in the song and he says, "Never seen someone so prolific on that first album. Coming off *Silk Degrees*, Paich was on fire!"

Paich played "Georgy Porgy" down on the piano, someone wrote out a chord chart and they just started jamming the groove. Jeff, Paich, Hungate and Luke cut live and captured a moment, according to Lukather.

About his part, Jeff told me back then: "'Georgy Porgy' is me imitating all the Maurice and Freddie White stuff (from Earth, Wind & Fire). It's imitating Paul Humphrey heavily; it's imitating Earl Palmer very heavily. When it comes to that groove, my biggest influences were Paul Humphrey, Ed Greene, Earl Palmer and the godfather of that sixteenth-note groove, James Gadson. That 'Georgy Porgy' groove I owe to them. It's the groove on 'Lowdown,' just a different lift of it maybe, a different tempo. I stole all those grooves from those guys, but I may lay the beat just a little bit different, depending on the song."

"I'll Supply the Love" was the other single, which peaked at 45 on the charts. At Toto's first big show at the Roxy in Los Angeles on February 8, 1979, the song featured a memorable moment for the audience that included Jeff's childhood friend Kerry Morris. In the villainous sounding instrumental interlude of the song, Morris came out onto the Roxy's balcony in a costume that had been Porcaro's. Jeff wanted Kerry to be a part of the big night somehow and the band agreed he should. From the audience standpoint, the costume resembled a giant chicken, but Kerry says it was an "ugly, warty bird."

"It was Jeff's Halloween costume from the year before," Kerry explains. "It was a big, kind of a dinosaur bird thing, with big ol' warts and stuff all over it, like Scred, the Muppet Lily Tomlin sang to. I put it on and did that little thing. It was supposed to be scary, but afterwards everyone asked, 'Were you the chicken?'"

Percussionist **LENNY CASTRO** was on stage with them that night, too. He had been some part of the demos and tracking for the first record as well. Castro first met Jeff in 1977 while cutting Diana Ross' *Baby It's Me* album at producer Richard Perry's newly opened Studio 55. Castro says Lukather was on the session as well. Back in those days, Castro says he often cut percussion live with the other instruments.

"I remember Jeff came in and as soon as we looked at each other, I knew him," Castro recalls. "There was such large familiarity when we first looked at each other. It was, 'Fuck, I know you. I've never met you, but we know each other.' When the session was over and we were packing up, he came over to me and Luke and he said, 'Hey, you guys want a gig?' Of course we said, 'Yeah, what's going on?' And he said, 'Boz Scaggs is looking for a guitar player and percussionist.' To tell you the truth, I didn't even know who Boz was at the time."

Porcaro told them what rehearsal studio to go to and when Lukather and he showed up at the appointed time, they all played with Scaggs. Castro says Scaggs said, "Great," and split, and Castro and Lukather were left looking at Jeff like, "Huh?"

"We thought it was an audition,'" Castro says. "Well, it was not an audition, because when we said, 'Jeff, what's going on, did we get the gig? Boz just left,' Jeff looked at us and laughed and said, 'You had the gig before you even got here.' As far as Boz was concerned, he got the word from Jeff and he took it. And that's basically how Jeff was with people. If Jeff said something, it was Bible. I'd be on a session with him and we'd go and listen to the playback—Jeff hated to do more than two or three takes. He just said it was a waste of time, that you pass it after you do the first one, the second one maybe, the third one, eh, after that it's all premeditated. He was not into that. We'd be in playback and he'd say, 'The drums sound great, percussion sounds good, everybody overdub, come on Lenny, we're going to go to the bar.' We'd leave the studio and the producer would go, 'Yeah, you're right. Drums and percussion are right there. Replace the bass, replace the keyboards, replace the guitar...' He had a natural sense of composition. He knew where to put licks, fills; he knew where to, on a chorus, just lean forward tempo-wise into it, things that people don't really notice on a track. He would create the excitement without people really knowing it. He led the band usually."

The Boz Scaggs tour was not long after the "audition" and some rehearsals. Castro laughs when he recalls that road trip, as it was Lukather's first tour and he says, 'The hang was pretty severe in those days because we were young and dumb and full of ..."

Castro says there were many nights of carousing: clubbing and drinking—and having fun.

"Jeff had done so much traveling that he wasn't really into doing the touristy stuff," Castro explains. "But he was always interested in younger musicians, especially in different countries. Whenever somebody would approach, he always found the time to sit down to give advice and help out those younger cats. It was a big thing for him to pass on his knowledge. He was really, really great that way."

With hours and hours of bus rides, what did he and Jeff talk about? "Girls, life, money, cars. He was heavy into Civil War history," Castro says.

"When we went to New Orleans, the first thing he wanted to do was go to the antique shops and go looking for Civil War stuff. He loved to talk about that whole era." (Author's note: "Unknown Soldier (for Jeffrey)" on *Toto XIV* was written by Paich and Luke because of Jeff's passion for the Civil War, Paich told me. Paich says he spent a lot of time researching the Civil War to write the lyrics so he could honor his friend's love of the period.)

Was there ever any friction between Porcaro and Castro? "We always got along. If anything, there was friction from me. I was always jealous about how many girls he could pick up," Lenny says with a laugh. "He could walk into a bar, look at a chick and the chick was gone. He had that suave kind of thing. He reeked of cool. The way he walked, the way he held his cigarette, the way he talked, he reeked of cool."

If Lenny ever felt bad that he wasn't an official member of the band, Jeff set him straight on that one day: "I got the gig with Stevie Wonder and I started working with him and I came back home. I was excited and went to Jeff's house and I was raving, 'Man, I just went on tour with Stevie Wonder,' and blah, blah, blah, and he just kind of sat there and looked at me," Castro recalls. "And then after I stopped raving, I said, 'Jeff, what's up?' He said, 'Well, fuck you.' And I said, 'What does that mean?' He said, 'I can't do what you do. If I want to go play with somebody, or do another tour, I have to go through record company assholes, managerial assholes, promoters, this and that. Thank your lucky stars you're not signed with us.' That had been a thing with me in the beginning. I had wondered why they hadn't asked me to sign, but when Jeff told me this, it made sense. He said, 'If anything bad happens, it happens to you. And you aren't able to fly around and do what you're doing.' After that, he wanted to know all the details about the Stevie tour."

That first album bore the cover art of the sword, Jeff's idea, a theme carried into many subsequent albums. Porcaro explained to me that it came from the song "Manuela Run": "It's from the opening lyrics, 'Don't look now, you'd better watch that sword that's hanging over you,'" he said.

Although the public seemed to accept this new band, for some reason reviewers focused more on the fact these phenomenal musicians were session guys than creating some great new music. And somehow studio musicians bore a negative connotation to some journalists. Some of the live reviews that they got on their first tour infuriated Jeff because some critics equated studio musicians with being rigid.

"If you read those reviews, those are people who thought that the Clash or AC/DC were tremendous because they jumped around. We didn't decide to be in a band because we wanted to be rock stars; we're just musicians who know how to play. So if somebody goes to see a show and they don't like it because we ain't moving around and sticking our tongues out and jumping around, then fuck 'em," Jeff said. "Because those same people get a big kick out of the most untalented, unmusical, out-of-tune, jive tunes, the worst lowlife playing in the world, which is some of our biggest acts today. We're just playing music and most people who write reviews don't have the ears to even hear shit."

He hated the negativity they got continually for being session players and argued: "Every studio musician I know can go on stage and play in front of people. My God, the pressure of playing in front of a bunch of punks is nothing like the pressure of a chart with Paul McCartney in front of you and you've got to do something right. What is that? You think the people who write about you and the people in this town are going to make you uptight and nervous compared to what we face in the studio? No way. See, because the people who write this shit don't have the faintest damn idea of what they're writing about when it comes to the studio thing. Not everyone can work in the studio," he continued. "It's a very hard job. There's a lot of pressure and it varies. It depends on where you set your sights, just like anybody in any field and what kind of project you want to tackle, whatever your aspirations are. For me to be able to walk into the studio with Fagen and Becker and for them to be satisfied with just one track out of ten I may do with them, is a great accomplishment, if you know Fagen and Becker and their music. It's a great accomplishment to be able to satisfy an artist by doing one take and not spending a lot of money."

And whether the critics realized it or not, the guys in Toto were working in the studios on some of the hippest, most iconic projects. In August 1979 Jeff got the call to work on one track on Pink Floyd's *The Wall*. At 5:32 minutes, "Mother" is the second longest track on the double disc. Guitarist/vocalist **DAVID GILMOUR** remembers how Porcaro ended up playing with them.

"We moved from a studio in France to L.A. to finish up the recording of *The Wall*. We had had two or three attempts at it, but we hadn't yet found a solution to how to deal with its unusual time signatures," Gilmour says. "I suggested that we get a drummer in to give it a whirl. Someone, probably (producer) Bob Ezrin, suggested Jeff. We met when he came into Producers'

Workshop Studios for the session," Gilmour continues. "He listened to the track, said, 'Yes, no problem,' lit up a big Hawaiian bud, sat at his kit and knocked it off very quickly. He had immediately seen the what-now-seems-obvious solution. I enjoyed the session enormously and thought him the best drummer I had ever played with," Gilmour states.

In 1979, Jeff was so busy that the recording of **PETER FRAMPTON'S** *Breaking All the Rules* had to completely adhere to Porcaro's schedule, and therefore was recorded mostly in the middle of the night. Frampton initially had a core group of musicians scheduled to record on the A&M soundstage using their remote truck for a live sound. He and producer David Kershenbaum decided to add Steve Lukather, and when the drummer didn't work out, Luke suggested they call Jeff. But as Frampton remembers with a laugh: "He was working around the clock, doing 10-2, 2-6 and 6-10, so when I spoke to Jeff, he said, 'I can start at midnight,' so we started the sessions of the living dead. We went from midnight 'til 8 in the morning. We got so much done during that first session that of course we asked him to come back to do the whole album and he was booked of course, so it was like, 'Well, I can do 3 a.m. on Tuesday.' The whole album was made like that. It was always light when we left the studio. And then he would leave us and go to his morning session. It was wild times at A&M Studios."

Frampton first met Jeff and all the guys in Toto in 1978, when Toto opened for him for one night in Hawaii. It was actually their very first show as Toto, and Frampton says they hit it out of the park. Even though Frampton had already been on tour for a couple of years supporting his number one album *Frampton Comes Alive*, which spawned the hits "Baby, I Love Your Way" and "Show Me the Way," as he watched the band from the wings, it scared him to death. He laughs as he says there was no way he wanted to follow them on stage that night.

But Frampton was thrilled when Kershenbaum suggested the two Toto members join him in the studio two years later. The legendary guitarist describes all the Porcaros as "down-to-earth, regular, modest players, as brilliant as they are. And that's what attracts me to people. They have an ego but it doesn't speak," Frampton says, adding that Jeff was always smiling in the studio. "Even if I played a track on piano and my chops weren't that great, but I had written it on piano and it was just he and I tracking it (because it was something I had just written), and I kept on making mistakes and we did a lot of takes, he would never say a word, and each take was just as good as the one before. I just remember him being so into the music.

That's what it was all about for him. It wasn't like he was a session guy. He didn't play like a session guy; he played like a band member and he was a musical chameleon."

One of the earliest times Porcaro shared his feelings with me about playing sessions was full of passion and very memorable: "When I was really into the studio stuff—before Toto started happening—one morning I would do Archies cartoons and in the afternoon I'd do a Helen Reddy album and that night I'd do a Tommy Bolin album," Jeff told me. "So there are those three spectrums. What's great about studio stuff is that you can walk in and do, say, a Streisand date where maybe I'd use a different drum set because there are live strings and it's all done live. At night with Bolin, maybe there would be a headband and deerskin boots and a completely different attitude and approach, which I always thought was like an acting gig. It's fun to change attitudes because your environment is always changing. It's like getting yourself psyched up; you're still the same person, but if I'm playing with Dolly Parton, I'm going to have a completely different attitude in my energy and in my playing than if I'm doing an R&B thing or something else. That's not something you can learn, but you can get a collection together of records of different styles that you can force yourself to learn, and if you sincerely enjoy any kind of music, you know what that attitude is. But say it's your first gig; you're starting out and nobody knows who the hell you are. A contractor or producer hires you for that artist and he's your boss. If you screw up, he doesn't ever hire you again because his gig is on the line, and that's the whole political bullshit about the studio system. Plus, there's the pressure once you're there and you have your first opportunity to play. Number one, you feel you want to be sure you have the kind of energy you want to give them. You want to give them your all and try to impress them, which usually ends up backfiring if you go in with that attitude. Your whole basic thing is just to keep time. I have fun helping with arrangements of tunes or suggesting song structures and knowing songs, instead of, like some guys I meet, no matter what instrument, still to this day, have no idea about a song or tune structure. You should have a real good sense of a tune or the song—verse, chorus, bridge, dynamics and stuff like that. Just keep trying to keep the best time and be as simple as possible. Some of the tracks have been done on the first takes and those are the magical moments," he told me. "I did a Jimmy Webb album not too long ago where almost every track we did was a first take. And there are those times when the rhythm section guys are tuned in really great and it happens."

JIMMY WEBB, songwriter of such iconic songs as "Up, Up and Away,"

"By the Time I Get to Phoenix," "MacArthur Park" and "Wichita Lineman," couldn't believe his eyes as he looked out the window of the control booth at Sunset Sound and realized Toto was his hired band for his 1982 album *Angel Heart*. Mostly, he was blown away that Jeff Porcaro was sitting behind the drums.

"Those guys were young, brilliantly talented, full of imagination and fun," Webb says. "I have a mental picture of Jeff playing the drums. It was on one of the real rockers, a shuffle. It was pretty fast. We played it and he sort of turned into this glorious angel of rhythm because he smiled through every track. On that particular track he had almost a manic grin on his face and they were really in the groove. We had learned the song and we went right through it. The other guys were excellent as well."

Webb says he knew David Paich from the time David was 12 and hanging around session dates of his dad, Marty Paich, from whom Webb says he learned a lot.

"He was a wonderful man," Webb says of David's dad. "Most arrangers guard their secrets, but he laid his out there. I would ask, 'How did you get that sound with the strings?' And he would say, 'Let me show you how I did it.' And he'd write out a few bars. I never dreamed in my wildest thoughts that this David Paich, this very young boy who very quietly observed our sessions, would become the monster piano player he's become."

When it came time to hire musicians for the album, Webb says they discussed if they could get some of the Totos, they would try to get the others.

"They were *the* guys," Webb says. "If we can get David, let's get Steve. Then it was, 'There's no way we can get Jeff.' I think what happened was I got those guys and Jeff called them up and said, 'Hey, how come I'm not getting to play on this album?'"

Webb describes making that album as a "wild ride." The near two-week project, was like Jeff said, nearly all first takes, but they rehearsed the music first.

"Jeff was a force of nature," Webb states. "There are drummers and there are drummers. Some drummers just drum and some drummers lead. They get up on their toes and make a lot of eye contact with everyone in the band and say, 'Come on.' They don't say it out loud, but with their whole attitude and their body language. 'Come on guys, let's do this and get on this M-F.' I used to watch him with my mouth wide open and he would come into the control room laughing and high fiving the other guys."

Webb says there was a lot of joking, silliness and fun, as well as rock 'n' roll philosophy during the breaks, and he recalls sometimes during the down time, Jeff would entertain everyone with "outrageously funny" Steely Dan stories.

Webb pauses. "I don't know how you could pack so much energy and fun into that one small body because when he played the drums, he kicked them; they were loud. Not to, in any way, be derogatory, but he was small. He was beautifully made, but you see these drummers with these big ol' arms like NFL linebackers and he didn't have that, but he got the same noise they got. And he was indefatigable."

Webb recalls a night in 1992 when he was in Barcelona at the Olympics during a dinner with all the Americans. He was sitting with Bette Midler, who was crying and he asked her why: "She said, 'Jeff Porcaro has died,'" Webb recalls. "It hit me like a freight train. I stopped drinking. I got up, I went to a car, I don't know whose car it was, and sat down in the back seat of the car and just wept. I remember Jack Nicholson—believe it or not—because this was atypical behavior for Jack, but he had followed me out there and he leaned out the doorway and took my hand and sort of shook it and when he left, there was a Xanax in my hand. It was one of the most tragic things that has happened to me and I've been in the business for 50 years. It was like sort of a light had gone out of the world—like some wild beautiful thing was suddenly not there anymore."

Aside from Webb's album, as a session player, one of the albums Porcaro placed in his "top five" was Tommy Bolin's *Teaser*, about which Jeff said: "That's kinda the way I played when I was in high school, kinda Jimi Hendrix. In the high school band we played a lot of Hendrix stuff, Faces, that was my acid music. And I loved Tommy Bolin and that kind of group. And a couple of months ago I found the cassette of that record and it blew my mind how funky it sounded and stuff, but I also dug it because it was real raw. I remember him being a solo artist and he's a great guitar player and he's the kind of guy with a great charisma, a great aura about him. It was the kind of thing like a *Band of Gypsys* feel; that's the kind of band I would always have loved to be in where you could use some of your R&B chops and some of your jazz influences, but really I loved playing *Band of Gypsys* music."

Toto's debut album sold over two million copies, despite the attack on their studio credentials and criticism for their debut record being too commercial. Then their 1979 follow-up record, *Hyrdra*, was criticized for not being commercial enough, even though they did end up with the hit "99." (By the way, for all you "Get Smart" geeks who might have thought the song was about Agent 99, the Barbara Feldon character in the original TV series, not so: "That was the funniest thing I ever read," Paich laughs.)

Jeff said they did not go into the studio with the intention of going in a different direction with *Hydra*. "If there was anything conceived about the second album," he explained, "it was the fact that we had done a tour after the first album and realized writing and production-wise that we would have to back off from a lot of things that we would do in the production of an album in order to perform it comfortably, instead of five part harmonies, we'd better stick to three if we're going to play live and go on the road to make those things easier."

He made it clear that their decision to pare things down was for them when he reiterated, "It had nothing to do with the reviews and the actual performance. The actual performance is the playing. None of us are tap dancers or anything like that," he said with a laugh.

Talking about the process, he said, "We go in and start playing. Sometimes there are no tunes written yet and maybe there's a chorus written and we just start playing. Like the tune 'Hydra' was just a big, long jam that we edited and it was fun and we said, 'Cool, we want to do this,' and we did it."

In 1982 **MICHAEL McDONALD** called Porcaro to work on his first solo album post-Doobie Brothers, *If That's What It Takes*. The keyboardist had made quite a mark as a member of the Doobies, writing such hit songs as "Minute by Minute," "Takin' it to the Streets," "It Keeps You Runnin'" and "What a Fool Believes," combined with his unique and immediately recognizable vocals. But even before all those credits, Porcaro recognized all that talent and McDonald is thankful for Jeff's recommendation, which actually jump-started his career.

"Not a day goes by that something doesn't remind me of some memory of Jeff because he figures so heavily in my career, my life and my friendships," McDonald says. He thinks the first time he met Jeff was when he was around 16 at a club called the Brass Rail in the Valley: "We were all playing different sets," McDonald recalls. "I played there with a band called the Blue Rose Band with Terry Furlong (who used to be with the Grass Roots), and Voltage played there. They were with a different girl singer, but they eventually became Rufus with Chaka Khan. Dobie Gray played there with a band. Delaney & Bonnie would play there, back in the days when record companies would give bands like that $60,000 to live on for a couple of years to play live and hone their songs, and that's what we were all doing. And Jeff's band was all high school kids and it was a fusion band as I recall. That was the first time I saw Jeff and I remember noticing him," McDonald says, adding that they didn't talk that night, but he noticed his playing and how he did a lot of cymbal work.

"The next time when I actually met Jeff, we played a casual together for the wrap party for the TV show 'Emergency,'" McDonald remembers. "That night he was talking about doing this album with Steely Dan, which turned out to be *Pretzel Logic*. And I remember at the time thinking, 'How great is this? This guy is so young.' He was maybe 19 at the time, maybe, and he was playing on this album with my favorite band in the world, Steely Dan. I was kind of enamored of them because they had already had *Countdown to Ecstasy* and I was asking him questions about the band. He was talking about the sessions and different people in the band. I was all ears."

They played the gig together, but this time, apparently it was Jeff who noticed McDonald. It was about a year later when McDonald got a call from Porcaro, who said he had had gotten Michael's number from a mutual friend and was calling to tell him Steely Dan was auditioning for a tour that McDonald had heard about that had kept getting cancelled.

"He said, 'I mentioned your name for keyboards and vocals, so if you can get down to Modern Music this evening, it would be great,'" McDonald recalls. "'Maybe you could audition with the band.' I threw my Wurlitzer into my little Pinto and drove down and rehearsed with the band and wound up getting the job."

McDonald says he got the job because he could sing the high parts and he went on the road. That's when he and Jeff became friends.

"I was always impressed with Jeff as a person," Michael asserts. "He was always self-assured and I admired his confidence. He had a genuinely good heart. For a guy who was so self-assured, I always caught him in moments where he was very kind to people. I would see him in moments with his grandparents back east. He always made a point to go see people or old friends. He impressed me that way. When Jeff passed away, there were thousands of people at his funeral and it wasn't because he was a great drummer; it was because he was a great guy."

McDonald says they didn't work the same days on the *Katy Lied* sessions because Jeff cut rhythm tracks and Michael came in to cut the vocals later, "But from time to time we would wind up at Denny Dias' house and just hang out with Donald, Walter, Denny and Denny's wife, listening to stuff," Michael recalls.

One moment Michael says he will always cherish was a Saturday morning, sitting in Jeff's apartment after their time with Steely Dan when McDonald had been with the Doobie Brothers for just a few months.

"He asked me how it was going with the Doobie Brothers," McDonald recounts. "He was doing this other album, *Silk Degrees*. I played him some rough mixes of the *Takin' it to the Streets* record and he was real supportive and he got a kick out of the fact that stuff was so sort of quirky. Then he played me the stuff he was working on, and it was 'Lowdown'; just rough mixes of Boz's stuff. We just sat there and I remember looking back at that many times going, 'Man, neither one of us had any idea what was going to happen next with either one of those projects.' It's just fun to think back on that Saturday morning with nothing much to do but play music for each other. It's a fun memory for me."

When McDonald left the Doobie Brothers and recorded *If That's What It Takes*, Porcaro played three tracks, including the hit single "I Keep Forgettin'."

"On 'I Keep Forgettin' there's a wonderful moment when he drops a stick on the vamp out and there's just one hi-hat beat that's not there and he just reached down and picked up another stick," McDonald says. "You wouldn't notice it; only if you knew it happened. I remember seeing the stick bounce across the floor, but he already had another stick in his hand and he was playing. We all liked that take. He was great to work with in the studio," McDonald adds. "All the way to the last few months when I saw Jeff and he worked with me on the *Take it to Heart* album."

McDonald describes how Jeff was so much fun in the studio: "He just always had this special tape of something he had in his bag that he wanted to play for you," McDonald says, "like tapes of great things like Beatles' outtakes or like the demo of 'Fool on the Hill' that McCartney made before he had lyrics. Something I loved about him is you'd go in in the morning with an idea of what you wanted to do and what you'd wind up with was something you had no idea you were going to do that morning, which I love," McDonald adds. "More times than not, those were the kind of days I would have with Jeff on sessions. And by the end of the day, if he didn't have a session, he'd still be hanging out. And on one particular day, we were on to another song and he had already done his part. He was just hanging out and he said, 'I think something would be good on this song,' and it was this gigantic African log that Emil Richards had. We ended up using some of Emil's rare instruments on the track. I think it was a track called 'You Show Me,' which was a Brazilian ballady song."

Porcaro had been done with his work by noon, and yet waited for Richards' instruments to arrive at A&M at 5:00, McDonald says.

"The whole idea of a shuffle and the typical rock 'n' roll drum pattern became different in his hands and became more sophisticated and groovy," McDonald says. "A hundred drummers could have played the same thing, but not that way."

Porcaro continued to do sessions even though he was fully committed to Toto. When they were working on a band project, he told me they would mostly work five days a week, in the evenings from about 7 p.m. on, explaining, "As long as I don't stay up too late, I can work during the day and do a session in the afternoon, and on the weekends."

Jeff asserted that recording in the band always felt freer than the session work.

"The way we work in the studio (with Toto) and record our instruments and arrange our tunes and produce our tunes is *for ourselves*," he emphasized. "As a sideman, you're there to satisfy the needs of the producer and artist you're working for. Which is fun for me. I mean, sometimes that's a relief from being in the group, you know?"

He said he had always heard if you split to tour, there would ultimately be a guy behind you to take away your session work: "So you're always risking the chance, when you come home, the people who call you won't call you anymore."

Mostly, he said he found that to be true when there were contractors involved, but not so much with the artists or producers. But Jeff was never too worried about his place in the food chain. He even recommended other drummers for gigs, and one drummer he particularly touted on the scene in the late '70s and early '80s was an amazing new drummer in town named **VINNIE COLAIUTA**.

While Colaiuta isn't quite sure how Porcaro came to know of him, Vinnie recalls his first meeting with Jeff when he happened to be a guest at a Tom Scott session around 1979 where Jeff was the drummer. That same year, Colaiuta had been the buzz around the drumming community as a relatively unknown nabbing an audition with Frank Zappa and recording Zappa's monumental *Joe's Garage*. After a take, Porcaro emerged from the drums and Colaiuta's bassist buddy Neil Stubenhaus introduced the two of them. Jeff remarked that he was a little tired and not quite "on it."

"The groove was just nuts," Colaiuta recalls. "It was sort of like a samba, kind of funk groove that Jeff just killed all the time. It just felt so amazing to hear it. It was like magic to me to hear it. There was so much heart and truth in it and when he said that, I thought, 'If this is tired, I'm not sure what it's like when you're not tired.' I think that just reflected his humility. I don't think I've ever met anyone as truly open-hearted and giving as Jeff. Both Jeff and Gadd were like that with me, but because Jeff and I lived here, Jeff and I knew each other better."

Vinnie says the relationship between the two drummers grew gradually. He can't quite recall the complete genesis, but he says they would attend each other's gigs and before he knew it, Jeff was calling to ask him to sub on a date at the Baked Potato, the local "cool" club. In fact, Colaiuta recalls one time when he was playing a gig at the Baked Potato and Porcaro was in the audience. While immersed in the music during a tune, Vinnie's eyes were closed and when he opened them, he saw Jeff beneath him. His hi-hat stand had broken during the song.

"The drums stood in the corner of the club and there was this little partition that went up waist high and then tables where he was sitting," Vinnie describes. "When I looked down where my hi-hat pedal was, I saw that somehow he had jumped across the partition and he was on the floor looking up at me, fixing my hi-hat. I just looked at him going, 'What are you doing?' And he just started cracking up and I started cracking up."

They got to know each other, exchanged numbers and talked on the phone. Recalling one phone call in which Porcaro went on a tirade about his recent trip to Miami, during which he worked with the Bee Gees, Colaiuta laughs: "He went off. He was going, 'Man, they had the click so loud it was deafening. I had to duct tape my headphones to my head just for the click. These guys—you wouldn't believe what they were doing, man: cutting tape and trying to line up all these beats and doing all these takes over and over.' He was complaining about it, really pissed off. They had put him through hell. I was thinking to myself the whole time, 'How is it you could be doing this to him? You've got to be seriously certifiably nuts to hire him and put him through that.' It just goes to show you the loony bins that have been in this business and run the show. Let's face it, whenever Jeff was on a record, it was the best feeling shit ever, so what exactly are you listening for? Are you listening for a groove or are you trying to have a machine do things? Even Jeff said perfect time isn't great feeling time."

Interestingly, Jackson Browne recalled Jeff telling him this same Bee Gees story. Porcaro talked about the experience: "Gadd, Kunkel and I think Bob Glaub went the week I went to Florida at their Middle Ear Studios, Biscayne Bay," Porcaro told everyone in the room at a *Modern Drummer* roundtable interview. "They would have a Urei click going and they wanted to make two-bar loops, so they would play the demo of the tune and they would talk about what they wanted the drum pattern to be in the verse, the chorus and the bridge, and then they would run tape. They had big giant reels of tape like I had never seen before. You'd hear it click for two bars and then you'd play the downbeat bass drum. You'd hear eight beats, hit a downbeat, stop, then Albhy Galuten and Karl Richardson would move the reels of tape by hand over the tape heads, looking at the meters, take a ruler, measure the tape and make marks. This took seven minutes. They'd go to talk-back and say, 'You're three milliseconds behind the downbeat, let's do it again.' So you'd wait for the tape to rewind, you'd hear eight clicks, you'd hit it, there would be seven minutes of measuring and you'd hear, 'Man, it's close, you're one millisecond over; you overcompensated one millisecond.' Each quarter note you would play for a two-bar loop was on one track, you'd play eighth notes on another track and sixteenth notes were on another track. You'd have to do hi-hat sixteenth notes one at a time, two bars with one on each track.

"This is when the Linn first came out and they didn't want to know about any machines; it had to be analog," Porcaro continued. "While this was going on, in the back room was a scientist whose name was Seth. They had these wood carpenter saw horses with clamps on them. Coming from the clamp was a big brass encased motor and it had a brass piece coming out with four Allen screws in it. Inside it, clamped with the Allen screws was a 5A Regal Tip drumstick and in front of that was an 8x12 tom tom on a stand, tilted just perfectly so if you hit middle C on the Fairlight, this arm would hit the drum harder than you could ever hit a drum. But then it would recoil and just when they would try to program it to come down again, they had these series of lights that went from white, yellow, green and red, and when it got to green, they would have to reach over and unplug it because the motors were $750 apiece and they would burn out. They were trying to get this to work, so on a Fairlight they had a bass drum on a stand that had two rods coming from underneath the riser, attached, bolted onto the footboard. One motor brought the pedal down and the other motor lifted it up so it could come back for another beat. They had two arms on the hi-hat and an arm on a floor tom, one on a snare drum and one on a mounted tom and the whole concept was, while Gadd, Kunkel and I were doing our thing, they had this scientist trying to get this robot to do what we were doing so they could have analog sounds and could program something and it would come down right on time. It was too expensive; they failed doing it. It just blew your mind, though, watching these people measure milliseconds, and after two hours you have a break with a headache and you're dizzy, and you go back there and there's this scientist trying to take over your gig."

Colaiuta recalls he and Porcaro had meals together as well, and the relationship grew into a friendship. Jeff was very generous, Vinnie says, and early on at sessions, if artists weren't thrilled with the sound of Colaiuta's drums, Porcaro let him use his. Then Jeff took it further: "One day he called me up and said, 'Hey, I can't make this session down at A&M. Can you fill in for me? My drums are already there. And it was for a Stan Getz record," Colaiuta recalls. "I don't know if it ever got released or the stuff ever got used, but Herb Alpert was there producing and it was just that Jeff would do that. He didn't care. He thought, 'Yeah, Vin could do that. I don't care. I'm just going to recommend him because I like him.' He always stuck up for me. He always defended me."

And that ardent defense occurred when Jeff felt that Vinnie was not treated fairly by guitarist/songwriter/producer **JAY GRAYDON**. Of course each party has a different take on the event, but for Jeff, the story that circulated—sometimes represented as a prank, sometimes humorous and sometimes dark—was definitely payback due to his sense of loyalty to Colaiuta. To Graydon, it was completely out of the blue and unmerited.

Graydon had issues with a young Vinnie Colaiuta's playing on the band Pages' third album (called *Pages*) that he was producing. In his estimation, Colaiuta "hadn't quite gotten it together yet. There were some tracks he played on that were real good, but there were some that weren't making it, so I hired Jeff on it," Graydon says, explaining that as he was in the middle of an overdub solo during the recording one day, he felt a presence to the right of him. "I look over and Jeff is pissing in my gig bag," Graydon recalls. "I put my guitar down, I grab him by the neck and I'm shoving him into the back wall of Sound Labs, screaming at the top of my lungs."

Graydon was furious. He says Porcaro cleaned it up for more than an hour. The story still conjures up negativity in Graydon. According to Paul Jamieson, Porcaro felt that Graydon was trying to ruin Colaiuta's career, which Porcaro was trying to help at the time: "Jeff was a payback kind of guy," Jamo says. "In fact, one of our favorite songs was James Brown's 'The Payback.'"

For Colaiuta, it's all water under the bridge; he's had an unbelievable career since that episode. At the time, though, he says he was thinking that he was part of the band Pages and therefore he was going to do the entire record, so he didn't understand the philosophy of using multiple drummers on the project. The band had rehearsed all the music and was a self-contained unit in Colaiuta's mind: "Later on, as I started doing more sessions, I started to realize how that whole game worked and that sometimes producers cast different musicians. I can look back at it now and laugh at it," Colaiuta says today.

Jeff felt the same way back then, as he stated to Vinnie at the 1990 roundtable: "You were in the band," he said. "Before this album went down, you were rehearsing with that band and the buzz around town was, 'Wait until that album comes out because that shit is progressive and cool. Dig this cat.' Vinnie was already every musician's hero who had heard him. Regardless of how many sessions he had done, everybody already knew about him. You had already seen him on 'Saturday Night Live' with Zappa with a yellow Gretsch set going, 'What the fuck is that shit?'"

After that, according to Graydon, he and Hungate ended up taking a bag of dog poop that Hungate had from his yard and went to the Toto rehearsal room and took Porcaro's drums apart.

"We put all the dried turds in the toms and snare and the wettest one in the hi-hat dish so every time he fanned the hat, he'd smell it, and then we put the bag of what was left behind the bass drum. Jamo got it out of there before the rehearsal started, but Jeff could still smell it," Graydon recalls. "The next day at Cherokee, the drummer was getting the drum sound and the drummer was hearing, 'zzzzzzzz,'and the engineer was going, 'What the hell is happening,' and he goes out and looks at the mic and everything is fine. He goes back in the control room and hears, 'zzzzzz,' so he goes back out there and there are a bunch of flies circling Jeff's drums."

Graydon admits his relationship with Porcaro was never the same again, although he worked with him and hired him, of course, because of his playing. Some of the artists Graydon produced for which he hired Porcaro include Al Jarreau, Manhattan Transfer, Dionne Warwick, Kenny Rogers and El DeBarge.

"He's a great drummer," Graydon states. "There's nobody who has ever played like him. Shannon Forrest comes the closest. Jeff was a fucking outstanding drummer. Why do you think I used him on everything I could and why do you think he played on tons of records? He didn't think he could play a shuffle. The song 'Nothin' You Can Do About It,' on the Airplay album is a shuffle. It's kind of what I call a funka-shuffle and 'Mornin'' (Al Jarreau) is the same groove. It's kind of a pop jazz feel, triplet feel that is in the league of a shuffle. There are a hundred variations of shuffles, and he never thought he was any good at them. I told him he was out of his mind. 'Rosanna' is the same groove."

Graydon recalls that when he walked into a session and saw he would be playing with Jeff, he knew just what the music would feel like: "I know every drummer's groove in town," Graydon asserts. "I know where every drummer puts the pocket. What was special about Jeff's pocket was that he put the snare backbeat just a little late—I'm talking about microseconds late—to be on the backbeat of the time. And then everybody else was supposed to play center time and that's what was supposed to make it feel really cool and it did. One time (keyboardist Greg) Mathieson was playing on the backside and going with Jeff and after the take Jeff said, 'Don't do that, man. You play center time and let me play that,' and I see why Jeff said that and it made sense. So when I saw Jeff (on a session) and I saw Hungate and Ray and Foster or Paich back in the day, I knew by the first, second or third take we're going to get a take that's absolutely—I humbly state—that's absolutely genius. That rhythm section was so amazing."

Jeff's admiration for Colaiuta was special. Through the years Jeff and I talked about how he looked up to Vinnie's facility and Porcaro confided his had limitations. He told me Frank Zappa called him several times to record and he declined, knowing he was not up to the task to sight read Zappa's very complex music.

"It's too hard for me," he admitted. "Once in a while there's a musical idea that my mind says, 'Go, do it.' But I don't have the facilities to do it because with some things you need to sit and woodshed and work out before you can do them," he said, also confiding to me that at times that he played out at places like the Baked Potato, he learned how to adeptly cover mistakes, trying to channel Vinnie, but in reality he was terrified and struggling. "When people say, 'Man, Jeff, go for it. You've got time, you've got groove, you can do things those guys do. Just woodshed, and don't be lazy,' well, I'd rather paint. Plus, I'm close to what those guys feel like as human beings—what they feel like spiritually and artistically—and if I could play like Vinnie, I would not be able to not use those chops. I know people who don't like drummers because they think they're too busy. I know if I had the chops they have how frustrating it would be to do sessions."

SHEP LONSDALE entered the picture around the time of *Hydra*, in 1979. He had come over to America from England in 1973 while working with American bands as a live mixer. After mixing for the Doobie Brothers and then touring with their opening act Charlie on drums, he was hanging out at Leeds Rehearsal Studios one day when some of the Toto crew, about to leave on the *Hydra* tour, said, "Why don't you just get on the bus. We'll find something for you to do."

He went along and handled odds and ends tech work until one show day Paich recognized him from seeing him previously at Sunset Sound when he was mixing some live Doobie Brothers Japan concert tapes. He asked tour manager Chris Littleton about him, realizing he was the same guy and said, "Why isn't he mixing our monitors? Our monitors suck."

The monitor guy relinquished the job to Lonsdale immediately and halfway through the tour, the sound mixer left and Lonsdale took that position. Then, when Jeff decided to build his studio in the early '80s, he enlisted Lonsdale's help. The Villa, which Jeff named it, was to be the exact dimensions of the Sound Factory, one of Hollywood's most popular studios. Paich had a keyboard studio at his place, but Jeff wanted an entire tracking studio where he could also record drums. The Villa was up and running by September 1983.

"That studio worked so well because of the dimensions of the room," Lonsdale explains. "And also the equipment that was in the room. There was an API 24 channel mixing console, Altec 'Big Red' studio monitors, Ampex machines, just the whole thing which worked really, really well for rock. (Producer) Val Garay had made an exact replica in Sherman Oaks called Record One and that's where Toto ended up mixing *Toto IV.*"

Since Lonsdale lived just around the corner from Jeff, he became the engineer at The Villa. Occasionally, Lonsdale says, if someone wanted Jeff to record and he didn't want to go to the session, Jeff would have the tapes dropped over to The Villa and work on the project there. Of course they worked on Toto records there, too. One notable session at The Villa was the Miles Davis overdub on *Fahrenheit*'s "Don't Stop Me Now." Davis had been at The Villa for a couple of weeks looking for material, as he had recorded Steve Porcaro's "Human Nature" prior to that. Miles arrived the morning after Toto had just finished recording the soundtrack for *Dune* at the studio the night before.

"So Jeff said (to Miles), 'Have the studio for two weeks and Shep will engineer it,'" Lonsdale recalls. "Miles came over and I had just finished cleaning up the studio from the night before. I had been up for about 18 hours and he looked at me and said, 'Who are you?' And I said, 'Miles, I'm your engineer.' And he said, 'I don't think so.' I remembered an interview he did where somebody asked him why he always dressed the way he did and he said, 'You should look like what you are.' I looked at myself and looked at him and said, 'Ya know what? Give me ten minutes I'll be right back.' I dashed home, took a shower, put some clean clothes on and came back. He looked at me and said, 'You must be my engineer.'"

For two weeks, it was Lonsdale, Steve P. and Miles Davis going through material and Davis telling stories. Jeff would pop in and say hello now and then. Lonsdale also remembers the time Donald Fagen came over to The Villa for Jeff to make a loop for a track for a follow-up to his solo album *The Nightfly*. Lonsdale says it became very complicated: "We had the drum sound, we were playing the groove and then they wanted to sample all the drum hits from Jeff's kit. So they said if they wanted to enhance something later, they could just digitally lock it up and they would have all the drums individually sampled," Lonsdale explains. "At this time, that wasn't a regular thing. It took a while and it was kind of boring. We allowed it to happen and we played the loop about 16 times and we cut up the tape and made a loop and we had the tape going around the studio, around mic stands and stuff, so we could play all the versions of the groove that they wanted and they could pick which one they wanted to use for their loop, and they narrowed it down to like four out of 12 or 16 loop sections. Honestly, you could have picked any one of them and they all would have worked and they all would have been great. Jeff just nailed it. The groove was just incredible and the feel was just incredible and it got to the point where it was just, 'What the fuck are we listening to?' Jeff just said, 'Hey, I've got something to do. I'm just going to pop out, you just carry on.' I was stuck in there for hours.

"They finally narrowed it down to two versions of the loop, so I cut those two versions out of the big loop and made the smaller loop so they could listen to those two. Then they said, 'Let's go and have dinner.' They went off to have dinner and they wanted to listen to it all over again. Gary Katz said, 'We've listened to these enough. Which one is it?' And the one that they actually picked...they had me stop the tape right after they'd listen to it and said, 'That's the one, just stop it right there.' So I stopped the tape and that's when they said they were going to dinner. I released the tape from the head so it wasn't just sitting on the head while they were having dinner and they came back and wanted to hear it and I said, 'Ok, let me...' and they said, 'No, we want to hear it now,' and I said, 'OK,' so I engaged the tape machine and hit play and they go, 'That's the one.' Actually, it was the one after the one they had picked, after all of that. And I'm talking hours! But they could have chosen any of them because they were all so good. And Jeff felt the same way. And when he came back in, I said, 'You won't believe what happened.' And he said, 'I believe it. I've done Steely Dan records.'"

Toto's third album, 1981's *Turn Back*, didn't even do as well as its predecessor, but Porcaro had an interesting perspective: "In Japan, our third album was number one, so there's a group of people who thought it was great shit, and they thought the second album was 'genius shit.' Our first album, which people in this country thought was great, those people didn't make much out of, so it's a matter of opinion."

Paul Jamieson and Jeff on their way to the Grammy Awards, 1983.
(Photo courtesy of Paul Jamieson)

TOTO IV

In 1982, Toto was under the gun. Columbia had made it clear as they went into the studio that this would be the last effort for them if it didn't fare well, so the pressure was on. Engineer great **AL SCHMITT** was brought on board. He had already worked with the likes of Jackson Browne, Linda Ronstadt, Barbra Streisand, Al Jarreau, George Benson and Steely Dan, and he says he had worked on a dozen or so studio projects with Porcaro by the time he was asked to work with Toto.

"There was a period where almost every day I showed up and there was Jeff," Schmitt recalls. "We got along really well and I liked Jeff, I loved the family, I liked Joe."

Schmitt says he believes they had another engineer lined up to work on the album, but it didn't work out, so Jeff suggested him. And he's so glad he did. Schmitt says "Rosanna" blew his mind the minute he heard it.

"I thought we were going to win a Grammy," he says. "A friend of mine had always wanted to go to the Grammys and he had said, 'Next time you are going to be up for a Grammy, give me a call, would you? I'll get tickets and we'll go.' After I heard those songs 'Rosanna' and 'Africa,' I called him and said, 'Go buy your tickets for the Grammys, we're going to win one.'"

They didn't just win one. The album and the team won six! At the 1983 Grammys, *Toto IV* was named Album of the Year. "Rosanna" won for Record of the Year and Best Vocal Arrangement. Toto themselves were voted

Producers of the Year. David Paich, Jeff Porcaro and Jerry Hey won for Best Instrumental Arrangement, Accompanying Vocals for "Rosanna." The record even won Best Engineered Recording, and Schmitt was one of the engineers who received a Grammy for the wonderful sound.

Schmitt says the band loved the sounds he got. As soon as he played back "Rosanna" for them, they were thrilled. A fast worker, Schmitt was getting his sounds as the band ran the song down. By the time they had done one take, he had his sounds down. Paich said to Porcaro, "Hey Jeff, when is Al going to get some sounds?" Hearing this on the talkback, Schmitt said, "I got sounds. Come on in and listen." They went in and he played them that take and they looked at one another and said, "Whoa!" They went back into the studio, played one more and the very next take was "Rosanna."

Lukather says Paich wrote "Rosanna," but explains that Porcaro influenced how the song came out: "Dave came in with 'Rosanna' on piano and said to Jeff, 'I'm hearing a Bo Diddley groove and Jeff said, 'No, I don't. Dig this,' and started what you now know as the recorded version," Lukather recalls. "We had all been listening to (Steely Dan) 'Babylon Sisters' and (Led Zeppelin) 'Fool in the Rain' and Jeff's permutation of those grooves... well, Jeff made it his own and that changed the song's history and also made it feel like it does. It has one of the most famous drum intros of all time in popular music. You hear that and you know what it is! Not many can do that!"

Jeff explained it this way: "When I first heard David Paich play the tune, the Bo Diddley groove was very obvious. Because the tune was a shuffle feel, I felt that the half-time shuffle thing would feel the best. The tune also reminded me of the New Orleans type second-line drumming. So the first listening of the tune brought forth all the old haunts from drummers to groups of that era that I had tapped from and stored away for this very moment."

Schmitt says each band member was the producer of the song he wrote: "Steve Lukather was in charge when he did 'I Won't Hold You Back,' but they would talk to one other about it," Schmitt explains, adding that Porcaro and Paich were definitely more in charge of the entire project.

Giving me an overview of their general manner of working way back then, Jeff explained: "We went in for ten days and cut tracks. We cut about ten songs and then we took two weeks off and started maybe working on some lyrics or maybe other tunes. Then we'd take some time off, then go back into the studio, cut a couple of more tracks, maybe do some overdubs and if the lyrics were finished on one tune, maybe we'd put on a vocal. On the tune 'Rosanna,' over a course of nine months, the track was cut the first week of the album, the vocals the third month in the album, the horns the fifth month of the album and maybe a couple of percussion things in the sixth month, and in the meantime, we'd work on other tunes. What's nice about that is then you don't get caught up in the same thing. You can step back from it, get away from it, do other stuff and we would do whatever we really felt like doing. There might be a day where it's scheduled to do the vocal, say, on 'Rosanna,' but when we walk in the studio, the equipment is there and we're just sitting down and everybody is getting sounds and we start jamming and it's, 'Forget about the vocals today, dig what groove we're in now and let's cut this tune.' It's just what happens."

"Rosanna" went to No. 2 on the *Billboard* charts and "Africa" was their first No. 1 hit. This album showed everyone what the band could do, despite the fact that critics still panned them for being session musicians—as if that were some sort of liability. It never made sense to Jeff, who would always tell me being able to play in the studio only made him that much better of a musician. How could that be bad? But some critics had it out for them, like *L.A. Times'* music critic Robert Hillburn. In one of their Grammy collection acknowledgments, Paich couldn't help himself and sarcastically thanked Hillburn for "all his support."

The seeds were sown for "Africa" in Jeffrey's mind at age 11, when he visited the African pavilion at the New York World's Fair with his family: "I saw the real thing," he recounted to me. "I don't know what tribe, but there were these drummers playing and my mind was blown. The thing that blew my mind was everybody was playing one part. As a little kid in Connecticut, I would see these Puerto Rican and Cuban cats jamming in the park. It was the first time I witnessed somebody playing one beat and not straying from it, like a religious experience, where it gets loud and everybody goes into a trance. I have always dug those kinds of orchestras, whether it be a band of all drummers. But I just love a bunch of guys saying one thing. That's why I loved marching band, and I said, 'Gee, somebody there's going to be a little drum orchestra where everybody plays one thing and you don't ever stray from it. You do it until you drop. You're banished from the land if you move from that one part.'"

When they were working on "Africa," Jeff set up a bass drum, a snare drum and a hi-hat, and percussionist Lenny Castro set up a conga. Jeff described it to me like this: "We looked at each other and just started playing the basic groove: the bass drum on 1, the '&' of 2 and 3. The backbeat is on 3, so it's a half-time feel, and it's sixteenth notes on the hi-hat. Lenny started playing a conga pattern. We played for five minutes on tape, no click, no nothing. We just played. And I was singing the bass line for 'Africa' in my mind so we had a relative tempo. Lenny and I went into the booth and listened back to the five minutes of that same boring pattern. We picked out the best two bars that we thought were grooving and we marked those two bars on tape. We made another mark four bars before those two bars. Lenny and I went back out. I had a cowbell, Lenny had a shaker. They gave us two new tracks and they gave us the cue when they saw the first mark go by. Lenny and I started playing to get into the groove, so by the time that fifth bar came—which was the first bar of the two bars we marked as the cool bars we liked—we were locked, and we overdubbed shaker and cowbell. So there was bass drum, snare drum, hi-hat, two congas, a cowbell and a shaker. We went back in, cut the tape and made a one-bar tape loop that went 'round and 'round and 'round. The Linn machine was available to us. Maybe it would have taken two minutes to program that in the Linn and it took about half an hour to do this, but a Linn machine doesn't feel like that! So we had an analog groove."

They took that tape, transferred it onto another 24-track for six minutes and Paich and Porcaro went into the studio.

"The song started and I was sitting there with a complete drum set and Paich was playing," Porcaro continued. "When he got to the fill before the chorus, I started playing the chorus and when the verse or the intro came back, I stopped playing. Then we had piano and drums on tape. You have to realize that there are some odd bars in 'Africa,' so when you have a one-bar loop going, all of a sudden sometimes Lenny's figure would turn around. So Lenny went in and played the song again, but this time he changed his pattern a little for the turn-arounds, for the fills, for the bridge, for the solo. We kept his original part and the new one. Then we had to do bongos, jingle sticks and big shakers doing quarter notes, maybe stacking two tracks of sleigh bells, two tracks of big jingle sticks and two tracks of tambourines all down to one track. I was trying to get the sounds I would hear Milt Holland or Emil Richards have, or the sounds I would hear in a *National Geographic* special, or the ones I heard at the New York World's Fair."

Jeff's dad played bass marimba and gong on the song, a session which

Jeff produced. Joe says Jeff was pretty tough on him: "After 60 seconds or so, Jeff would stop and say, 'Dad, hold back, you're rushing.' Can you imagine? He's telling his father to lay back," Joe recalls of the experience. "He put me through the grind. I had to be right on.'"

"Good for You" was touted as one of the strongest tracks on the album, but Jeff dismissed it as just a "rock 'n' roll thing." When I asked about the drum fill in the middle of the song, he called it a "weird-feeling fill—that's all it is," he said. "The reason it's a weird-feeling fill is because it was one of those spontaneous things; what you hear on the record is the first time I ever played that fill."

Describing the atmosphere in the studio, Schmitt says: "There was a lot of joking going on, but also a lot of focus on what they were doing," he states, adding that they were extremely dedicated because they were acutely aware that this was the last album on their contract.

On the personal side of things, Schmitt reveals that he was a single dad of 8- and 11-year-old boys during the recording of *Toto IV* and recalls Porcaro's kindness: "Jeff got both Nick and Chris drum kits. And he would take my 11-year-old, who was staying with me at the time, to his house and play video games with him. My kids just adored him."

Schmitt says he loved being around Jeff, too, when they would cut other artists and Jeff would get there early to set up his drums.

"We'd chat for a minute and get some sounds on him and he was just so warm and friendly all the time," Schmitt says. "He made you feel you were important. He always had a great smile and he always rolled great joints."'

Porcaro named Schmitt as one of his very favorite engineers in an interview we did: "Al Schmitt recorded all the rhythm stuff for *Toto IV* and not once for that or for any other album, the latest thing being a Ruben Blades album which is five years after *Toto IV*, did I hear him say, 'Show up an hour early for the session, can I hear the bass drum? Can I hear the snare drum? I gotta set my gates. Can I hear the tom toms?'" Porcaro told me. "Al is the kind of engineer—and I remember Roy Halee, who I worked with on a Paul Simon record in New York, was the same way—who listens to musicians play and as you're running down, he's hearing how you play. It cracks me up how most engineers never go out in that room to hear what your instruments sound like. They just stay in that control room—'Snare drum don't sound good, man. Let me gate this and do this and get a Wendell Jr. so it can trigger it.'

"Al Schmitt and Roy Halee and George Massenburg will walk out in a room and listen to the sounds," Jeff continued. "What if I'm using a piccolo-high pitched snare drum and I'm in a big open room? They walk around and they may move some overhead parabolic reflectors, they may move some baffles that are far away, they may move some mics to get a tighter sound, but they listen and they sit around the rest of the musicians and they sit near you, in front of you and behind and on the sides and they get your sound. Hopefully you have an understanding with the producer, arranger or artist of what that sound is and supposed to be. This is a rock 'n' roll track, rock 'n' roll sound, it sounds great in the room, reproduce it for me. The technology is there for you, do it. That's the way it should be, but of course you run into others who say, 'Muffle your toms, there's sympathetic ringing,' and you just came from a studio where your drums were happening."

NIKO BOLAS was also someone Jeffrey loved as an engineer and a person. Bolas came to work on the Toto records through engineer Greg Ladanyi. As the assistant and then house engineer at Record One, Ladanyi had Bolas work with him on Toto. Once Bolas got to know the guys, he would work with them in concert with Ladanyi and independently.

"Because there was such an incredible amount of work to do on the *Toto IV* record, everyone had his own studio and everyone had their own slave reels," Bolas says. "They would go off and do their overdubs and they'd come back and my job was to sub-mix everything they did to a couple of stereo pairs so we were able to get a handle on everything."

Niko says he always saw Jeff as the creative force behind Toto, explaining: "He wasn't just the drummer, he was the helmsman. He was kind of captain of the ship. You'd get three or four crazy ideas bouncing off the wall—all of them brilliant—and there was this voice of reason that would slow everybody down and take things one at a time."

Lukather agrees: "Jeff could persuade us to do about anything or when *the* take was done," he says. "Sometimes he would say, 'That's *my* take; you guys go fix your parts' and he was right and we would do that," Lukather says with a laugh. "There were some things he missed. Byron comes to mind," Lukather recalls, referring to Jean-Michel Byron, the fourth lead singer they hired after the recording of *The Seventh One*. "Jeff really had to talk us into that and then in the end realized, 'uh oh…' after the fact, like we all did. No one is 100%."

"Jeff is the guy who taught me the adage 'It takes less time to play it than talk about it.'" Bolas says, then explaining that the crux of a song is the drums and melody: "The thing about all of the Toto tunes is the groove," Bolas says. "You can replace, take away, try different ideas, but you can't get rid of the groove, and that's all Jeff. 'Africa' was written based on that groove and then Jeff's thoughts and imaginations about Africa. The music, in general, with records—the melody and the groove are primary, and all the other music is secondary in that it's there for us to appreciate and enjoy, but the ultimate litmus test of anything and where you will always find Jeff at the top ten, is where you're walking down the produce aisle in the grocery store. Whatever you're hearing, I guarantee you you're only really hearing the groove and the melody. Jeff was the consummate leader in that," Bolas states, adding that Jeff didn't just groove in the studio, but he grooved during playback. "Jeff was the first guy to dance in the back of the control room. He made it alright to groove."

Groove. That is probably the most-used word in this entire book. It's certainly the most uttered by everyone to describe what Porcaro brings to the music. I wrote this in 1988, and it still holds up: "I'm driving in my car, thinking about what I'm going to write about Jeff Porcaro. The volume of the radio is nearly off while my mind is preoccupied, but suddenly I am prompted to turn the music up. What I've heard, almost subliminally, is a groove that feels so good—I laugh when I realize it's Boz Scaggs' 'Lowdown,' and the subject of my preoccupation is playing drums. I know that I heard that drum track from an almost inaudible radio because I couldn't *not* hear it. The song ends and I change the station. The next song that blares from my speakers is 'Pamela' from the newest Toto album, *The Seventh One*. It's that feel again, and it becomes obvious that that's what I want to convey about Jeff Porcaro. Hours later, I'm sitting in a restaurant. In the midst of a conversation with a friend, something I can barely hear in the background catches my attention. It's 'Georgy Porgy' from Toto's first album, and I wonder why I haven't noticed any other music that's been played in the restaurant all night. Maybe it has to do with the fact that no one plays a groove like Jeff. If you've ever seen him play live, you know it's him because he commits his body and soul to the feel of the music."

David Hungate left the band before they went on tour to support *Toto*

IV and Mike Porcaro took over on bass. At the time, Jeff said it was the obvious choice. He had worked with his brother a lot in the past. Plus, Mike was in the original high school band and then played with them in the live Boz Scaggs band.

Around the time of the release of *Toto IV,* Jeff, Paich and Lukather were called to work on the Michael Jackson/Paul McCartney duet "The Girl is Mine." The session took place at Westlake Studios with Paul and Linda McCartney, Michael Jackson with Emmanuel Lewis in tow, George Martin, engineer Geoff Emerick and producers Quincy Jones and Bruce Swedien. The band also consisted of David Foster and Louis Johnson. Paich says it was "unbelievable" and when the call came in it was definitely a "pinch me moment." While they were in the studio, Paich recalls someone began to play Stevie Wonder's "I Was Made to Love Her" while testing the mic and McCartney started singing it. Paich says Paul was singing it great, but sounded like Paul. And then Jackson stepped up to the mic and killed it, dancing and spinning around. In between takes of "The Girl is Mine," Paich says he hit a low chord like the last chord in "A Day in the Life" and Paul leaned into the mic and said: "You guys remind me of the lads who used to travel in a van in the early days."

Paich remembers that Linda McCartney was shooting photos right over his shoulder and describes her as "very cool," adding: "Linda razzed Jeff one time when he rolled a joint," Paich remembers. "She took it from him and told him what a terrible joint roller he was. There's a difference between how English people and American people roll joints. English people put tobacco in their joints."

After that song, Jeff worked on Michael Jackson's "Beat It," from the upcoming album *Thriller*. Recording engineer **HUMBERTO GATICA** worked on that track and recalls that he received a drum track programmed by Michael Boddicker, and Jeff came into Sunset Sound Studio 2, where they were alone together working to replace the programmed track.

"All the *Thriller* material was cut with a machine to design the concept and the beat and direction, but we all thought we needed to have a real, steady best drummer to play the groove for Michael and give him the live feel," Gatica relays, adding that the part was simple, but Porcaro took it to the next level. Together they designed a better bass drum part and feel. "He made it very, very special and it was a very defined feel that he put on it," Gatica says. "We recorded it different ways to see which way it would appear better in the final mix."

Gatica recalls that Jeff loved the part, and recounts that as Jeff experimented, he said (calling the engineer by the nickname Quincy Jones gave him), "'Hum, check this out.' And we tweaked a little bit the direction and he got a little more comfortable with the instrumentation that was around and what the machine was doing, and I think we got the part in two or three takes. Then we chose together what was best and did a composite of the drum part, and Quincy loved it."

By that time, Gatica says he knew Porcaro very well. He had met Jeff through a friend of his, television composer John D'Andrea, while D'Andrea was working on a project for which he hired Porcaro. Gatica recalls: "Jeff was already working with Steely Dan. In fact, sometimes he would be coming from a session with them and we built a relationship where he loved the way I recorded his drums. He liked my Latino personality and we became very simpatico with one another. Every time I had an opportunity to suggest a drummer, I would suggest him. Then I started to work with David Foster and I met Steve Lukather and all of a sudden I met Paich and David Hungate and Steve Porcaro. I was asked to engineer the album that won all the Grammys, but I could not do it because I was doing an album with David Foster at the time. Jeff was one of the great drummers and nicest people. He was the best. And creative. And he was accurate, and he was fun, and he was friendly; he had an amazing personality," Gatica adds. "I love him, he was sweet, he always had a smile on his face."

During that same year, 1982, Porcaro cut Don Henley's "Dirty Laundry." When asked what he did on the song, Jeff stated simply: "'Dirty Laundry' is just me laying it. It was an electronic track, meaning it was sequenced. That Farfisa organ part is a sequence going down, so I was just bashing. I played 1 on the bass drum, 2 and 4 on the snare. I'm just pounding. It's just a groove."

DANNY "KOOTCH" KORTCHMAR, who co-wrote the song with Henley and played guitar on it, says the song would not have been the same without Porcaro's contribution. Kortchmar asserts that Jeff was the obvious choice. After writing the song on Farfisa organ, Kortchmar had Steve Porcaro come in to tweak it and had Jeff play along with the LinnDrum machine.

"And of course he kicked the crap out of it and added another dimension to it. It was always going to be him because he knew how to blend with everything," Kortchmar declares. "This was the early days of the drum machine. A lot of guys were terrified of it and didn't want anything to do with it. Jeff embraced it. He was not afraid of it because, of course, there was no way a machine could replace Jeff. So he played along with it and kicked the crap out of it."

Jeff later played on "New York Minute," from Henley's 1989 album *The End of the Innocence*. Co-written by Kortchmar, Henley and Jai Winding, this tune contained a lot of fancy stick choreography from Porcaro. Kortchmar says it opens with brushes.

"It's still brushes at A, then the next verse it's one brush and one stick. Then at the chorus it's both sticks," Danny says, describing how Porcaro goes back to brushes after that, back to one brush, one stick, then both sticks through the chorus and bridge. "Then there's a trumpet interlude and the next verse he goes back to brushes," Danny says. "Then he goes back to one brush, one stick and then back to two sticks and ends the tune that way. He dug having that kind of a challenge. If you listen to that track, what he did on it was exquisite."

Kortchmar says he first met Jeff on a session sometime in the early '70s and remembers thinking, "This guy looks familiar," Kortchmar recalls. "Who's this guy?" It hit him that it was the drummer on "The Sonny & Cher Comedy Hour."

"I looked at him and thought, 'That drummer is killin'.' Then I forgot about it for a while and then we did a date and I said, 'Are you the guy,,.?' And I embraced him immediately and I said, 'You're so great.' And he was so young and just the sweetest fellow," Danny recollects. "And I was so glad, thinking, 'Gee, I'm playing with the guy who was kicking so much ass on that show.'"

Describing the Jeff he came to know after playing with him on many projects through the years, Kortchmar says, "Jeff had an attitude. It's not that he thought he was better than anybody else, but he did not suffer bullshit lightly."

Recalling one such incident, Kortchmar relays: "It was Neil Sedaka's comeback," Kortchmar remembers. "Elton John had rediscovered him and it was a gig at the Troubadour—Neil's big return. We rehearsed, we rehearsed and everybody had a book. The day of the big gig, we showed up at the Troubadour for the soundcheck and Neil goes, 'Okay guys, here we go fellows, open up the book...' Jeff goes, 'Huh? Where's the book?' Neil says, 'You don't have the book?' 'No, I don't have the book.' 'Where is it?' There's sweat pouring down Neil's forehead," Kortchmar recounts. "Jeff did not have the book and he was not about to take responsibility for not having the book: 'I don't have the book.' We're all looking at Jeff. He could do this in his sleep. I think he enjoyed fucking with Neil Sedaka. We had to do stuff like that to keep from going crazy. Jeff had a little bit of a sadistic streak," Kortchmar confides, adding another anecdote: "I heard a story where he was working on the Streisand movie *A Star is Born* and there was a break toward the end of a day. Jeff says, 'I gotta go make a phone call,' and he disappears and goes home. They break and Monday morning he comes back and someone asks, 'Jeff where were you?' And he says, 'Ah, I just got off the phone.'" Kortchmar laughs.

Danny also had the opportunity to hire him on projects he produced, like Ivan Neville's *If My Ancestors Could See Me Now*. He points out a song in 6/8 called "Sun": "He thought really hard on it and worked really hard on it," Kortchmar says. "The way he interpreted the drum part on that, he kicked the crap out of it. He's playing along with one of Ivan's loops, a sexy percussion loop, and there are a lot of changes. It was very creative."

Kortchmar claims Jeff didn't like to hang out much after hours.

"Everyone hung out more than him," Danny says. "He would go home earlier than everyone else, even though he had the best weed. My pad at that time was in L.A. overlooking Lake Hollywood and everyone came by my pad and listened to music, wrote music, played songs, and had a great time, but if Jeff came by, he left early. He was always the first to leave. So he was a combination of a full-on hipster—there was no one hipper than Jeff—and Ozzie Nelson. That's how he was brought up. He was a very balanced fellow. He had a wicked sense of humor and an absolute hipster vibe that I miss so much. Just like everybody who knew him. We all think he's about to walk into the room."

Eventually Toto went on a world tour with Mike Porcaro on bass to support the success of *Toto IV*. Lonsdale recalls one incident at the beginning of their first of three nights at the Budokan in Japan when the large sword with the rings that Jeff had designed that was in back of him on stage began to sway back and forth, instead of turn like it was supposed to. Jeff was the artistic director and he was furious. Lonsdale recalls that he was screaming into his snare mic that night. Lonsdale says Jeff lost it, and Lukather says that by the second night at the famous venue in Japan, Jeff's design was history.

In 1983, because of the one track on *The Wall* that Porcaro had cut in '79, when it came time for David Gilmour to cut his second solo album, he hired Jeff to go to Boulogne-Billancourt, France, to record *About Face* at Pathé Marconi Studio.

"When I was thinking of players for my *About Face* album sessions, Jeff was the only drummer I wanted," Gilmour explains. "I put him together, in Paris, with the bass player whose playing and sound I really loved, Pino Palladino. Putting down the backing tracks with these two brilliant players is one of the musical highlights of my life. It's hard to describe the look on the faces of the producers, engineers and techs in the control room while Jeff and Pino were laying tracks down," Gilmour says.

Jeff told me once that the recording of *About Face* was one of his favorite projects: "I loved working on that record," he said. "It was a fun record. I liked the songs and there were grooves on that thing. I also played little percussion parts on it too."

In 1983, Jeff also cut the iconic "I Love L.A." for Randy Newman, who remembers Porcaro as "a great drummer and a great guy."

While people think the song is L.A.'s theme song, it really is meant to be tongue in cheek, Lukather explains: "It's Randy's take on L.A. and how jive it all is," Lukather says with a laugh. "Randy is an old hero of ours and a good guy—total pro—and like all the sessions I got to do with Jeff and the guys, too many to count, we had a blast."

Producer **RUSS TITELMAN** recalls the session at Warner Brother's Amigo Studios as easy and quick "which was sometimes not the case on other tracks we did," he says. The basic tracks were cut live, and of Jeff, Titelman says. "He had such great taste. He was a perfect drummer, but it always had some kind of deep groove and deep feeling. There are a lot of guys who can be real perfect, but it can be real stiff."

They cut the entire *Trouble in Paradise* album and also did the video of "I Love L.A." with Newman. Recalling the session, Lukather says: "I remember Randy playing us the song. He handed out the charts. His were a little more detailed than most record sessions, but plenty of places to add 'our thing' and he sat at the piano and sang it. We loved the song, as we are all from L.A.—well, most of us, anyway. All of us lived here, anyway. Once we heard the hook and that Randy wanted a crowd chant on 'we love it,' we insisted it be us doing it," Lukather continues. "We cut the track pretty quickly and then started doing overdubs and we overdubbed all of us screaming 'we love it.' You can hear Jeff's voice real clear in there—all of us, really. And we were all cracking up."

Memories are a little unclear as to exactly who was in the crowd in the room yelling—which they overdubbed several times to make it sound big—but for sure it was Luke, Paich, Porcaro, Russ Titelman, Lenny Waronker, Lenny Castro and Nathan East. Meeting bassist East for the first time was a special memory from this session, at least for some of them. Lukather says he had never met Nathan before that day, but Nathan says he had worked with Jeff prior to the Newman session. He and I traced it back to the Melissa Manchester session in 1981 for the cut "Slowly" off of her *Hey Ricky* album.

The first time **NATHAN EAST** walked into the studio and saw Jeff at the drums, he thought, "I'd better bring everything I've got today because I'm with my favorite drummer," East recalls. "And it met all my expectations. It was heavenly. Even Jeff's count-off before the song starts is amazing. He just had this groove and he would start clicking his sticks together and it felt so good and before you even got to one, you had a running start. He didn't have to say anything, but if you looked over and you were getting the big smile, you knew you were bringing it."

Reminiscing about *Trouble in Paradise*, East says it was a thrill to work with the Toto guys and describes the sessions: "Randy Newman would come in, laid back, no high pressure and he'd play the song. It was usually a song or two a day we'd get through," East recalls. "We'd go over to the piano (while he played) and everybody would just make notes and the songs had different tempo changes. One verse would be short and one verse would just be piano and voice. It was really a creative process."

Whenever Nathan would see Jeff in the studio, both he and Jeff would light up "because we knew we wouldn't have to go to work that day," East says. "And with all those guys, because it's fun and you're laughing and joking and it's the biggest mutual admiration society on the planet."

East remembers working early on with Porcaro with such artists as Joe

Cocker at Village Studios, Barbra Streisand and Barry Gibb, and George Benson, "Like 'Lady Love Me (One More Time)' that David Paich wrote for George Benson, that Arif Mardin produced," East recalls. "To this day I hear that record on the radio and I hear the joy and I remember the big smiles we had when we recorded it."

Paich recalls that George Benson session as magical, describing it as a "big, warm blanket. Everybody knew everybody and it was an easy song to play. I think we cut it in one or two takes. Everything was right."

Nathan says Porcaro was always generous with his recommendations and then there was that one time Jeff came up with a crazy idea. There was this new Japanese group that wanted them for their showcase in Japan. It was at a time when money was flowing nicely in the music business and the Japanese were (and are) very enamored with American musicians.

"They called Jeff and they were asking if he could come and if he could bring me," East recounts. "It was in December around Christmastime and Jeff thought, 'Wow, I don't really want to be away from the family. I'm not really feeling like going over to Japan.' It was a two-night showcase, so it was leaving one day, going and doing the showcase for two days and coming back. So it was four days. So Jeff just gave them the biggest price he could think of and he thought he was giving them a price for him and me combined. He said, 'Ok, it will be 30 grand if we go.' And that's what they gave each of us and he couldn't turn it down—and they put us in first class. And I'll never forget, but we were the only two in first class going to Japan, with four flight attendants waiting on us. And we laughed the whole flight home."

East says Jeff wasn't only the best drummer, but the best friend, mentor and coolest human being, stating: "You look up the word 'friend' in the dictionary and there's Jeffrey, and the thing about it is he was that way with every single person. I don't care if you were the roadie or the tech. Those guys got more love than the artist. I'm thankful and grateful that I was blessed to walk this earth at the same time as Jeff. It's like winning the friendship lottery for whatever time we had together."

Speaking of *Hey Ricky* and **MELISSA MANCHESTER**, where Porcaro and East met, the singer-songwriter won the 1983 Grammy for Best Pop Female Vocal Performance for "You Should Hear How She Talks About You" from that album, one of the five tracks on which Jeff played. Manchester assumes producer Arif Mardin was responsible for the selection of musicians, which also included Lukather on two cuts, one of which was "You Should Hear..." Manchester says before Jeff ever played on any of her music, she, of course, had heard of him.

"In those days there were star performers and star musicians and each section of a rhythm section had their top tier player and Porcaro was at the top," Manchester says. "I had the opportunity to play with him and Steve Gadd a number of times and always felt honored. The experience of making records in those days was so organic because you were dealing with live bodies; you weren't dealing with machines," Manchester goes on. "It was really a collaboration; a musical conversation all the time, and because it was spearheaded by Arif Mardin, who was so magnificent, it was really exquisite, really."

Manchester, who gained a reputation as a balladeer, admits she was new to that kind of synth-pop music. The record company and management encouraged her to give it a try, so she says she put her trust in Mardin and the players and decided to "try the adventure." Admittedly, she was not present for the tracking, so she had little interaction with Porcaro, but says they passed each other in the hallway on occasion and she says she could tell how people felt about him.

"I would see him kibitzing with the musicians," she says. "Everybody loved him; everybody knew about him."

Despite the fact that they weren't in the studio together on the project, Manchester feels his musical contribution was invaluable: "He held down the groove so incredibly," Manchester reflects. "The construction of the rhythm section and the construction of the song is so rock solid that even though the production may be a reflection of those early '80s times, it's still a record that I think is going to live on because it is so well produced, so cleanly produced and because you had live musicians and Jeff holding it down, anchoring it. Even though it was a pop song, he brought so much soul to it. You can't diminish or dismiss the fact that a live person was playing the drums and a live person at the top of his game, playing the drums. And he was part of a room full of superb musicians. I have more and more appreciation for those musicians and for those times and those tracks regardless if they were novelty songs or big ballads or pop tunes or dance songs because live people put it together and that means there was an actual conversation. There was a consciousness of a unified purpose."

Jeff (and Luke), along with Paul and Linda McCartney in full Kabuki makeup for the filming of Paul McCartney's *Give My Regards to Broad Street*.

POST-GRAMMYS

In 1983, Jeff was psyched about a new film soundtrack project: *Dune*. In the liner notes for the 1997 extended reissue of the soundtrack, David Paich wrote about bringing a demo of music to his first meeting with director David Lynch in Mexico City. He hoped to procure the project not only for himself and Toto, but also for his father Marty, who orchestrated and conducted for the Vienna Symphony Orchestra (along with Allyn Ferguson). Paich dedicated the 1997 release to his father (who by then was gone) and Jeffrey. Aside from the original work done in Vienna, the music was recorded mostly at Jeff's studio The Villa, while the synthesizers were recorded at Paich's The Manor.

"We did a lot of snares, percussion of every kind, and most of the instruments came from Emil Richards' amazing world percussion collection," Shep Lonsdale remembers. "Bowed bass parts from Mike and all the guitars from Steve, so all in all there was a lot going on, along with work on Toto, which never really stopped no matter what. Jeff was heavily involved with most of what was going on, up until it got crazy. When it got to calls about what kind of guitar sound David Lynch was after, like a flag on fire in a hurricane on a distant moon, he would often go into the house. It ended up being a great sound, even if it did take some time. One thing that Jeff did throughout the time I worked with him was to leave artistic comments 'drawn' on how he felt about what was going on around him. At the end of the sessions, on all projects, I would find these caricatures on track sheets, pages on legal pads, envelopes, napkins and anything else that was lying around. They were amazing and would often be dead on. I never threw them away. At the end of the day, when I was making the slave reels and documenting the day's sessions, I would put the drawings in the bottom mic drawer. He knew I never threw them out, and he knew they were with the drum mics. I often wonder what happened to them."

Jeff must have been particularly prolific with the pen during *Dune*, as the project was wrought with chaos, so much so that Lynch eventually pulled out, and the film received poor reviews. Toto's involvement in *Dune* may also have had an unfortunate effect on their own career, since it prevented them from striking when the iron was hot and recording a follow-up album immediately after they won all those Grammys. The other ill-timed situation was the necessity to change lead singers, as drugs had reportedly taken a toll on Bobby Kimball's voice. Between not touring after the mega hit of *Toto IV*, waiting to record another Toto album and having to change singers, momentum was lost.

Late in 1984 Toto hired Fergie Frederiksen, who had recently worked with the band Louisiana's LeRoux. They recorded *Isolation* at Jeff's studio, The Villa; Paich's The Manor; and at Record One. Instead of incorporating some of the elements that made their preceding album a hit, they went in another direction, and didn't win over radio. At the time, of course, Jeff was extremely pleased they had chosen a more rock-oriented path.

"This is the first Toto album done with Mike and Fergie," Jeff said, at the time of its release in the fall of 1984, not knowing it would also be the last album with Fergie. "Now we have a new bass player that we went on the road with, which is Mike. Mike was the bass player in our high school days. (The song) 'Carmen' is a good example of the kind of feeling stuff—like the old Hendrix *Band of Gypsys* days. That's the kind of feeling of a song that we did back in high school. The whole year making this album, we were not in the frame of mind to do groove stuff. I think the attitude was more of... because I listen to the album and I think, 'God there's about four tunes where the tempo seems real close, but in our live show we always felt we were missing the amount of these kinds of tunes that are on this album for what we like to play. We like to play all sorts of stuff, and when you have a show where half of it's the groove stuff and not a lot of rock 'n' roll tunes unless they're real old, it's nice to have some of that."

"Stranger in Town" actually reached No. 7 on *Billboard's* rock chart (and No. 3 on the Hot 100). Jeff worked with Paich a lot on the third verse, and he told me: "Originally the song was going to be 'watch out for this killer'; the guy is walking around and he's a killer," Jeff said. "Then it was, 'Let's make it more ambiguous. Let's give the guy some heart and soul.' You can read so much into the song, which is what I like about it. Especially with the video, which helps out the understanding of the song. It's people's fear of something good, say a religious guy, or a new rock singer, or a new idea: some people really fear it and aren't into it, and others look at it and don't see the evil that other people see."

During the recording of *Isolation*, Jeff and Luke got called by Paul McCartney to work on his *Give My Regards to Broad Street* project. Paich says he got a very excited call from Jeff from England. Jeff had played the basic track for "Mr. Friendly" for Paul, which had no vocal, and Paul started a vocal improv, making up words as he went along, "like he would on 'Twist and Shout,'" Paich says. "Jeff said he wished he had had a tape recorder because it was as if Paul McCartney was Toto's lead singer."

David Paich got married on December 1, 1984. Sometime during the year, Jeff called him up to inform him that he was going to be his best man. Just like that! Jeff told him he would walk him through it and be there for him. Paich explains they spoke in shorthand and could finish one another's sentences by then. Road manager Chris Littleton organized the bachelor party to be held at the notoriously questionable and sleazy Tropicana Motel in Hollywood, which featured mudwrestling, the furthest activity from Paich's inclination. Littleton thought it would be a hoot for the groom-to-be to partake in the hoopla, but Porcaro, knowing full well how modest and shy Paich is, devised a Plan B to have a quiet drink, just the two of them, at a bar. Jeff rode with David in the limo to the Tropicana, trying to convince him to take a detour to the bar, but Paich didn't want to disappoint everybody waiting at the motel, so he and his best friend went on and Paich, the good sport, partook in the event while everyone whistled at him.

On the big day, band members and engineer Greg Ladanyi were in the bridal party, while Steve Porcaro refused a spot in the bridal party to be a designated bodyguard of sorts, so he could oversee the groom in case he became too anxious and needed calming down. Paich describes the event itself as a "blockbuster" which they had at a Hollywood venue called The Palace. They had two bands, and Paich says there were probably 300-400 people in attendance—he's not even sure if people were just coming in off the street.

The next year Toto went on tour in support of *Isolation*, and Scotty Page was blown away when he got the call to go out on the road with them, playing saxophone, rhythm guitar and cowbell. Throughout the years, as he worked on his musicianship and in such bands as Seals & Crofts (post-Porcaro) and Supertramp, Jeff was always the yardstick, the benchmark against which he evaluated his performance.

"I was excited and scared to death," Page recalls. "I had to learn all the music and I'll never forget going to that first rehearsal. I lost sleep. Talk about woodshedding music—I spent about ten hours a day on that music."

The first thing Jeff did at rehearsal was hand Page the cowbell. Now he'd really be tested.

"I was really scared," Page admits. "Knowing him and time, I thought, 'Oh my God.' I had learned to eat, drink and sleep with metronomes. I was a fanatic. He was the one who had really gotten me into thinking about time," Page explains, adding that Porcaro had taught him how to work with the metronome back in those early days. "He said, 'When you're playing with it, don't think of each click on the downbeat, but put each click on the 2 and 4, leaving the 1 and 3 silent,'" Page explains. "When you do that it completely changes the feel and your focus of attention. That simple trick profoundly changed my playing."

After Page finished the first song on cowbell at the first rehearsal, Porcaro went over to him and put his arm around him and said, 'Yeah, Page!'" Page says he felt a huge sigh of relief. And off he went on tour with the band, ending up on Bus B with Jeff, Lenny and Lenny's wife at the time, Paulette.

"It was heaven because it was hours and hours of conversation," Page says, describing conversation as mostly sharing music, which he says consisted largely of three artists: Jimi Hendrix, Steely Dan and Marvin Gaye's *Greatest Hits*.

In Japan, Page was the target of a Jeff engineered prank in the early hours of the morning, around 2:00 a.m. Page was on the phone with his wife back in the States. It was the era when there were no cell phones and long distance calls from a hotel phone cost an arm and a leg. Jamieson, Lukather and Jeff went to Page's door and knocked. Lukather was yelling for Page to help with Jeff. Page, thinking it was an emergency, told his wife to

Jeff drew all the family cards.
St. Patrick's Day card for Jeff's grandmother drawn by Jeff, circa 1968-69.
(Courtesy of Joleen Porcaro-Duddy)

An arts and crafts project Jeff enjoyed in junior high to which the family devoted a wall.
(Courtesy of Joleen Porcaro-Duddy)

A rendering of Jimi Hendrix by Jeff, circa 1970.
(Courtesy of Joleen Porcaro-Duddy)

Jeff's cartoon hipster, circa 1971.
(Courtesy of Joleen Porcaro-Duddy)

Civil War solider rendering, circa 1971.
(Courtesy of Joleen Porcaro-Duddy)

A senior high school art project.
(Courtesy of Joleen Porcaro-Duddy)

Jeff's kooky Martini Man.
(Courtesy of Joleen Porcaro-Duddy)

Later, Jeff did a series of pieces based on Steely Dan songs and gave his brother a couple of them. This one, based on "King of the World," believed to be ink and pencil, depicts the narrator "on this old ham radio."
(Courtesy of Steve Porcaro)

Joleen, Mike and Jeff in the garage studio at the Valleyheart Dr., Sherman Oaks house circa 1973.

(Courtesy of Joleen Porcaro-Duddy)

Jeff and Joleen in the Valleyheart Drive house, December, 1973.

(Courtesy of Joleen Porcaro-Duddy)

A fishing trip during 1972 Maine visit. L-R: Steve, Joe, Jeff, Uncle Al Geronda, Eileen's sister's husband, and Mike.
(Courtesy of Joleen Porcaro-Duddy)

Jeff moving out for the first time and Mike helping him.
(Courtesy of Joleen Porcaro-Duddy)

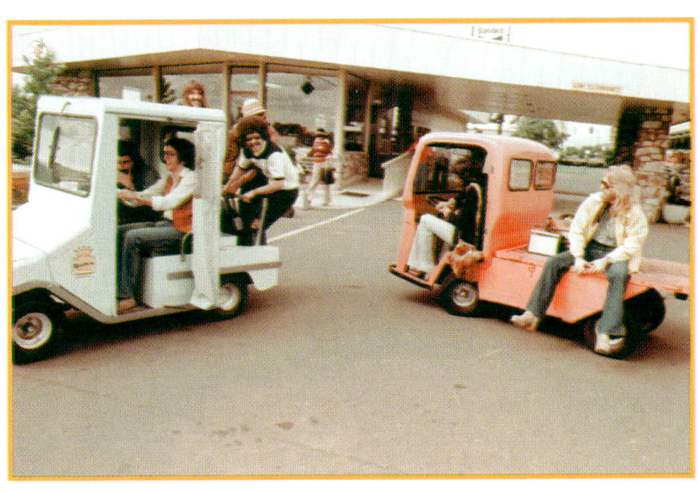

On tour with Seals & Crofts, 1975
(Courtesy of Michel Rubini)

Jeff on tour with Steely Dan, mid '70s.
(Courtesy of Barney Hurley)

At the Los Angeles Greek Theater, summer of '76, the Porcaro family on a very special night before Jeff, Steve, Mike and Joe (just for this show) will take the stage with Boz Scaggs. L-R: Mike, Joleen, Jeff, Steve, Joe, Eileen.

(Courtesy of Joleen Porcaro-Duddy)

Boz Scaggs 1977 American tour.

(Courtesy of Barney Hurley)

Jeff and David Paich in a limo on a Toto tour circa '79 or '80.

(Courtesy of David Hungate)

Jeff during Toto's *Hydra* tour in Japan, spring, 1980.

(Courtesy of Barney Hurley)

Toto video shoot for the single "99" from *Hydra* (1979).

(Courtesy of Mike Baird)

Jeff during the filming of the video for *Hydra*'s "St. George and the Dragon."

(Courtesy of Barney Hurley)

Jeff was really proud of organizing this Christmas card photo shoot to surprise his folks. It's a rare shot without his glasses. Mike is at the top; next row down, L-R: Steve Duddy, Steve Porcaro, Jeanette (Steve P.'s first wife). Front Row: Joleen, Steve and Jeanette's daughter Heather and Jeff.

(Photo by Maraphotography.com)

Historic session at Westlake Studios for "The Girl is Mine," from *Thriller*. L-R: George Martin, Quincy Jones, Bruce Swedien (front), Michael Jackson, Jeff Porcaro, Steve Lukather, Paul McCartney

Jeff at the drums, 1982.
(Photo by Rick Malkin)

Jeff toasts David and Lorraine at the Paich wedding, Dec. 1, 1984.
(Courtesy of Paich family archives)

Toto aboard the bullet train in Japan with talk show host Dick Cavett during the Isolation tour, 1985.
(Courtesy of Barney Hurley)

Jeff at Olympen in Lund, Sweden, January 22, 1987 when the *Fahrenheit* tour hit Europe.
(Photo courtesy of Jens Ekberg, jensekberg.com)

Daddy giving son Miles a drum lesson.
(Courtesy of Susan Porcaro Goings)

Jeff with son Christopher on his first day of nursery school, 1987.
(Courtesy of Susan Porcaro Goings)

Jeff and Jim Keltner enjoying time together at winter NAMM 1983, Anaheim, California.
(Courtesy of Barney Hurley)

Another fun NAMM meet-up, some Steely Dan alumni: left to right: Jeff, Jeff Baxter, Denny Dias, Elliott Randall, Walter Becker.

(Courtesy of Elliott Randall)

Jeff and Jamo with Bernard Purdie, one of Jeff's main influences, at a Los Angeles NAMM convention.

(Courtesy of Paul Jamieson)

Jeff and Vinnie talking with Keltner looking on at the end of the 1990 *Modern Drummer* round table at author's San Fernando Valley home.

(Photo by Lissa Wales)

The guys in the group Toto love **TIGER** be
and one of their first questions was, "Do v
get to fill out those lifelines we've seen?" Tr
answer is **yes**—and here are Steve Lukather
and Jeff Porcaro's, in their own handwriting

JEFFREY THOMAS PORCARO
JEFFREY PORCARO Nicknames: "Artful dodger
Color Hair: Brown Eyes: Green Height: 5'6" Weight: 135 lb
Parents' Names: Joe & Eileen Birthplace: Hartford Conn
Birthdate: 4-1-54
Brothers & Sisters' Names and Ages: Mike - 24, Steve - 22,
Joleen - 19
[illegible]ments Played: Drums
[illegible]es: Art - Painting & Drawing

FAVORITES:
Color: Blue Dessert: Chocolate [illegible]
Drink: Chocolate Malt Singer/Group: [illegible]
City: New York Actor: [illegible]
Food: Pot Roast Actress: Jill Clayburgh
TV Shows: Twilight Zone

Shirt Size: Small
Shoe Size: 8½
Ring Size:

Have Any Pets? Chiquita - my kitty

Personal Ambition (Happiness, Marriage, etc.) [illegible]
Professional Ambition (Director, Writer, etc.) Actor

[illegible signature]
Signature

A questionnaire Jeff filled out for Tiger Beat early on in Toto, with some interesting answers in his own handwriting.

(Courtesy of Joleen Porcaro-Duddy)

hold on, put the phone receiver down on the bed and went to the door only in his underwear.

"I run over to the door and look through the peep hole and see Jeff being held up by his arm by Lukather, and Jeff looks like he's passing out or something," Page recalls, explaining he opened the door, and the guys grabbed him, ripped off his underwear, threw it back in the room and closed the door, which locked behind him. "They ran down the hallway and all they could hear was me yelling under the door to my wife, 'Hang up, hang up.'" Page recounts.

There he was, stark naked, screaming in the middle of the night in a five-star hotel, afraid his wife would stay on the phone on the other end waiting for him to return, racking up hundreds of dollars in charges. Luckily, there was such a ruckus in the hallway that somebody opened their hotel room door to see what was going on and threw Page a towel so he could make his way down to the lobby to get a key to his room.

The next day, he told his bandmates he thought the prank was hilarious, explaining that if he didn't laugh about it with them, they'd pull something else on him. And then he was part of a prank they pulled on Fergie when they thought he was getting a little too full of himself: "We took his hairdryer and unscrewed it and took all the shrimp heads from catering and stuffed them in his hairdryer and screwed it back on," Page says, laughing. "He put that in his suitcase and it smelled so bad."

Other memorable tour moments for Page include one night on the U.S. tour when the busses pulled into a truck stop in the wee hours of the morning and the "A" bus was, as he put it, "lit:" "We go in to get some food and here we are with our colored hair and it's 4:00 in the morning and there are all these truckers, and we have long hair and we look like a bunch of goofballs," Page recounts. "We sit down to get some food and there's a little old lady, probably in her 80s who's been working in this place probably for 50 years. Everybody knows Jane or whatever her name is and she walks up to Luke and says, 'What would you like, sir?' And Luke says, 'I want a hot douche enema.' Jeff and I are going, 'He's going to get us killed.' You shoulda seen the truck drivers, all flipping out. Lukather, the stories! He was like a little kid. I love him to death. Jeff and I would talk about it all the time—'Lukather is going to get us killed.'"

But Page says the times were fun, and keeping time on stage was the best part of it.

"When people ask me what was the best thing about playing with Toto, I tell them playing cowbell on four songs with Jeff Porcaro because the groove was so deep. I sat right next to him on the bandstand. It was better than sex," says Page, who then hired Jeff to play on multiple projects of his after that tour, such as *Push Back the Walls*.

When Lukather and Porcaro showed up to see Page play with Pink Floyd at a Los Angeles concert the following year, "It was such a thrill," Page says. "There's nobody who influenced me more than Jeff Porcaro. Every day I practiced, he was my secret driver, my guru."

Talk about pranks, Porcaro definitely had the devil in him. Just ask fellow drummer **MIKE BAIRD**. Jeff got him fired off a session due to their crazy antics. Well, it was pretty mutual. But Jeff started it. It all began when Baird moved over to Jeff's cartage company, R&R Express, and one day Baird showed up for work at what he recalls was Western Studios.

"And there are these incredibly graphic drawings on the head of the floor tom of a guy holding this giant dick with shit oozing out of the end of it, and I forgot what it said," Baird recalls. "The floor tom was really my ash tray—where I set my drink and my cigarette ash tray, and I was going, 'What the fuck?' I'm pretty sure Jeff had come to the warehouse and seen my stuff there and decided to do it there. So I was, 'Alright motherfucker, game on.' I wasn't the artist he was, but he was in the next (studio) room and they hadn't picked his shit up, so I took a marker and drew on his floor tom and drew me—this fat guy—sitting on his face while he's eating my ass. And it went back and forth and back and forth for probably a month."

But then Baird got hired to do a session for a religious artist, and he told his cartage guys to make sure to change the heads. When he got to the studio, the artist was leaning over the partition and Baird, in his jovial manner, gave his usual salutation: "'Hey everybody, how's it going? ' And she turned around to me and looked at me like I literally was the anti-Christ, with her eyes like golf balls," Baird remembers. "She looked at me and walked out of the room. I sat down at my drums and the producer came out and said, 'The session is over. We're going to pay you for your deal.' I said, 'I told the cartage guys to change this shit. I didn't want anyone to see this, but obviously they didn't.' He said, 'Oh no, she literally thinks you're Satan.' I filled out a form and split."

Baird thinks the first time he met Porcaro was around 1974, pretty much at the beginning of Baird's career at Western Studios. Baird had a session in the front room and Jeff had one in another room.

"This guy comes walking towards me on a break and he says, 'Are you Mike Baird?' and I say, 'Yeah.' And he says, 'Where the fuck did you come from?' And I say, 'South Gate.' And he says, 'Where the hell is South Gate?'"

Of course he knew who Jeff Porcaro was already, although he didn't know what he looked like until then. With the introduction Porcaro made, Baird says, "It put me back on my heels." And that was the beginning of their friendship.

"So dig it," was how Jeff prefaced the tunes he played one day for his guest on his stereo after he called Baird to his Hesby home. Then Baird recalls: "He puts this track on and I'm listening to it and I'm thinking, 'This kinda sounds familiar. What the hell is it?' And I'm looking at him and he's looking at me and he's shaking his head and his eyes are nice and big and he's looking like, 'Yeah, yeah, yeah,' and he finally goes, 'It's you!' And I went, 'It is?' And he said, 'Yeah, that's you, man, dig it.' And he goes to another track that I played on," remembers Baird of the day, but with no recollection now of which tracks they were. "And then he takes that record off and finds another record. He did that about three times and I said, 'Okay,' and I started looking through his stuff to find something that he played that I thought was awesome."

Of course Jeff didn't want to hear it, and told him "fuck that shit." But finally Jeff played Mike a Steely Dan track (that Mike can't remember which) of which he was proud and said, "I want you to dig this. He said, 'Look at the clock,'" Baird recalls. "And the clock on his wall was a quartz clock so it ticked to each second and he put the song on. Those were the days of no click, so the time was your time. And he goes, 'Look at the clock, man.' And I look at the clock and every tick is a downbeat. And I go, 'Wow!' And he goes, 'Yeah, dig that shit, dig that shit.'"

A rare moment for Jeff to sing his own praises, to be sure, since one of the most quotable (and ridiculous, of course) utterances out of his mouth came in my 1983 interview, when he told me, "My time sucks."

L to R: Lenny Castro, Steve Jordan, Jim Keltner, and Jeff at the recording session for "Lea" from *Fahrenheit*, 1986.

(Photo courtesy of Paul Jamieson)

TEMPERATURE CHANGES

With *Fahrenheit*, Toto's next album, Fergie was gone and Joseph Williams came on board as lead singer. Jeff put his buddy Niko Bolas on the album cover. (He's the guy walking down the street looking at the girl.) The album yielded a hit for the band again: "I'll Be Over You."

One of Jeff's favorites from the record was "Lea." Bolas recalls a phone call he got one day from Porcaro while Toto was recording Fahrenheit and he was in another studio working with **STEVE JORDAN** on a Neil Young album. Bolas says Jeff was always the first one to suggest someone more perfect than he to play a track, so when he called, he asked him to bring Jordan over to record something at The Villa for a Toto track on *Fahrenheit*. Paul Jamieson, who was with Bolas in the studio at the time, drove Jordan over to Jeff's house/studio. Porcaro was in charge of "Lea." Lukather says Jeff had always threatened to have other drummers play drums on Toto tracks, but it had never happened until then. Steve Jordan *did* play drums on "Lea" and Porcaro played percussion along with Jim Keltner and Lenny Castro, whom he secured for the percussion loop that was created for the song.

Jordan discloses he was so flattered because, of course, it was Jeff's band and "he wanted me to play drums, holy cow!" Jordan was blown away because Jeff had just gotten a new set of Gretsch drums and insisted that he play them. And Jordan was happy to see Lenny Castro, with whom he went to high school in Brooklyn. "And of course," he adds, "we all idolize Jim. It was crazy."

Playing on the Toto record was a thrill, Jordan says, and so much fun. He explains he was a fan of Jeff's—and all of the Toto guys, actually: "They were all doing stuff before I was. Let's just talk about Jeff's playing. The reason I became a Jeff Porcaro fan is because he was unlike any other famous players at the time. When Steve Gadd played on something, Harvey Mason played on something, Bernard Purdie played on something, you knew it was them because of their style or some trademark thing. When Jeff played on something you didn't know it was Jeff because Jeff played the music first. He always played the song."

Jordan mentions how Steely Dan would hire individual drummers for particular tracks, but when they hired Jeff, they used him for an entire project "because he played the music," Jordan emphasizes. "The music always came forth as the priority. You never really focused on what the drums were doing. You just were moved by the feel. Everything felt great. He never played something that didn't feel great. He plays the song and the main thing is you have to make it feel good, so boom, he's got that down. That's all you need. You don't have to say, 'Hi mom, I'm doing this fill I'm famous for right here to let you know this is me.' He never did any of that. That's why he could play on 'Beat It' there and 'Lowdown' here and be a chameleon. That's the essence of the musicality of Jeff Porcaro."

Jordan describes Porcaro as bending over backwards during the whole time at the "Lea" session: "'How you doing, man, is everything ok? What do you need? Do you need something?'" Even as he was leaving for the airport to take the redeye (so he could get back to New York for the Letterman show), Jordan recalls Jeff asking, "You need a couple of bucks, man? Are you straight, man? Let me give you a couple of bucks, man, make sure you're cool."

Lukather says Jeff also programmed a Fairlight synthesizer on two songs on *Fahrenheit*: "It's Not the Same without Your Love" and the title track.

Around the same time, in 1986, **SERGIO MENDES** hired Porcaro for the first time. Mendes says there was a point in time in the '80s that every musician began to tell him he needed to work with Jeff Porcaro. He particularly remembers Nathan East mentioning Jeffrey to him. Mendes recalls coming to the United States in 1964 and auditioning musicians at Shelly's Manne Hole in Los Angeles, where he met Emil Richards and Joe Porcaro. He wasn't surprised when he began to hear about Joe's son, and he finally called Jeff in to work on *Brasil '86*. He says he was instantly fascinated with Jeff's style, versatility and taste.

"You know, not all drummers can play the Brazilian music," Mendes asserts. "It's different than your usual shuffle or rock 'n' roll. It takes a different kind of musicality and Jeff just nailed it."

Despite the fact that Mendes admits he does not become great friends with all the musicians on his sessions, he and Porcaro struck up that rare friendship, explaining: "I call it the magic of the encounter. Those things are hard to explain. We clicked with each other. He was like a young brother to me."

Mendes began recording the Grammy-winning *Brasileiro* in spring of 1991. His wife and singer **GRACINHA LEPORACE** recalls it was finished up at the end of the year. Porcaro played on five tracks: "Indiado," "Lua Soberana," "Kalimba," "Barabare," and percussion on "Senhoras Do Amazonas."

"Everything he played, he brought joy, excitement and a fresh approach to the music I was doing, above all," Mendes states. "Working with a great musician, they bring their own language. Nobody can speak that language except them. I remember on *Brasileiro* I had a song I recorded in Brazil with a drummer on it and I said, 'Jeff, I would like you to play on this song,' so he listened to this song and said, 'Sergio, what do you want me to play on this? This sounds great.' That was Jeff. 'What am I going to add here?' He had that wisdom; that taste. He knew when things were great and he ended up playing percussion on that song."

The album came out in June of 1992. Leporace recalls, "He was at the house a couple of weeks before he died to celebrate the release of *Brasileiro*. He brought a beautiful bottle of wine for Sergio, and Jeff loved tequila. He brought a bottle of tequila that he went on to drink—not the whole bottle," she says with a laugh. "And the kids were there. We had a son that was about the same age as his oldest."

Porcaro was also very much about his friends. He would include them on his sessions whenever possible. Lenny Castro recalls he'd often get crazy calls from Jeff: "What're you doing?" Castro might reply, "Well, I'm just about to take a shower," or, "I'm eating dinner." Jeff would say, "Get dressed, get in the car, and come down to the studio—NOW! Bring your tambourine or a bongo, or something."

Castro remembers one evening in 1987 he was about to eat dinner when Jeff called from a David Benoit session at Ocean Way Studios, saying, "We need you, come down here." Joe Porcaro was also on the session. Lenny ended up on three tracks for Benoit's GRP debut album *Freedom at Midnight*, which went to No. 5 on the *Billboard* jazz charts

As for jazz pianist **DAVID BENOIT**, this album was the first time he ever worked with Jeff (although it wouldn't be the last). When the album producer Jeff Weber suggested they use him, Benoit's initial reaction was, "Do you think he would do it?" Benoit was awestruck by Porcaro's bigger-than-life reputation. He didn't even think the drummer would take the call.

"To me, Jeff Porcaro was huge," Benoit says, emphasizing the word huge. "He was the founder of Toto and the greatest studio drummer ever. I was nobody. I figured he wouldn't even want to do it. I was nervous and intimidated to meet the great Jeff Porcaro. And when I met him, he had this way low voice, and he said, 'Are you kidding? I've been following your career,' and he knew all about me and he was real happy to be there, and so the vibe was so great."

Benoit had heard that Jeff always arrived at the studio early, unlike other first call drummers who arrived at the very last minute, and sure enough, he was there two hours before call time.

"He was real conscientious about that. And the other thing about him, was despite his stardom, he never charged more than double scale," Benoit says.

Benoit reveals that, without a doubt, the drum track for "Freedom at Midnight" is the best of any recording he has ever done: "It was the most exquisite, perfect drum track," Benoit says. "A couple of observations: it was one of those special days where the planets did align. We had a great engineer, Allen Sides, who had recorded Jeff over the years and he always loved drummers who he didn't have to EQ or change the sound. He just put some great mic's up and Jeff's kit, just right off the bat, sounded fantastic. We recorded it live, there was no overdubbing, and there was one little fill I did, halfway to the piano solo, and it was like an upbeat thing. Jeff caught that fill with a little upbeat hi-hat thing and I don't know how he did it. How could he know I was going to do it? He was so attuned to what was going on around him. I really felt like it was never about him. It was about the music and how he could service the music and make it great. He really heard what was going on. The other thing about Jeff was, if he didn't like something, he was very clear about it," Benoit continues. "I remember a couple of years later I brought in this keyboard. It was an okay Rhodes sound and he said, 'That Rhodes sound, I don't know, gotta work on that.' He had such a high standard for how things should sound."

The producer on that Benoit record, **JEFFREY WEBER**, had had his first encounter with Porcaro not long before that project and shortly after *Fahrenheit* on an experimental project with Scotty Page.

"Scotty had an idea to do a recording in the round using a binaural head microphone," Weber explains. "This was a microphone where the pickups were in the ears. It looked just like a human head, but the ears had microphones in them so when you listened back, you would be listening back like with your own ears. It got really deep because certain engineers would make a mold of their ears and put it on this microphone, so it would be exactly as you would be hearing it as if it would be you. I was producing the live-to-two-track version of that."

There were two records involved: *Push Back the Walls* and *The First Dance*. An all-star cast of musicians was assembled, including Steve Lukather, Bob Glaub, Bill Payne, Lenny Castro, the Heart Attack horns and, of course, Porcaro, along with five engineers at RCA Wally Heider Studios in Hollywood.

As a sidebar, Weber laughs as he recalls a fight broke out when someone burst into the studio insisting that the head belonged to him and they couldn't use it: "In the meantime, the band had put a cigarette in the mouth of the head, some powder under the nose, a scarf around the neck, and it was hilarious," Weber recounts, explaining that the engineer who brought in the head, whose name he can't recall, ended up in an actual physical fight that ended up out on Sunset Blvd., resulting with the guy running into the Cinerama Dome.

In 1989, Weber had his first opportunity to use Porcaro on his own live-to-two-track project for an artist named Emily Remler.

"Emily Remler was a female jazz guitarist ala Joe Pass," Weber says. "She was the sweetest, nicest woman, but she was a drug addict. She would shoot up on the top of her hands. When I met her, all her face make-up was on the top of her hands to disguise her tracks."

Weber assembled an all-star band, including Jeff, and they recorded what Weber describes as "a more electronic record than she had done before. She was happy, she was straight, she was in a new relationship with a trombone player from New York, and she was over the moon with this record on Justice Records," Weber says. "She had left to go on tour in Europe and two weeks later she was found dead in a hotel room in Sydney, Australia. The newspaper said it was a heart attack. I don't really know."

Explaining why he, as a live-to-two-track or live-to-multi-track producer, would hire Porcaro for his projects, and even sometimes hold off his projects until Jeff was available, Weber says, "I'm an audiophile, which means I'm an asshole. Every single instrument is crucial to me, because we do live two-track recording with no mixing, no editing, and no overdubbing. The idea was to capture a performance rather than manufacture one, so every single chair had to be astonishing and fearless. The fact that you would say 'Hey we're doing this live to two tracks, whatever you're playing, you're playing,' you can't have a musician playing tentatively or be afraid. Not too many musicians are like that. Jeff Porcaro—been there, done that. They had to bring it. All those guys from Toto could do anything; they could play anything. They didn't need to rehearse. It came out of them like breathing. It came out smooth and yet it had the soul and the feel. It was so extravagantly amazing."

Weber says Porcaro always arrived at the sessions an hour early to make sure everything was perfect with his equipment: "He wanted everything to be right," Weber says. "He wanted you to get the best from him. But the other side of it was, as a producer, you better damn well know what you wanted, because at the same time, he didn't suffer fools. You couldn't say stupid things like some producers do like, 'Make this more red,' or 'Make this more magical,' because at the end of the day he would lose his temper. Or you couldn't say things like, 'Oh, that was really great, let's do one more.' I learned very early on when you hire the great guys, let them do what they do best and get out of the way. I tell them I hired them to be them."

As a producer, Weber wants the musicians to be emotionally invested, so while he gives them a chart, he welcomes their input, observing: "If they're going to just play the notes, a musician like Jeff Porcaro is going to be uninterested super fast. A perfect record does not a perfect record make," Weber says, lamenting that to this day, every time he makes a record he wants Jeff on it.

The big thing that happened after *Fahrenheit* was that Steve Porcaro quit.

"We were all bummed when Steve left the band," Lukather says. "It really affected me a lot because if it weren't for Steve, I wouldn't be in the band."

According to Steve P., the decision was inevitable and he believes they were all relieved when he told them. He admits he had struggled in the band from day one.

"Jeff was such a pure musician as far as a drummer goes; it all came so easily to Jeff. He was so fucking talented," Steve P. says. "I was a way different kind of musician. I was way into the technology. That was my niche."

Steve P. felt his talent didn't come as natural as his brother's, and he'd observe, for instance, they would be on a Pointer Sisters date for producer Richard Perry, and Perry would be trying to find the right key for the singers. Describing the scene, Steve explains: "For some reason, I was cutting the track on a Wurlitzer live with the guys out in the studio," Steve P. recalls. "We had chord charts that I had no problem with. We'd run the track a couple times and I'd gotten the changes under my fingers and had a few licks sussed out. Richard, being a great producer, would want to make sure the track was in the perfect key for his singers. He was known to suddenly shout out, 'Up a half step!!' during the count-off! As if it wasn't bad enough having to transpose the chart on the fly, suddenly I'm trying to play my same licks in Eb from D, or whatever the case was, an entirely different universe physically on the keyboard. While I'd be struggling to pull it off, I'd look up at Jeff, who behind his drum set would just sit there giving me a look, like, 'Get your shit together!' He, of course, was ready to go."

Jeff's brother says he was hired in Toto to program for Paich and to cover Paich's overdubs live: "Just like I did for Boz Scaggs," Steve explains. "String ensemble parts, Minimoog parts. You don't have to be a great keyboard player—synthesizers and string lines. So technically I was fine for all that and they really kinda always just wanted me to do that: program for David, play his overdubs live and shut up."

After the first album Steve P. figured if that was to be his role, he'd be the best "synth guy" there was, and he immersed himself in it. He admits it didn't come easy: "All the advance sequencer stuff I was trying to do, you needed to play with a click," he says. "You needed to be in a band with a drummer that was okay playing with a click and there was the rub. That was kind of starting to happen in the business anyway. Long after I was out of Toto, the last five years of Jeff's session career, he'd show up at sessions where he'd have to play with a click and he hated it. It became the norm, but when I was trying to do it before it became the norm and Jeff was still always hired because he was the human clock and he took great pride in it, he hated it. From day one, we butted heads."

As an aside, Steve shared his observation that what he found so funny about Jeff and what added to the complexity of their relationship, was Jeff hated the technology when it came to anything that had to do with Toto, but outside of Toto it was a different story: "He didn't want to know about it. He hated the triggers, click tracks and all of that stuff," Steve says. "He loathed it. But at the same time I could call him any Sunday and he would come over in two seconds to the Manor and play pads and play to a click and do whatever I wanted him to do if it was my own thing, as long as it wasn't Toto."

While *Fahrenheit* did all right and the tour went well, the band was struggling to hold on to its record deal. Steve P. says there was an immense amount of pressure from the record company to come up with a hit and to stay musically current while times they were a-changing into grunge and punk. Toto's revolving lead singer situation wasn't helping matters any.

"We were coming home from Japan and all everyone had been talking about when we were talking about recording a new album was how we had to 'scale things down.'" Steve P. says. "It became very unpopular to have a keyboard player in your band, let alone two, and doing all that orchestral stuff. So they were talking about how we had to lose all that stuff and get down to straight ahead rock n roll. They were talking about losing the stuff that was my reason for being in the band."

So on the plane home from Japan, Steve very calmly told the guys that he would be happy to program for Paich and go on tour again, but he did not want to be a band member. For him, it was self-preservation. He felt under-appreciated and no longer wanted to spend two weeks on a part like he had on the "Rosanna," solo, for little regard. He also felt quitting the band would help preserve his relationships with the band members and his brother in the long run. He had seen all too many members in other bands sour on one another and didn't want that to happen.

"We actually got along amazingly well for a very long period of time. We really were friends and hung out a lot outside of any band business. We were always at each other's houses; we were always going to Jeff's house. We were each other's best friends," Steve P. says.

Around the time of *Toto IV* Jeff had told me the same, and that even though they were all very strong personalities and sometimes had their "own opinionated trips," it was never an issue.

"We're in a group together because of one reason and never, ever through childhood or anything had scenes musically," Jeff said. "We all enjoyed playing the same kind of music, so little arguments never come across or we never would have put a band together. We're a band who knows each other real well. We all grew up together and everything and working with members of my family is not a problem, either. In fact, it grooves."

Steve P. admits he began to worry that was not going to last: "And my thought at the time was I have to see these guys every Christmas, family holidays and I don't want to wait until we hate each other," he confides. "They were all pissing me off at that point."

But Jeff and Mike were blood and Steve would definitely have to see them at family functions. Steve says seeing Jeff once he left went fine because it had been handled well and without drama. There were no long discussions about Steve's leaving. As was usual, Jeff kept his feelings close to the vest, according to Lukather: "When he started opening up about something hurting his feelings, it was rare. A lot of times, he brushed it away. Same with Dave. They didn't meet the feelings head on. I was more the wear-the-heart-on-the-sleeve kind of guy. But it was less traumatic for everyone because Steve left, but he didn't leave. So was Jeff upset? It was hard to be upset when nothing really changed."

Looking back, Steve P. says he believes the band was fairly relieved when he quit because they understood the musical climate and knew they had to become more of a rock guitar unit as they were fighting to hold on to their record deal. But with all that said, he recalls Paich being the most visibly upset.

After Japan, **GARY GRIMM** began working with Jeff as his tech, continuing with him for the following tour on *The Seventh One*, and also accompanying Porcaro on some sessions. Grimm was also responsible for setting up the percussion rig for Lenny Castro on the first tour and Luis Conte on the second. Jeff knew of Grimm, a drum performance graduate of Cal State Northridge, from when he had worked at Valley Arts Music Store and becoming the drum shop manager the last couple of years he was there. Valley Arts wasn't far from Jeff's house, and he'd go in there from time to time. Grimm began to gain a reputation for tuning and started making his own drums. Porcaro came into the store one day and invited Gary down to Leeds Rehearsal Studios, where Toto was rehearsing, and asked him to bring one of his drums.

Toto's production manager Tom Kiphut also knew Grimm, as he had also been production manager on Stevie Nicks' *Rock a Little* tour, on which Gary worked with Rick Marotta. This was just before Toto went out that spring, so when Jeff was looking for a new drum tech, Grimm was the guy. Gary says when Kiphut called him up to tell him that Jeff wanted to know if Gary wanted to work with him, he almost dropped the phone. "It was like I had won a million dollars kind of thing," Grimm says with a laugh, and goes on to describe the gig like it was worth that as an experience.

The job was to begin after the two-week break following their return from Japan, so immediately upon their arrival, Grimm started learning Jeff's set-up. He laughs as he relays the following story: "I didn't get this at the time, that's how green I was, but Joe (Porcaro) called me up and said, 'Hey Gary, I'm having a problem with this electronic pedal, would you mind taking a look at it?' I said, 'No, not at all. Do you want me to come over?' he said, 'No, if you don't mind, I'll come over.' So what he was doing was he was checking me out to see how we lived: 'Is this guy a slob? We don't know him.' It was all cool, but I didn't get it. I was like, 'Yeah, your pedal's fine, here you go.' His dad was protecting his son."

Gary didn't have a lot of time to learn both Jeff's and Lenny's set-ups and says he felt shy about calling Jeff, but finally got up the nerve: "I said, 'I'm going to go set up your stuff at Leeds and would you mind maybe coming by for 15 minutes and going, 'Yeah, that's good or no, that's not,' and I can make the proper markings.' And he said, 'Naw, you do it, It'll be great. You'll get it.' He was just really great. He had total faith—it was just, 'It'll be great, don't worry about it.' And of course I was worried about it. I was like, 'Oh crap!'"

Grimm says Porcaro was always that chill. And to this day, he says Jeff was "in a league of his own." Gary begins to choke up as he says, "He's just special. He just had room for you. First of all, he respected you. He wouldn't hang out with you unless he respected you to do his gear. He was very generous, just being there for you, just him being him," Gary says, explaining he was not just an employer; he was a friend.

Despite the report of being chill, Porcaro could explode sometimes, although Grimm says he was never the recipient. Looking back at that visit from Jeff's dad that day, he recalls that Joe was trying to warn him when he told him, "You know, Jeff can kind of get upset sometimes," and I said, "Okay," and he said, "But I want you to know that he totally respects you and it would be nothing personal."

Grimm's first gig with Toto was in Puerto Rico and he laughs when he recalls how it took him about four hours to set everything up via two Polaroid photographs that he discovered in one of the equipment cases. One was a far shot from the back and one was a far shot from the front. There were no close-ups. He remembers doing the line check and playing the Purdie shuffle when he felt Jeff's presence behind him. "I immediately stopped and he said, 'No, no, keep going,' and I was like, 'Um, no, yeah, whatever.' And he got up there and he said, 'Are you guys ready for my line check?' And they said, 'Yes,' and he hit everything. It lasted about 30 seconds and he said, 'Great, I'm fine, see 'ya later. Gary, let's go hang in the dressing room.' We went into the dressing room and he said, 'See? I told you that you were going to be great.' He asked me how I did it and I told him about the two Polaroid photos and he was kind of blown away."

Fast forward to an amazing memory Gary has when the band played in Ludwigshafen, Germany. The day before was a day off in Bern, Switzerland and the band decided to switch rooms with their band backline techs, monitor engineer, front-of-house engineer, front-of-house lighting guy and production manager, unbeknownst to them. After he checked in, Jeff called him and asked him how his room was, and Gary went on about how amazing it was and Jeff asked if he could come check it out?

"I said, 'Of course, come on up.' He came up and told me what was going on, so I asked, 'How is your room?'" Grimm remembers. "He said, 'Well, I'm looking at a wall next to the elevator I think.' I said, 'Here, take my room,' and he said, 'No, no, no, no.' He wanted me to come down later for dinner and I couldn't do it; I was just dead tired. I didn't go. What a dumb thing to say! Of course now I would. I was so green and shy at the time. So he asked me to have breakfast the next morning. He said, 'Everyone is going to go skiing. Let's you and I have breakfast.' I went down and had breakfast and of course he was dressed to the nines. He was always dressed perfect."

"'Ya know that song we do in the encore, 'I'll Be There'?" Porcaro said to Gary, referring to the only non-Toto song they did in their show at the time. "I said, 'Yeah.' He said, 'You can play that.' I said, 'What?' He said, 'Well, you can play that.' I said, 'Well, yeah, I suppose I could.' He said, 'Well you're gonna play it tomorrow. Get a pair of sticks you like and it'll be great.' The rest of the day I was walking around town and this and that. I was excited but at the same time it was, 'Are you kidding me?' I got a tape of the show and listened to the song, wrote out my little form chart and I was ready. The way Jeff was set up was sideways at the front of the stage so people could see him and he could see the band and no one had to turn around, and David was at the other side, same thing, kind of like a half circle. They did the show and walked off and then came back and Jeff sat down and I thought, 'Maybe he forgot.' The moment the song started, which is him playing the floor tom, he remembered. He looked at me and said, 'You're playing this song. Are you ready?' I said, 'Yeah.' He said, 'Come on.' He just got up and I ran in and played it. It was fun and it was good. Lukather, as they do, came over and was screaming at me, 'Grimm, this is great!' I got up and went back and Jeff was, 'No, no, no, you're taking a bow,' and it was, 'Oh my God, it's a whole thing!' Later David told me that it was great but that Jeff hadn't told them he was going to do that, and they were all surprised. I said, 'I'm glad it was okay.' And he said, 'Yeah, we're all glad it was okay.' He said that's one thing Jeff would do, if there was a drummer like Bissonette or someone, he'd just tell them, 'Hey why don't you just sit in,' but he wouldn't tell the rest of them."

On tour supporting *The Seventh One* in 1988.

(Photo courtesy of Barney Hurley)

THE SEVENTH ONE

Engineer/producer **GEORGE MASSENBURG** was very disappointed to hear that Steve P. had left the band. He and (keyboardist/Little Feat co-founder) Bill Payne were really looking forward to his synth work on the record. It turned out, like Luke says, Steve P. was there anyway. But Massenburg notes he didn't offer much creative input: "He would play what he heard and that was that."

Steve P. admits he approached the album as if he were a hired hand because of the situation. Gone was the desire to be ridiculed for giving too much of himself.

"They would see me spend, for instance, two weeks on a 'Rosanna' solo and they would come up to me—all of them—and say, 'Quincy Jones hires you and you do three songs in an afternoon,'" Steve P. recounts. "'David Foster hires you and you do the synth on two songs in less than three hours. Why can't you just do that for us?'"

So he did.

Nonetheless, Massenburg was excited to be on the project. He had already worked with Toto on *Fahrenheit*, although he is not credited. He was brought in to mix "Don't Stop Me Now," a tune written by Lukather and Paich on which Miles Davis played. When it came time to record *The Seventh One* in 1987, the way Lukather remembers it, Jeff was working on some sessions with Massenburg and Payne, and they pitched themselves to Jeff.

"Jeff brought them to Paich's studio, The Manor—his house in Sherman Oaks—and they said they were the right guys for the job," Lukather recalls. "They sold us and we said, 'Well let's try it and see,' and it worked out great. Jeff said to me and Dave (Steve P. had just left the band), 'Man, George gets the great sounds and it would be great to have a real musician like Billy help push us a bit.'" Lukather continues. "We all loved and respected Billy and George, and I had worked with George on Earth, Wind and Fire's *Faces* record and some other stuff and loved the guy. (Our depraved humor was well-matched, ha ha.) We were all fans of his, well both of them. It seemed like a cool, off-the-beaten-path idea, and it worked really well. *The Seventh One* is one of my favorite Toto records and sold multi-platinum worldwide, and is still a fan fave as well."

As Massenburg recalls, Jeff and he went way back to when Massenburg first came to Los Angeles in late 1975. He already knew about Porcaro: "I knew he followed in the footsteps of my then-favorite drummers Jim Gordon and Jim Keltner, so I really wanted to work with him," Massenburg says.

Massenburg hired him on his first project, Valerie Carter's debut solo album *Just a Stone's Throw Away*. He says what was great about Jeff, like any great drummer, is he played the song, and he describes his vivid memory of Jeff listening to a playback: "One of the pictures I get of Jeff is visual: Jeff with his arms folded, listening to a track and sticking his tongue in the cheek of his mouth."

Jeff told me *The Seventh One* was the first album Toto had recorded where they actually heard a vocal going on while they cut. He said they tried to do as much live rhythm tracking as possible. He said on "A Thousand Years" and "These Chains" he listened to the demo cassettes through headphones while recording the drum tracks, explaining the process: "It was like playing along to a record, which I did when I was learning how to play. I did that on those particular tunes because the demos were great, the two guys were singing, so it was definitely the right tempo, and production of the demos was such that I heard all the parts. So I played along. The only other track that's not live is 'You Got Me.' That track was a demo that David wrote for Whitney Houston, We heard the song and said, 'We should do this in Toto.' The song felt great; it was all electronics, drum machine and stuff, and we decided to add real drums, percussion, real horns, guitar, etc."

"Mushanga" was one of Jeff's favorite tracks on *The Seventh One*, and

Lukather says the part Porcaro played dictated the song. Porcaro told me that he had fun on that track "because walking into the studio, I knew what the thing was going to be, but I wanted to think of a new beat for me—something different," he said. "I didn't want one of those situations where, after I heard what I did, it ends up that I stole it or I'd heard it before in some sort of context. It was fun doing that beat. Now that I know it, I wish we could cut the track again. It was one of those things where I had to figure out the sticking a certain way; there are no overdubs."

When I asked him to explain the beat, he replied with a laugh, "No, this beat of all beats, you cannot explain. It's impossible. I sat for an hour trying to explain it to my dad and he was cracking up because it involves hitting every drum, the rim, the head, the hi-hat, and it's all this split-hand stuff. It's basically a simple thing once you do it, but it's confusing to figure out for the first time—at least for me. As soon as I got it, it was, 'Quick, let's cut the track.' We just cut it with David and me and I went into a trance and tried to remember it, because a lot of it had to do with me just getting comfortable with my sticking. The track came out great, but then after we cut it, I finally got the beat down and started adding more things, like playing quarter notes on the hi-hat and things like that."

On that album, Porcaro said he liked "These Chains" because it was an exact rip-off of Bernard Purdie on Steely Dan's "Home at Last" from *Aja*.

"It's not exactly the same beat, but that was the sole inspiration, just like with 'Rosanna,'" Jeff said. "I like 'Stay Away' a lot, the rock 'n' roll thing with Linda Ronstadt, and I like 'Anna' a lot, and the whole damn album."

Massenburg remembers one night Jeff and he smoked some pot and decided to dissect time: "I've always been very research oriented," Massenburg says. "We usually played to a click track, so we wanted to discover what the minimum latency was—the degree of shift in the click—what you could hear in a groove in terms of shift if you moved the click by these small increments. We got really high and we started to hear a difference in groove at about 500 microseconds, which is 20 times finer than anyone had ever reported, so I've lived with that all these years. That's more than the delay or latency in converters. To really understand what you're hearing or what the groove is, you have to feel the groove and make corrections for it. More than anything, that's what I learned from Jeff: how to find the groove. Since then, I've been less likely to use a click track to cut a track."

Massenburg admits that things would get out of control in the studio with Toto. He even brought a blowgun to the studio and would let it loose on a target on the wall when things got nuts. Sometimes he says he just would not endure it, recounting one day: "We're starting the mix, we think we've finished the last overdub and it was a struggle because Joe Williams was having a little bit of trouble making the guys happy with his vocals. When we really identified that, we were starting the mix, we were in Studio C in the Complex and Billy (Payne) and I are in the control room and the guys are in the studio and they're standing around this 4x4 baffle," Massenburg recalls, and begins to describe an ensuing bunch of partying. "I packed up and left."

He concedes the group has a lot of strong personalities with a lot of suggestions, but mostly, he says, good suggestions and "You would always listen to Jeff. Jeff would never, ever have what you would consider to be a command—'We have to do something else. We have to do a different kind of thing.'—unless he was absolutely, positively sure we were headed down the wrong path and it needed to be corrected," Massenburg recalls.

Massenburg says he also appreciated the time Jeff would put into getting sounds.

"We chased down big sounds and I think that's one of the hallmarks of the record," Massenburg asserts.

Massenburg remembers going up to Skywalker Ranch with Jeff to record Cher's 1990 album *Love Hurts*: "Peter Asher hired (producer/engineer) Nathaniel Kunkel and me, and Jeff to play all the drums for a new Cher record," Massenburg recalls. "We sorted out an approach where Jeff would play big drums on the first pass and cymbals on the second pass so we didn't have to apply room compression to cymbals. It would just be pure drums in this giant acoustic space and then we'd come back and do cymbals."

He also recalls a moment in the back of the limo on the drive up to Skywalker: "I turn to Jeff and say, 'You know that tune you did on the Boz record there's like a disco hi-hat part.' And he looked at me and raised his eyebrows like only Jeff could do and I said, 'Where the fuck did that come from?' and he said, 'Joe Wissert.' That was one of the few times that Jeff made it clear that that wouldn't have been his choice. It was not central to the sound of the record and should never have been done. Jeff had a better idea of what worked than most producers," Massenburg says, adding that

Jeff often communicated by a raising of the eyebrows. "And you knew if you didn't get a response, you had just said something so transcendently stupid that you should just go get a drink of water," Massenburg says with a laugh.

Massenburg says Jeff wasn't the kind of guy to sit down and talk about his philosophy; it would come out through sound bites: "One that really stuck with me, and one I used every session, is 'When in doubt, lay out,'" Massenburg relays. "You're playing a track and you're not only responsible for yourself, but you're responsible for all these other musicians who are, aside from being very well paid, have a schedule that they need to keep; they need to get to the next gig. You had to be responsible for your decisions. They would have an idea, but the filter was not only in listening back does it sound good, but does it challenge the song, does it fit for the song and is it good for my colleagues, and will we be able to get out of here in three hours with three or four tracks?"

Looking back now, Massenburg reflects on Porcaro's chronic complaints about his left arm: "As early as '85, '86 and '87, whenever you'd work with Jeff he'd say he wanted to get tracks quickly because his left arm hurt," Massenburg remembers. "We all sort of accepted that as Jeff being Jeff and that's what he needed. We didn't realize that that was an early indication of heart issues and circulation issues."

He said after Jeff would do a take, he would come in for the playback and announce: "That was a good track, I don't know how many more are in me. My left arm really hurts," while flexing his left arm.

But Jeffrey had always had issues with aches and pains with what he described as his small hands even gripping the sticks. Early on, he was ordering special sticks without lacquer and because of the pain after playing a show, he had finally figured out a post-concert ritual that worked for him: "The best thing, is after you play, I dip both my forearms and hands in ice, ice cold water like pitchers do," he told me. "That has been so unbelievable. There's always been a question of hot/cold, whether it be a sprain, a muscle cramp, tendonitis—somebody says cold, somebody says hot. Now they're saying cold. What causes cramps is the swelling of everything and all of a sudden something snaps, the elasticity is gone, it's tired, it's fatigued. So what I do is immediately is soak it in ice water and the swelling goes down. Then I go and take a boiling hot shower, a cold shower, one last dip in the ice, wrap up, a sweat shirt and I wake up in the morning and I don't even know I even played, except for my calluses, my bruises and cuts."

Although he seemed to get a handle on the issue, it always stuck in the back of his mind. Jamo says he only thinks he saw Jeff nervous once, but I know otherwise. Toto was on tour in Alabama and drummer Roger Hawkins and the entire Muscle Shoals Rhythm Section showed up to see the concert. They came backstage before the show and Jamieson says when they left to take their seats you could hear a pin drop in the room.

"They were their idols," Jamieson says. "He didn't tell me he was nervous, but I sensed it."

Jamo obviously didn't realize that Jeff was very nervous every night he played, which he confessed to me in an interview: "I get dizzy and queasy when I first sit down," Porcaro admitted. "I still have a psychological thing about number one: am I going to play good, and number two: am I going to cramp still, even though I think I have all these magic things (solutions)? Nothing scares me more than cramping, because if I cramp, I'm shot. If my right arm cramps like it used to, up until I was 21, I can't play for three weeks, not like I do, and that's loss of revenue and loss of a lot of stuff."

In late 1990 Porcaro worked on **RICHARD MARX'S** *Rush Street*. Their relationship went back to the '80's.

"When I moved from Chicago to L.A., I was 18. It was '82. I came out here from the encouragement of Lionel Richie, who was doing his first solo record and hired me as a background singer on 'You Are' and a couple of other things. He said, 'Anytime I'm in the studio, you're welcome to be here,'" Marx recalls. "I took him up on that incredible, gracious offer and basically spent six or seven months nearly every day in the studio watching him make that first solo record. He had left the Commodores and like those of us who are solo artists and not tied to a band, he realized he could pick from the greatest candy store of musicians he wanted. So he had Joe Walsh play on a song and different people and he began to wade into the different musicians."

Marx says by Richie's second album, *Can't Slow Down*, on which he also sang backgrounds, Richie was using Lukather, with whom Marx had become friendly.

"He was just a couple of years older than me, whereas everybody else was a lot older than me. I was really the kid in town and up until then, he was the baby. And I was really lucky, he was so welcoming and gracious,"

Marx says. "And of course, I was a big Toto fan. So Luke introduced me to Jeff at a session and Jeff was so super cool. He was the coolest cat in the room."

Marx remembers that Jeff and he would run into each other at sessions and see each other in hallways and chat. Then Marx says he recalls bumping into Jeff at a session somewhere after Marx had had a couple of hit songs and Jeff was so thrilled for him.

"It was almost like pride," Richard says. "It was, 'I've known this kid since he was fuckin' 18 and now he's having hits left and right.' He was so happy. Even though he had nothing to do with it, he was so genuinely happy for me. It was the first time he had seen me in a while and he gave me a big hug in the hallway and it knocked me out of the park and he made a point of saying, 'And you're doing it with really great stuff.'"

Recalling how Jeff came to work with him, Marx recalls: "I think it started with him kidding me about not having hired him. I mean I knew he really didn't give a shit, but...," Marx didn't finish the sentence, but it was as if he was saying it still meant something to him that Jeff said it. "This was after I had had some hits. And I had my go-to guys, especially on the first album. I was using John Keane, J.R. a little and Tris Imboden, so I kinda had my guys. It didn't even occur to me to hire Jeff because, first of all, I thought, 'Oh, he doesn't need the work,' and I had my go-to guys. But it started with him giving me some shit one day about it in the hallway, in a playful way, as he was saying goodbye to me. He kind of leaned into me and said, 'Ya know, it wouldn't kill you to hire me for a gig, man.' So I said, 'You're on. I'm cutting in a few months.'"

Altogether Porcaro recorded five tracks with Marx. Four were recorded right away and of those four, three—"Hands in Your Pocket," "Calling You," and "Superstar" —ended up on Marx's 1991 album *Rush Street*. "One Man" was held for Marx's next album, *Paid Vacation*, released in 1994 after Jeff's death. "Chains Around Your Heart," also on *Rush Street*, was recorded a week after the first four.

"I think what people consider the greatest drummers on earth are those who play the song and are all about the song and not their performance," says Marx, reiterating what everyone else has said about Porcaro. "He was masterful, but he was such a pro in that way, and that's why he was so successful. He got his mind around the song."

Marx says he saw Jeff lose it once, though, and it really was all in the name of creativity, even though for a moment it caused some tension. He recounts that they were in the midst of cutting "Superstar" after they had worked it up: "It was like the third take and I was singing along with the guys; I don't think I was playing. I was sitting in the vocal booth and calling out different production things because I was producing the record, too, and we got to like the middle of the second chorus and I realized the bass part was not what we had worked out," Marx recalls. "I was trying to be very conscious of everyone's time and energy and didn't want to waste a take that I knew we would have to do over because I knew it wasn't right, so I called, 'Stop, stop, stop,' and Jeff got so pissed off for a second. He said, 'Man, I was in such a fuckin' groove. It's like you jumped up and down on my dick, man.' He got over it immediately, but it was the only time I had a problem with him. It was because he was so into what he was doing. It wasn't like he was being a diva; it was just he was so in the moment of the groove."

After the session, Marx pulled Jeff aside and apologized and Jeff said, "No, I'm sorry I said anything; it was like I was in a hypnotic state."

Marx also gave Porcaro arrangement credit on that song, and when questioned about that fact, Marx said this memory was hazy since the session had been nearly 30 years ago, but adds, "But my best guess is that he helped me sort out the section coming out of the second chorus going into the solo," Marx surmises. "I remember wanting a sort of frenetic sounding segue between those sections and we kept trying different drum patterns and then he suggested what you hear, and then (bassist Leland) Sklar and (guitarist Mike) Landau worked their parts around it."

When the initial four songs were cut and they were saying their goodbyes, Marx told Jeff he had a ballad for the album that he really wanted Jeff to do the following week on Thursday. Jeff was scheduled to leave on a family vacation the Wednesday before the planned session.

"I knew I had to wrap up the album and I'd have to get somebody else, and I said, 'Oh man,' and he said, 'Can you wait?' And I said, 'No, I can't,' He looked at me with that shit-eating grin look of his and leaned right into me and said, 'Give me 24 hours and let me see if I can work this shit out, man,'" Marx recalls. "Sure enough, he called me that night and said, 'It didn't go over that well. I'm in the dog house a little bit tonight, but I talked her into it. We're going to go Friday.'"

Taking a moment to talk about Porcaro's quiet charisma and indefinable energy Marx added, "I absolutely loved him."

Marx held "One Man" off the album because the ballad "Chains Around Your Heart" was not a hit and he didn't want to put another slower-tempo song on the album. While making *Paid Vacation* a year and a half later, he thought it fit with the material better, so he decided to mix it.

"I had forgotten in that time it was Jeff that played drums and not only is he counting it off, but I'm hearing him yelling something funny to me and stuff. It had only been six or eight months since he had died and it was brutal. It was beautiful, but it was weird hearing his voice," says Marx, who dedicated the song to him on the album.

In what was surely one of our last conversations, Jeff proudly told me he had just worked with **BRUCE SPRINGSTEEN**. He relayed the whole story to me, and how he had gotten the call from producer Chuck Plotkin, who booked him for the session in September 1989 at One on One Recording in North Hollywood. He got to the studio along with bassist Bob Glaub and keyboardist Ian McLagan before Springsteen arrived, and they asked what they were going to be cutting.

The reply was "Viva Las Vegas."

"Viva Las Vegas?" they asked in disbelief.

"And then Springsteen came in and played us his version of 'Viva Las Vegas' on acoustic and it was unbelievable," Porcaro said. "Then he went in with his Telecaster as part of the rhythm section and sang and played. The four of us cut 'Viva Las Vegas' and it's a great rock 'n' roll track."

Porcaro told me that the song, recorded for *The Last Temptation Of Elvis*, a UK-only various artists album produced by British music magazine *New Musical Express* and released in February 1990 in support of the Nordoff-Robbins Music Therapy Center in London, took about four or five takes to complete.

Bob Glaub can still envision Jeff listening to the playback of "Viva Las Vegas": "He would dance in the studio listening to the playback if something felt great," Glaub says, adding quickly. "Well, something always felt good if he was playing it. But he had this distinctive kind of several little steps he'd do with the different kind of grooves and I have a very vivid memory of listening to the playback and watching him dance and play air bass."

"A cut above the rest," is how Springsteen describes Porcaro when he granted me a rare interview for this book, to talk about hiring Jeff for his album *Human Touch*. Springsteen says it was one of the first times he was going outside of the E Street Band to look for musicians and when he was going through some of the Los Angeles musicians, Porcaro's name, of course, came up.

"Once we started playing, it was evident he was at the top of the game, incredible feel and all the things you look for in a drummer, he had in spades," Springsteen asserts, confiding while he tried working with other great players, for the rock music on *Human Touch*, Jeff was most perfect. "His ability to keep time was staggering, first of all," Springsteen attests. "He was an incredible, incredible time keeper, so his grooves were just deep and beautiful. And then his ability to fill without losing his time was just spectacular. He had these beautifully constructed fills that he would do around the drums and then he would come back just right on the money. It was just at a level, just like I said, heads above everybody else. He was an amazing performer."

Describing how he presented the songs to the musicians, Springsteen says, "I might have had demos of some, but then on some, the usual way, I kind of go out there and start strumming some chords, and we find a groove. I present the arrangement and at the time I was working with Roy (Bittan), my pianist, so we would get in the studio, find an arrangement and do it all by ear, basically."

Springsteen says he's definitely "the boss" on a session, but allows some creativity on the part of the players—"within limits," was how he put it—explaining, "I have pretty specific ideas of what I want to hear, but if somebody is bringing their own to it and it's working, great, and when you have the great musicians, they do do that. Generally they rarely have to be told what to play; that's why they're great," Springsteen says. "They're playing it so tastefully and they're attuned to what you're doing. Occasionally something might need a little shaping, but it's usually pretty minor, but to my recollection the playing was very exciting.

"Jeff was a career high as far as having fun playing with another musician outside of my band," Springsteen adds.

They spent at least three weeks together on that record, and Springsteen says while Jeff was extremely professional, he was also very sociable, describing the hang: "He was just a pleasure to be with," Springsteen says. "He had a million tales about the L.A. studio scene, all of which were entertaining and fascinating to me because I had never been a part of that kind of scene. He was just a lovely guy, to the point of where I asked him to come out on the road with me. We got along so well and his playing was so powerful. I was looking for another drummer for that particular tour and he was certainly first in mind."

As we neared the end of our conversation, Springsteen opened up a little bit more: "The impact his playing made on me was quite deep. He really was a very, very unusual musician. The level of what he did was just at the top. I have one of the greatest drummers in the world with Max Weinberg, but Jeff was just unique. People say you can't get a lot of emotion out of studio players but it's not true. The truth is the guys who are great are great because they bring that also and in Jeff's case, he certainly brought that with him—emotion in his playing. If you listen to the drumming on that record, I think it's spectacular."

Bassist **RANDY JACKSON** also played on *Human Touch* and says: "That particular session was amazing because Bruce had never worked with me or Jeff. We recorded a bunch of songs a bunch of different ways. I can't remember how many songs we did. I know we did a lot more than what made the record."

While many know of Jackson as a longtime judge on the hit TV show "American Idol," Jackson has played and recorded with such artists as Madonna, Mariah Carey, Celine Dion, Jon Bon Jovi, Michael Bolton, Bob Dylan, Billy Joel, Journey and a long list of others. He was excited to have a chance to work with Springsteen.

"Bruce is the quintessential artist, and most true artists have an idea of the canvas they want to paint on and what they want to paint, so when you're a session guy you're always there to try to fulfill those needs and get closer, if not on the head, of what they want and maybe offer a little something different," Jackson continues. "Jeff was so unbelievably talented that he could drive the bus all over the barn. You could say, 'I want this to sound like Braunstein meets Heifitz meets Paganini meets Mikos meets Metallica,' and he'd go, 'Right. Got it, let's go.' There are a ton of musicians that go to all these music schools and can play a billion notes, but is it accompanied by any feeling?" Jackson asks. "Because really, what you're trying to portray as a drummer, musician or artist is a heartfelt feeling with someone else's music. And that is something that you're really born with, that sort of innate quality to be able to inflect that emotional feeling, because it's emotion at the end of the day. It's very rare that drummers are really listening to the singer and really playing the accompaniment and listening to the whole arrangement and the band, playing together," Jackson continues. "It's an innate thing you're born with that you're not an egotist on the drums—'listen to me, I can do this, I can do that.'"

Jackson says he really enjoyed seeing Springsteen's process: "We'd play something and he'd say, 'No, let's try it a little bit more like this.' It's almost like trying on shoes," Jackson says, explaining Springsteen would often play a demo and discuss the feel.

Jackson says during breaks they'd always be telling jokes and cracking each other up, "and cracking Bruce up," he remarks, adding, like Springsteen mentioned, during down time Jeff and he would share their tales about the recording sessions they did: "We'd tell him how back in the day we'd do three or four a day. Jeff did six sometimes; I was doing other things, like I was an A&R guy for Columbia at the time," Jackson says. "I remember Bruce really enjoying hearing about that. I also think he really enjoyed getting some different guys in who were different from the E Street Band—who are all incredible and have created a legacy—but it was just a different look. I really appreciated, and I know Jeff did also, Bruce letting us into his sandbox. Roy Bittan from the E Street Band was also on those sessions and Jon Landau, the greatest manager in the world, was always there, and Jeff and I made this comment once: 'Wow, it's kinda cool, man, we've been let into the inner sanctum.'"

PART THREE

While on tour, Jeff hung out with original drummer from Bob Seger's Silver Bullet Band, Charlie Martin, circa '84.

(Photo courtesy of Paul Jamieson)

STORIES

Porcaro seemed to have his own inner sanctum, but it was a bit of an illusion. He was so cool, so hip, and yet so accessible that you couldn't believe it if he let you in, but he did to so many. There are so many stories of virtual strangers calling him up and asking for meet-ups and or visits to sessions and I've never heard of one that was turned down. Paich says there are countless drummers who owe their careers to Jeff—and I know not just drummers. There is no shortage of stories about Porcaro's kindness and generosity.

Kerry Morris remembers how Jeff came through at a difficult time for him sometime around 1976: "He let me stay at the Hesby house for almost three months. I had a falling out with the family, so I was living on the street. He said, 'Man, you need sanctuary. You gotta move in here for a while,'" Kerry says, adding that Jeff was always attuned to someone's feelings, always asking, "You okay?"

One day Jeff and his family went to Disneyland, and Morris' friend was the drummer playing in the Tomorrowland Terrace band at the time. Kerry mentioned that to Jeff before he went to Disneyland and Morris reports: "Jeff didn't know the guy, but Jeff noticed that his drumhead broke. So between tunes he went down (to the stage) and asked him, 'Hey man, do you need a drumhead?' And he said, 'Yeah, you got one?' So Jeff went out of the park, went to his car and got him a snare head and brought it back in and gave it to him, so for the rest of the day he could play. The whole time, this guy knew it was Jeff. I heard that from my friend."

In 1982, Jeff loaned drum tech Paul Jamieson $10,000 to buy his first home. Jamieson had worked with him from the end of 1975 to the late '80s. They were great friends, or as Jeff called him, "my cat." Paul also remembers how special Jeff treated his parents when they visited from Detroit.

"He had met them a couple of times when Toto played in Detroit and he loved my father," Jamieson recalls. "He got a limo to pick them up at the airport. I had Raider season tickets and Jeff went to probably a dozen games with me over the years at the Coliseum. The limo dropped me and my old man off at the Raiders game, took my mom and girlfriend to my house in Studio City and picked us up after the game. My old man told me it was the fourth time in his whole life he had ever ridden in a limousine."

Porcaro and Jamieson were big football fans. They went to Super Bowl XVII together at the Rose Bowl in Pasadena in 1983 (Washington Redskins vs. Miami Dolphins). Jamo says they were both boxing fans, particularly the middleweight division: Tommy Hearns, Sugar Ray Leonard, Marvin Hagler, Roberto Duran, Wilfred Benitez. And they had a lot of laughs together. One of Paul's favorite memories of Jeff was down in Miami when they went to do the follow-up album to the Bee Gees' *Saturday Night Fever*. The first day of the two-week stay, Jeff handed him his credit card and told him to rent a car.

"I went and got a Mustang convertible with a four-speed. He doesn't know how to drive a stick shift," Jamieson recounts. "We come out of the studio at midnight to go back to the hotel and get into the car and he says, 'What's this shit?' And I said, 'It's a stick shift.' He said, 'You know I don't know how to drive one.' I said, 'Right. I'm going to teach you.' He starts giving me a hard time, so we pull into a Winn Dixie parking lot and he gets into the driver's seat and he stalls it out about 20 times. He just had this mental block. This guy could play eight notes with his right foot and the hi-hat like a ballerina, but he just could not do this. And after about 20, 30 times he started yelling at me. I drove to the hotel and the studio the next day and took it back and got one with an automatic."

Jamo's other favorite story was during their Paris stay while Jeff was working on David Gilmour's solo album, revealing the practical joker that Jeff was: "I'm there with Pink Floyd's guitar player and Toto's drummer. I'm 32 years old and I want to go to the clubs and find some French babe. Gilmour's married and Jeff was with Susie, so I'm on my own," Jamieson relays. "I kept asking Gilmour about a club. He kept saying, 'Ok Jamie.'—for some reason that's what he was calling me instead of Jamo. He said, 'I got you sorted Jamie, I got you sorted for Wednesday.' Wednesday comes. A couple of times during the day I remind him, he says, 'I got you sorted, Jamie.' So we go to leave, it's midnight. Every day we had taken a taxi there to the studio and every night Gilmour had driven both Jeff and me back to the hotel. We go to leave and Jeff jumps in the back seat of Gilmour's four-door Jaguar, and I had always let Jeff ride in the front and I had gotten in the back. I didn't think twice about it. So we're driving, and in Paris they have these giant parks the size of Central Park. We're driving through this park and Gilmour says, 'I got you sorted, Jamie.' And there's a bunch of hookers. We pull up, I'm in the passenger seat, Gilmour rolls down the window and starts speaking French to one of them. She's got her back to me, blond, with this fuzzy fur coat on like Pebbles Flintstone. She turns around, opens the coat and she's nude. She has the biggest pair of fake tits I ever saw in my life. Then I look down and her dick is twice the size of mine. Gilmour and Jeff just started laughing. The two of them were in on it. Every time I see Gilmour, he brings that up."

Jamo also recalls the memorable meeting on the *Toto IV* tour between Jeff and Jamo's childhood friend Charlie Martin, who had been the original drummer in Bob Seger's Silver Bullet Band: "They had done the live record at Cobo Hall (*Live Bullet*) which was a big record for Seger, and they were starting to break everywhere. They were on tour and had two weeks off, so they came home. Charlie was driving his car and it broke down on the freeway, and in Detroit the freeways are underground. It was at night and he was walking up the ramp to get help when some drunk ran him over and crushed his legs, and he's in a wheelchair for the rest of his life. Jeff loved his playing, and I invited him to the Toto gig. After the gig we had a big party at the hotel, and he and Jeff met that night. I'll never forget, Charlie was doing wheelies in his wheelchair on the dance floor like he was dancing."

Jamo says he learned a lot from Jeff. Once on a session he asked him, "When you do a date, what's your job?" Jeff answered simply, "To keep time and play to the singer." Another time, they were riding in Jeff's 450SLC Mercedes and Carly Simon's "You're So Vain" came on the radio. Jamieson went to change the station and Porcaro stopped him, saying, "No, put that back." "I said, 'You like that song?' Jeff said, 'That's Jim Gordon, that's a perfect drum track. I learned something that day. He said, 'Watch how he lays back here. Watch how he pushes here.'"

Jeff's kindness towards band drummers he was replacing in the studio was incredible, said Jamo: "The kid was in the studio with his nose against the glass watching everything Jeff was doing and Jeff would immediately go up to the guy when the band wasn't playing and do whatever he could to put the guy at ease," Paul says. "He would say, 'Hey I'm not here to steal your job. I need your help,' and he would do as much as he could to involve the guy in the process. He went out of his way to make him feel good and ask him, 'So what about the chorus?' or this part or that part? I thought that was a real endearing thing about him."

Jeff felt that replacing someone wasn't always easy to do with grace. He told a story about how he was called to do a job for a band in England and was given the impression they didn't have a drummer, but when he got there, he encountered the uncomfortable situation with the drummer arguing with the band about why he couldn't play on the album. Porcaro told Rick Mattingly (in an article called "Getting Replaced" in the April, 1992, issue of *Modern Drummer*) sometimes the drummer is actually good enough to play on the records, but in this case, after hearing the band's demos, he realized why he had been called in for the job. Nonetheless, Porcaro sat with the band drummer at dinner "and hung out and talked about, 'yes, isn't it a drag, but...,' and I explained to him what I thought the producer was looking for, not making it an uptight situation. And after I talked to him about what he was doing on one particular track that I thought maybe they weren't satisfied with, I managed to convince the producer and leader of the band to let him play on that song."

Porcaro went on to say he would tell band drummers not to take it personally. Sometimes it was just a budget thing; he could get the job done faster, or he was even just hired because he was a "name." But ultimately, Jeff said, it was the producer's responsibility to explain to the band members that Jeff was hired to put them on the charts and he was doing this to make that happen, so they all needed to get on board for the big picture.

Jeff was willing to lose out on work completely because of these kinds of principles. Gary Grimm recalls a situation where he was with Jeff when he was called to replace a drum track that happened to be Vinnie Colaiuta. Gary doesn't remember who the producer or the artist were, but he remembers Jeff's response vividly because he had always heard about these instances: "Jeff got in there and he was real polite and real professional and said, 'Ok, play me the track,' and then he said, 'You know, there's nothing I can do to do any better than that.' And he said, 'Come on Gary,' and we left."

In another twist, Porcaro wasn't above replacing himself. Jamieson says Jeff's humility was rare in the studios. If he believed there was someone who could do the session better, he would tell the producer to get that other drummer.

Mike Baird is just one drummer with whom I spoke who is evidence of that: "He'd just stop in the middle of a session and call and say, 'What are you doing?' I'd say, 'I'm just hanging.' And he'd say, 'OK, be at Record Plant. You gotta play on this track. See you here,'" Baird recalls. "Then I'd get a call from the cartage company saying they were on their way there with my stuff. I'd say, 'What's going on?' And they'd say, 'I have no idea, we just got a call from Jeff saying to deliver your stuff.' I showed up at Record Plant. His drums are there and they're miking my kit. He comes out and goes, 'I just told the producer, 'The person for this track is Mike Baird. You gotta use him.' He was the one who had the date, but he told that to the producer and the producer said, 'Okay.' And he sat right next to me the whole fucking time. And then they go, 'Okay, that sounds good, Mike,' and Jeff goes, 'Great. Hey, thanks a lot,' and then walks off. And it's like okay, what the fuck just happened? The cartage guys come back in, break down my stuff and that was that."

Another example of Porcaro's passing his work over to someone else was early in 1991, when he worked on Warren Zevon's *Mr. Bad Example* with producer Waddy Wachtel. Wachtel recounts this story as one of the wonderful moments of the album when, after hiring Jeff to record the album, which "he plays just beautifully on everything of course," it got to the track "Things to Do in Denver when You're Dead." Jeff looked at Wachtel and said, "This has to be Keltner. This is so Jim."

"I said, 'That's brilliant.' We called Jim and got him in," Waddy recalls. "If Jeff is telling me that the right drummer for this is not in the studio at the moment, and he's someone I love dearly, I said, 'Ya know, you're probably right.' And it was the perfect groove for Jim to play."

As Keltner describes it: "Jeff would do the unthinkable. Nobody else would ever do this. He would call from the studio himself and say, 'Hey Jimmy, you gotta come down and play on this track. I can't.' I'd say, 'What do you mean?' And he'd say, 'I can't feel it. I can't make it work, but you can.' I was so amazed he would do something like that," Keltner relays with a laugh. "So I would go, just because I wanted to hang out with him, because he was one of my closest friends. I remember that night very well and I remember being up on the drums and I have a memory of him standing there, watching me playing, laughing. I always made him laugh when I played."

Wachtel thinks they probably cut "Mr. Bad Example" the same day, which Keltner also played instead of Jeff.

Talking about how Porcaro played for the song, Wachtel says, "If you just listen to the album *Mr. Bad Example*, the first song, 'Finishing Touches,' is an entirely different treatment from the next song 'Suzie Lightning,' and then 'Model Citizen' and each one. He's a great accompanist, aside from being a great technician. He's a song guy. A good musician is a song player. That's why when he heard 'Things to Do in Denver When You're Dead,' he just looked at me and said, 'Wad, this has Keltner all over it.' And he called him."

Continuing to talk about the different cuts, Wachtel says, "On the song 'Finishing Touches,' we wanted an extremely tough drum sound, so he couldn't use cymbals and we had open microphones. If he had used cymbals, we all would have died. We had the microphones wide open in the room to get this drum sound we wanted. Then on 'Suzie Lightning' there is some of the most exquisite, beautiful drumming you have ever heard," Wachtel adds. "The same on 'Searching for a Heart.' He played them like he wrote them. He really did. He was so dear to my heart."

So many artists and players have commented how Porcaro played for the song. Obviously that was paramount to songwriters as well. While I didn't have the opportunity to have an extensive interview with the Grammy, Oscar and Golden Globe winner Carole Bayer-Sager, she answered some questions via e-mail. The composer, whose material has been recorded by such legends as Michael Jackson, Celine Dion, Barbra Streisand and Frank Sinatra, recorded a solo album, *Too*, in 1978 on which Jeff played on one track, and *Sometimes Late at Nigh*t in 1981 on which he played on six. Bayer-Sager says she met Jeff via David Foster and she remembers him as a great drummer. "I always felt lucky if I could get him on any of my sessions. He had great sensitivity. He could play on ballads as well as up-tempo tracks. He was also a great guy. I was always happy to see him."

With all the stories of Porcaro's kindnesses, what you don't really hear are stories of Jeff leaning on other people or sharing feelings of sadness. Jeff very rarely showed his emotions. I questioned every close family member and musical cohort as to whether they ever saw Jeff break down. I asked Joe and Eileen if they ever had to comfort their son in the wake of a death or any other emotional trauma, and Eileen said the only time she could recall was as a little boy when he would hurt himself or get a scrape like little boys did; nothing else, nothing later on in life. To me, Jeff sounded like an alien until Joe explained an event in his own life at about the age of eight that changed his own emotional displays and probably influenced his children.

"When I was a kid back in New Britain, Connecticut, there was this Irish family next door and we heard the mom had passed away, so I went over there," Joe remembers. "The Italians in those days, because there were no funeral homes, when somebody passed, the casket was in the living room for a whole week and there were people screaming and wearing black. I remember when my uncles passed, the screaming and the crying all week long. When I went to this Irish family's home, there was an accordion and a violin and people were dancing and laughing and people were stoned. It was a celebration. They weren't freaking out. It stayed with me all my life. When my mother and father passed, of course I was sad, but I didn't cry. That one scene changed my life forever about that stuff."

Joleen weighs in that she thinks Jeff was just controlled because they grew up in a house where peace was of paramount importance. Joe's childhood had been somewhat rocky and it was very important to him that the household be calm and without drama. Jeff, as the oldest, was the arbiter of tranquility: "If we got angry we had to go to our room," Joleen says. "It was, 'Go ahead, be angry, but you're not going to scream in the house in front of everybody and cause a scene.' Jeff's saying was always, 'Don't blow it.' So if you started having a temper tantrum or a hissy fit he would say, 'You're blowing it.'"

Of course, it couldn't always be controlled, considering there was a challenging dynamic between Jeff and his youngest brother Steve. Joleen recalls the last family vacation they took to the East Coast for a cousin's wedding when she was about 12 and Jeff was 19, and they spent a week in Maine and a week in Connecticut.

"My mom and dad were out visiting friends and all of us kids had stayed back with my Uncle Vinny and my Aunt Josie. I don't know what Jeff and Steve got into it about, but I just heard a big commotion in the house and Aunt Josie going, 'Knock it off.' Steve would get emotional because that was the thing. Jeff would make all of us cry because he was like our older brother who we looked up to, so if he just talked to you in a disappointing voice he could make you cry. It's not like he ever called me any names or anything, it was just that voice being disappointed in you. You loved him that much that you didn't want him disappointed in you, so you would get emotional. And Jeff was kinda hard on Steve because I think Steve came along and he was so frickin' cute and apparently cracked people up from the minute he came along. He was just one of those really cute babies who got a lot of attention for that, being the youngest boy and all of that, so who knows, maybe there was a little jealousy."

The other time she saw her two brothers go at each other was because Steve had gone into Jeff's closet and "borrowed" a shirt without asking: "Jeff won best dressed at Grant High School his senior year," Joleen discloses. "The kicker was that he wore the same pair of pants every day, but he washed his pants every single night so they weren't dirty, nasty pants, but girls added patches. It started out as just patches and then embroidery got added. Then he had tons of denim shirts and girls would do the same thing with intricate embroidery or they'd sew those really cool trims and patches. So Jeff saw a spot in his closet missing a shirt that Steve had taken and there was a big scene. And it was like, 'Oh my God.' That would be nothing in my household today, but for us growing up it was, 'Oh my God.' I think somebody left in tears, and it wasn't Jeff."

From 1980 to 1983 Joleen was Jeff's personal assistant. She took over when Jeff discovered that his previous assistant was stealing money from him and she describes it as a lot of fun: "I was 19 at the time and he was 25. Normally I wouldn't get to see him that much except Sunday brunch, but now I got to see him five days a week," Joleen says. "When you're in that situation, you're hearing so much stuff, or Kerry Morris is there and they're talking about this, that and the other thing and they might include you and you're experiencing so much of your brother's life that you wouldn't be experiencing if you were at another job."

Joleen says working for her brother was wonderful; that he was "so chill." She says she always described her job as what a wife would do: keep his place tidy and make sure she had all of Jeff's favorite eats stocked. Sometimes he'd be on a session, so she'd just settle into her routine, which she outlines as follows: "I'd get a paper bag and start in the front hang room with the fireplace and I'd empty all the ash trays and make that room look perfect. He had a cleaning lady once a week, but I'd go through the house and just make it look perfect," Joleen says, adding that she did his laundry and he was a fanatic about everything being ironed.

Next was a trip to the accountant, where she picked up an envelope of cash, and she would go to the nearby Gelson's Market to get Jeff's staples, which consisted of a couple of bottles of a red wine called Valpolicella, Häagen-Dazs coffee ice cream, salted cashews, and Milwaukee miniature pickles. She discloses that when Jeff remodeled his home, he stocked his fridge with all the worker's favorite juices and soft drinks. When he was home, Jeff asked Joleen to bring her golden retriever, Lady Di (named after Lady Diana) to work with her because he loved the dog so much.

"We called her Lady, but Jeff would still call her Lady Di," Joleen recalls. "It was so sweet."

Jeff loved dogs. Cats, too. He had a jet-black cat named Chaquita with what Joleen recalls were amazing yellow/gold eyes. He had several dogs through the years, one of which was named Toby, a Blue Merle Shetland sheepdog named after their childhood collie Toby from Connecticut. The second Toby ended up with mom and dad Porcaro when Jeff was traveling too much.

Family was always paramount to Jeff. Starting in the '70s, Joe and Eileen began a traditional Sunday brunch at their home, which Joleen earlier referenced. It was an easier time of day to get the family together as opposed to an evening dinner, and all the boys would make it if they were in town. Joleen laughs as she recalls these gatherings: "My mom and I would be in the kitchen and I would be helping her. This was when I was still in high school and it would be, 'Who is he going to bring to brunch this morning?' Whatever chick he went out with Saturday night and stayed over with him, showed up. My favorite part was looking out the kitchen window and seeing what girl Jeff was bringing and especially what she was wearing. But bless him, most guys would throw some chick in a cab and say, 'See ya,' but he would bring them to Sunday brunch with the family and we treated everyone he brought over as if he were going to marry them because he treated them that way. At least that's how I saw him treat girls."

Joleen says Jeff was always the first one at the brunch and the last one to leave. His family was always important. He called mom and dad all the time. She says there wasn't a time she was at her parent's house when a call didn't come from her brother whether he was at home or on the road; unmarried or married, he called religiously.

Niko Bolas holding baby Nico in December, 1991, flanked by daddy.

(Photo courtesy of Susan Porcaro Goings)

KINGDOM OF DESIRE

Fatefully, this, Jeff's last album, was in every way, made by Toto like brothers. The songwriting was a group effort between Paich, Lukather, Mike P. and Jeff. They went back to their high school roots and wrote as a unit, and then went to Skywalker Ranch in Northern California as a unit, where they made music together, ate together, lived together, laughed together, played together and enjoyed one another.

After *The Seventh One,* Toto was on the hunt for a new lead vocalist, which is where Lukather says Porcaro talked them into the colossal mistake of hiring Jean-Michel Byron. Lukather explained the process: "At the time, the Byron experiment had failed miserably and we didn't know what to do. We had to go back and lick our wounds a little bit. Jeff and I were always talking on the road, and Dave, too, and we wanted to get back to basics where Mike, Jeff, me and Dave could sit in the room and just write some music together, from scratch. We went into Leeds, set up the gear and were jamming for a week or two," Lukather recounts, adding that making everybody a part of the process brought a new energy to the band. "Prior, we were all fighting to get our songs on the record," he admits.

Lukather says everybody was in a good mood, just hanging out with his high school buddies. On top of that, they were all making equal money: "a good reason to be in a good mood." At least 75% of the record was created that way, he recalls, and it came out more hard-edged than some of their previous work, noting: "I thought Dave and I were going to share the vocals 50/50, but Dave just kept wimping out on me. He kept going, 'No, you do it, you do it.' Everybody thought it was me pushing it, but it wasn't that way at all," Luke says with a laugh. "It was also that I would stay in the vocal booth until I got a vocal, until my fuckin' lungs were on the floor. This is before you could fix anything; you had to give performances."

Lukather says going to George Lucas' Skywalker Ranch with producer/engineer Greg Ladanyi in Northern California to record the album was wonderful.

"We had a great time," Lukather says. "It was a lot of fun. We partied together, we ate together, we hung together, we laughed together. There were no other distractions. We were able to be like kids again. The music was going so well that the days were so productive and it was really sounding good. We were getting a song a day and doing a ton of overdubs and we were writing, so within two weeks we had pretty much 80% of the record."

They returned to Los Angeles and did the bulk of the rest of it at Record One. They brought in "ringer" background vocalists as Luke called them, including Richard Page, Steve George, Bobby Womack and John Fogerty to sing the "high shit." That's where Steve Porcaro laid down his parts, again much like a sideman, and he happily complied to "do what you do on sessions," Steve P. says. Steve Porcaro would come in and tweak things and overdub quickly and leave, and that was his role, maintaining a distance. And his relationship with Jeff flourished at the end while they were no longer a part of Toto together.

Lukather says he learned to play golf while they recorded at Record One. When he realized Jeff was showing up at the studio two and three hours early and playing a golf computer game, Lukather went early to play with him.

"This was an old-school cathode screen computer video game and we'd just sit there, smoke a joint and play golf until everyone would show up," Lukather says. "We'd have a laugh until everyone got there. It became a thing; an endless golf game."

Lukather recalls a little-known experiment on the track "Gypsy Train": "One time we tried double drums with Tommy Lee and Jeff," he says. "It didn't work because it was just too much fun, though. Tommy and I were hanging *hard* back then, and Jeff really liked Tommy, as do I."

The song "Kingdom of Desire" was cut at A&M Studios in Hollywood. Kortchmar, who wrote the song, says he remembers playing it one day for Jeff, during a session they were on together: "All of us played all our tunes for each other when there was a break when we were in the studios. I played it for Jeff and he said, 'Oh this is great, I want to ask the guys. It would be great if we did this tune.' I said, 'Alright, great, terrific,' and then I kinda forgot about it."

A few weeks later he got a call from Porcaro: "We want to do this tune; you gotta come over here."

Kortchmar acknowledges that the mood and lyrics of the song are darker than Toto's previous work, but he was thrilled they wanted to cover it and then they asked him to produce it. He was floored that they actually named the album after it.

"Kick Down the Walls" was another song Toto cut for *Kingdom of Desire* that Kortchmar wrote with musician Stan Lynch. Lynch was still the drummer of Tom Petty's Heartbreaker's at the time they recorded the song. Of all the songs on the album, Jeff was least enthusiastic about this tune, so it was cut from some versions of the release. A re-mastered version is included on *Kingdom of Desire*'s box set.

"(Stan and Danny) had played it to a drum machine and brought it in and then Danny brought in the track and we started overdubbing. Then Jeff said, 'Let me just overdub to this because it's really good,'" Lukather recalls. "He did it in one take like he often did and everyone was jumping up and down in the studio. With Jeff it was, 'Just roll the tape in case,' and then he would just completely devastate it. There was just a little knowing wink at the end and he liked an audience, when there were cats in the studio giving him the positive energy. That was one of those moments. Stan, who's a drummer, was blown away."

Niko Bolas recalls cutting the drums at Bill Schnee's studio: "I remember we worked a bit on a different kind of sound for Jeff—lots of compression, which he loved." He also believes it was there that Jeff bestowed upon him some monumental news. Niko was just sitting in the studio when Jeff walked in and announced, "Hey man, I'm naming my boy after you," and walked out.

"It blew my mind. I was flabbergasted, humbled, honored, and excited.

Who knows how to explain it?" Bolas reveals, disclosing that in Greek tradition, he rode out to the Porcaro house to ask to be a godfather, bringing a food basket. "I put it on the back of my Harley and rode out and spent the morning at the house. I have a picture of me holding little Nico at the time," Bolas recalls. "Jeff's whole thing was his family," Bolas says. "Everyone loves Jeff and can romanticize all the studio stories because we all want to be that cool. But the reality is, when someone is that cool, they don't need to be anything. Jeff's whole trip was his kids. Once he got married, he was all about family. He would come into the studio and say, 'Dig what Christopher did.' Everything with Jeff was, 'Dig this.' And when Christopher was born, Jeff was on a pink cloud and he stayed that way for all his kids. He was, 'Dig Miles, Dig Nico.'"

Bob Clearmountain mixed the record at A&M and Lukather recalls one night in the studio—April 29, 1992—when the L.A. riots broke out in reaction to the acquittal of four policemen who had been on trial for the beating of a Black man named Rodney King.

"It was, 'Run for it, get back to your house, L.A.'s on fire,'" Lukather recalls. "We were going, 'What the fuck?' It was pretty scary. We all went running for the hills. Everyone ran home. That was a doozy of a what-the-fuck moment."

Lukather says they were pleased with the album, but the record label buried it. They asked for the record back, but the company wouldn't return it. It was the last record Jeff made with the band. By the time *Kingdom of Desire* was released in May of 1993, Jeff was gone. He left us on August 5, 1992.

PORCARO WEIGHS IN ON PRODUCERS, ENGINEERS AND ARTISTS

Jeff at Hotel Sheraton, Copenhagen, 1988.

(Photo courtesy of Carsten Weide)

Jeff asserted that there are many kinds of producers.

"We talked about the kind of producer Gary Katz is," Jeff said. "Let's take a Richard Perry. Richard Perry is very well-versed in music, has a very good musical background and is a musician and a singer. Richard's sessions may rely on having an arranger there and Richard does a lot of big commercial hit records and so his job for a drummer, you may get a lot of dictation from him as a producer, very set. There may be more pre-production time with the acts that he produces. Richard will give you musical freedom for ideas and once again, will let you know if a track is acceptable or not. He may be a little different than Katz, but very much alike."

Porcaro said that Quincy Jones knew exactly what he wanted in the studio: "And on like Michael's *Thriller* stuff there might have been some sequencers, a lot of pre-production, so they will definitely have dictated, 'I need this performed.' And that's not all the time with Q. Sometimes Q will have a rhythm section. It depends on the project.

"Then there are producers who I call figurehead producers," Jeff continued. "They should be executive producers. They may be there in the studio but they're leaving it mainly up to the arranger or the artist and there may be a self-contained band," Jeff said, adding that sometimes a producer might be one of the band members, so they work with the band and they are musicians as well. "And the thing about producers, it depends on the job," Jeff continued. "He may have more control on one job you work with him on than another because maybe the artist he's working with is more dominating as far as what he wants—and maybe rightfully so. Not that the producer doesn't have the same talent, but the producer is there to help the artist and oversee."

As for engineers, Porcaro said they are extremely important for drummers and he was very outspoken about their role: "A lot of them have their own different thing. They have special mics they use, some have certain studios they like, some have certain consoles, certain boards—having an API or a MCI or a Neve. Some have particular preferences in monitoring systems. What everybody has to realize when it gets down to the nitty gritty, they're making things on such a curve that you often miss it on your average stereo and hopefully you'll sound good.

"Some engineers are very good, but they're very set in their ways: 'This is the only way I get drum sounds.' There are certain engineers I work for who will even have snare drums: 'This is my snare drum.' Now, some of the drums may sound great and there may be something special, but there's always what size stick and who is hitting it? You may use the same mic and put the same EQ and have your same level and record in the same room, but it's still going to sound different. Maybe the drum is a versatile snare drum, but played harder or tuned anyway, the engineer still likes it for every reason."

Jeff went on to say there are engineers who completely don't like tom toms and when the Simmons electronic drums came out there was one engineer who loved them: "He said, 'Man it takes so long to get these tom sounds. With Simmons I just have to throw it up and it's there.'

"You also have engineers who are only used to a dead room, and you put them in a live room and they go nuts," he told me. "Some may be experienced enough to make that change; they don't care where they are, they're very versatile."

As for artists, Porcaro disclosed the drummer's function varies for each artist and "how brilliant they are, varies. And how fun the music is to play, varies," he said. "But the artist is the most inspiring thing for me. First of all I'm being paid a high wage to go work for him. Or I'm being paid a high wage to go play for the producer who suggested me to the artist, 'This is the guy to use.' But it depends on the session."

Jeff admitted he was very sensitive to the mood of the artist, confiding, "It gets me if I walk into a session early and I hear the record company or the management or the wife or the father or kids bugging the artist before he plays. I get upset. Or if I see the artist doesn't have what he should have, it becomes a personal thing to me because it's important that the artist be comfortable and he has what he wants and all that is on his mind is to do his thing. That's important and if the artist gets you, the musician, excited, and you're performing for that person, then you're going to get something good. I don't care what style it is, you're going to get something good."

Jeff told me he had encountered every possible scenario with an artist: moody artists, funny artists, artists who were sick, some with colds, some with addictions, some who were nasty—you name it.

One prime illustration is the story about Jeff working on the Ricki Lee

Jones *Pirates* recording session. Although he discussed it elsewhere, to my knowledge, I'm the only one who ever got the full details of that famous episode in Jeffrey's life:

"Her first album, I got called in to replace a certain famous drummer's drum part and I replaced it; it was the last thing done and I replaced it, it was brushes. She remembered that and she wants me to do her whole next album. I get hired and I get a tape a month before the sessions of Ricki's demos. What a great thing," he began. "The producers are Lenny Waronker and Russ Titelman. I go to the session; it's Chuck Rainey on bass, Dean Parks on guitar, Russ Ferrante on piano, Lenny Castro on percussion and Ricki Lee Jones playing piano and singing, and me on drums. It's Amigo Studio and the drums are in a glass isolation booth with glass going across so I can see everybody in the main studio. I have my headphones on and we start going over the song. After the first pass is through, Ricki Lee in the phones goes, 'Mr. Porcaro, I know you're known for keeping good time, but on these sessions for me, I can't have you do that because my music lyrically, when I'm telling my story, I like things to speed up and slow down. I like people to follow me.' When she said it, there was something in her voice that sounded weird, but that wasn't predominant in my mind. The first thing that entered my mind was Seals & Crofts, who liked to have their bridges up, but not radically, and then I thought of Ice Capades: you have to watch for timing like a circus. So the natural thing to say to Lee Hirschberg, the engineer was, 'Can I have more of Ricki's vocal and keyboard in my ear?' We start again and I'm listening. I'm pretty good at listening. She stops halfway through. She says, 'The time is too straight. You gotta loosen up a little bit. Did you notice on this one line I'm speeding that line up and I need you to speed up with me.' I go, 'I'm sorry.' I go, 'Lee, can I have just a little more of Ricki's vocal and take my drums down in the phones just a little bit.'

"We start again from the top and I hear her again and she's intentionally speeding up, it seemed like emphasizing it, and I'm following and that's cool. She slows down again and I thought I was slowing down. And she stops again and says, 'Try to get out of your...' And I got the impression she was saying, 'Get out of your perfect, being a perfect studio musician routine and be an artist for me,' or something like that," Porcaro continued. "When she said that, the blood rushed up to my head. Like I've said, I'm always nervous when I play for anybody, especially when they are critically acclaimed and are supposed to be the artistic statement of the times. I get real nervous because I don't want to be squaresville; I want to be hip. I looked out into the studio and all the guys in the band I've known for years, they know me, they all looked at me—we all looked at each other and they had this look on their faces like 'What's going on here? This is strange.' We did it one more time and it was so strange. I think it was Lenny Castro who went into the control room who said something to Russ and Lenny like, 'What's going on? Call a break or something real quick.' Anyway, there was a break called, for whatever reason. Ricki is still at the piano, I'm sitting at my drums going, 'What the fuck?' and I'm staring at her. She's not looking at me; I'm just looking at this person hunched over the piano, playing. She's playing a different song I have on the demo. Chuck Rainey's still sitting down. Lenny Castro comes to visit me and says, 'Man, something is weird.' And I say to Lenny, 'She's fucking with me.' I didn't want to go to Russ and Lenny Waronker, so I told Lenny (Castro) to tell them they'd better pay attention to what's going on if they're too busy in the control room and to call off the dogs or I'm skating. I'm not going to take this. I mean, I'll take criticism, but I won't take stuff that I think is unnecessary.

"So she's playing. It's still the break. Everybody's still talking. She doesn't have headphones on. I have headphones on, Chuck Rainey has headphones on and we're playing along with her," he went on. "It's a shuffle groove and it's grooving like a motherfucker. Lenny and Russ hear it in the booth and say over the talkback, 'Ricki, put your phones on.' She puts her phones on. She's still playing. She goes, 'Yeah!' Big smile on her face, and I go to myself, 'Oh, thank God, because this is grooving.' Let's move away from this first thing and do this because we're having fun. I'm thinking, 'Oh great, the beginning of a two-week project, at least we're moving on,' So we start running the track down and I come up to this fill. It's a simple fill; it's triplets over one bar. It's written out on my music. I play the fill and she stops. She says, 'You have to play harder.' I say, 'OK,' with a smile. We start again. I have brand new Remo Ambassador heads on my drums. My toms are sounding nice. I go to play the fill again. She stops. 'You gotta play harder.' Everybody looks at me. I go, 'OK, let's do it again.' We start again. One bar before the fill, I hear louder than hell in my phones, 'We're coming up to the fill, remember to play hard.' I hear a voice, telling me to play hard! I whack the shit out of my drums, as hard as I've ever hit anything in my life. While I'm hitting them, she's screaming 'Harder!' I stop. She stops. My drums have dents in them so if you hit the drum lightly they will buzz. And I'm pissed and I'm steaming inside. And I think, 'Nobody, and in what I perceive in her frame of mind, talks to me that way. This business ain't worth this garbage coming from that garbage.

"Lenny Waronker goes, 'Let's do it again.' I know he's in an isolation booth away from everybody else. We start again and everybody is looking at me. We're coming up to the fill. She goes, 'Okay, play hard.' And I take my sticks like daggers and I do the fill except I stab all my tom toms and I land on my snare drum. Both sticks are shaking, vibrating, bouncing on the snare drum. I get up, pick up my gig bag, and it's complete silence," he recounted. "I slide open the sliding glass door, I walk past her, walk into the hallway, get in my car, turn it on and drive home. I get home and the first call I get is Lenny Castro: 'Wow it's insane here.' 'What's happening?' I ask. 'She's gonna sue you. She has all these musicians here and you split.' I said 'Let her sue me. Nobody, but nobody, can talk to me that way. And if I'm the wrong cat, I wish Lenny Waronker and Russ Titelman had broken up the thing and said, 'Ok, let's call the session early and do some pre-production,' and pulled me aside and I would have been the first to say, 'Hey, you don't have to give me two days' notice. Find somebody else, I'm the wrong drummer, I'm sorry, I wish I could have been a better drummer for you guys. I did the best I could.' They let a situation go on way too long, especially for me who worked with them before. I thought I demanded a little more respect."

Castro explains how he knew from the beginning it wasn't going to be good; that Jones had said some negative things about Toto being stiff session guys in the press, even though Castro had been in her first road band: "I'm sure Lenny Waronker and Russ Titelman had heard about all that nonsense and I always wondered why would they hire these guys when they knew there was bad blood, but they did it anyway," Castro ponders. "And what happened, happened. I knew it was going to blow up and it did. There was a door through my iso room that led to the parking lot and Jeff came through that and the next thing you know, I hear the car start and he's gone. Lenny and Russ come running in to me, and say, 'Where's Jeff, where's Jeff? You gotta go get him back,' And I said, 'You hear that car? You hear that? That's him going home.' The screwed up thing is that they tried with two or three other rhythm sections to do that song. Carlos Vega was in one version and I think Art Rodriguez was in another and then Gadd figured it out and it was so simple—she wanted an implied triplet shuffle, but she didn't have the brain to communicate it."

After Jeff heard from Castro, he got a call from Gary Katz: "He heard about it," Jeff relayed to me. "He was with Warner Brothers at the time and she was with Warner Brothers as well, and he said, 'I tried to cool her out, man, because she's out to get you. She wants to sue you.' I said, 'Let her come get me.' I didn't hear anything for a couple of years. She never sued me or anything. I get a call I think it was last year from James Newton

Howard. He was producing the Ricki Lee Jones album and he goes, 'You won't believe this, but she wants you to play on two songs.' I go, 'Does she know who I am?' What I didn't know—I perceived it, but maybe what I didn't take into consideration or should have understood a little better—was maybe she was going through some hard times when I got messed with, that we all go through and maybe we all handle our hard times differently. The way James Newton Howard explained to me on the phone is maybe she doesn't remember that situation too well. I said, 'Well, whether she does or she doesn't, I'd love to play for her. I hold no grudges and I know you the producer, and I know you knowing that story, you won't let that happen. If I'm wrong, you'll just stop the session because you're responsible for the session, and move on to doing an overdub while you find a drummer for the next session.'"

Porcaro chuckled as he described the day of the session: "I get there, I'm booked for two days, two songs. Ricki says, 'Hi Jeff, good to see you again. You seem to have lost weight.' Actually I had gained 30 pounds since the last time she saw me, so for a second, I thought 'She's fucking with me.' But I thought, 'No, because she's gorgeous, she seems more together than the last time I saw her, things seem beautiful.' The plan was to do one song per day. We were booked for six hours a day. We did the first song, two takes. 'Thank you, see you guys tomorrow.' We did the second song, three takes. The whole band, including people who were there when I stabbed my drums with the sticks, she goes in front of everybody, 'Jeff, I really have to tell you this, no drummer has ever played so great for me and listened to my music so closely and what I'm saying with lyrics and followed me so well like you, and I just want to thank you for the tracks.' I almost broke out laughing because she had told me, 'Mr. Porcaro stop playing like such a studio...' and I played no differently for her last year than I did when I was keeping too good of time."

There were situations that "bugged" Jeff—that was a word that Jeff liked to use—and he definitely had his limit on how much he would put up with. He pointed out it amounted to self-respect: "In this business, you have to put up with temperaments sometimes, but you should never have to put up with abuse," he told me in 1983. "I say that not from having an attitude, but as a person, you should be treated as one. You also have to put up with rumors and people talking, but you can't let those kinds of things get to you. You can't worry about what people think. I've seen situations where it's a guy's first session, and a producer or artist destroys him in front of a lot of well-known musicians, who the guy was very excited about being there with. And I've seen guys cry in the studio," Jeff told me. "People can get affected that way, but you can't let someone do that to you. They're just people, and you've got to put everybody in perspective."

Dean Parks professes, even on a session, Jeff looked out for his cohorts: "Jeff was the kind of guy who was a champion of 'Stop the bullshit,'" Parks says. "When things would get sleazy, dishonest or uncool, Jeff would rise up and bring it to light. During a break he would give a heads up to the other players about the character of an employer or contractor who was being sneaky, like, 'This is kind of a snake, we don't really dig this guy now; this guy is uncool.'"

For the most part, Jeff let things slide, his brother Steve says, explaining: "Jeff mostly was in a real good mood, in a positive mood. He was living his dream, from a real early age, from six months before he graduated high school. Right out of the gate. I'm sure there were moments of sadness, but did he show it? Jeff led a really blessed life. I did a Barbra Streisand date and I knew she was in the booth. It was very rare that I was on a live session, I was very much an overdub guy; 98% of the stuff I did was by myself overdubbing. At one point in the session, Albhy (Galuten) says, 'Barbra wants to talk to you.' So I walked into the booth and I go, 'Hi,' and she was just looking at me, up and down and finally said, 'Yeah, you are Jeff's brother. You look just like him.' It was funny, she just wanted to see Jeff's brother. And that's not the first time stuff like that happened. Jeff had a whole lot of fun and he lived his dream. He was on fire, playing on all these great records and everyone who worked with him loved him."

Working with Streisand was always a source of pride that Jeff mentioned to me and Joe told Beatosblog.com how after Jeff died, he performed with her: "I saw Barbra walking towards me after the show and I thought to myself that maybe I did something wrong during the show, I didn't know. Instead, Barbra came up to me and gave me this big hug and she said to me, and I will never forget it, that she 'loved' Jeffrey and that she is 'going to miss him.'"

THEY WEIGH IN ON HIM

Jeff with Peter Frampton at A&M Soundstage, 1979, recording *Breaking All the Rules*.

(Photo courtesy of Peter Frampton)

"Making music with Jeff was a dream because of the feel he created—and I'm sure everyone you've spoken to said the same thing. He had the inherent Porcaro feel; it goes back to dad, I would think. Jeff chose the right instrument, even though I'm sure he could have chosen any other instrument and he would have been the same on any one he chose." – Peter Frampton

"Porcaro was the best all-around studio drummer I ever worked with. And I worked with all of them. The reason I say that is because what he did on *Toto IV*, what he did on the Steely Dan records, he played for Streisand, he could do anything. He could play jazz, he could play rock 'n' roll, he could play that pop sweet stuff, he could play brushes; he could do it all. And he did it with such a great temperament. Everyone liked Jeff. I don't know anybody who didn't like Jeff. He was just such a cool guy." – Al Schmitt

"He had the best time of any drummer I ever worked with." – Humberto Gatica

"He did stuff that very few people could do and still bring feel to it. He was an extraordinary musician." – Danny Kortchmar

"He was a master of whatever was required." – Russ Titelman

"He was elegant in his playing, and musical." – Sergio Mendes

"I really felt like it was never about him. There are other drummers where it's about them, but it was never about Jeff. It was about the music and how he could service the music and make it great. He really heard what was going on." – David Benoit

"There are a slew of fantastic drummers in this town. But there was only one Jeff Porcaro and he brought so much more than just the ability to play the drums. He lifted a session. He made it amazing. We did the most difficult recordings on the planet, and the most rewarding because you're playing in the moment." – Jeff Weber

"Jeff very adroitly paid attention to the very best idea for the song. Jeff's thing was 'when in doubt, lay out.' If you're not sure what to play, lay the fuck out." – George Massenburg

"He was a great team player and if we were struggling with a section, he was never the guy just sitting there waiting for someone else to figure out what to do. He would always make a suggestion like, 'What if I did this on the kick drum,' or 'What if I laid out here.' He was always suggesting things and showing he gave a shit; that it wasn't just another gig." – Richard Marx

"His grooves were things of beauty." – Bruce Springsteen

"His timing was so steady you never had to think about it." – Dash Crofts

"The great thing about Jeff was he was very inventive." – Jackson Browne

"He'd always get everything in one take. He was a monster." – Leo Sayer

"First and foremost was Jeff's energy and enthusiasm. As an artist, you would gain a sense of confidence working with someone who you would feel was a kindred spirit. Jeff found the heart of what you were trying to do. I know enough about Jeff to know that that was not true of every session he walked into, but if it was something he was emotionally tied into—music that touched him—he loved to help interpret it. He made it his own piece. It had his signature on it. He danced a song. He sang a song. He paraded your own song in front of you through his eyes, through his own interpretation." – Boz Scaggs

"His enthusiasm was always obvious. That's what I loved about him. He would sit for the rest of the session while we overdubbed stuff. Most session players who worked as much as he did were fairly jaded: 'Tell me what to play and let's get it done.' But Jeff would get into the idea of the song with you and if it wasn't going well, it was, 'What if I did that?' or, 'What if I played this kind of pattern?' I always appreciated that." – Michael McDonald

"He was the most feel-good guy ever, big smile of course, and then the sweetest guy." – Nathan East

"He did not have to put his style on something. He let the song dictate what he was to do. He played the song purely." – Steve Jordan

"Jeffrey walked in the room ready not only to play, but play what you wanted or needed from him, with a smile and an enthusiasm, rarely matched and never surpassed, for me. There is an emotion to playing music, not just the notes on a piece of paper. Jeffrey read all the notes just fine, reluctantly maybe, but he brought more joy and excitement to a recording session than any other musician I worked with. What did I love about Jeff's playing? Two succinct things: I could always tap my foot when Jeff was playing, which is my tell-all, and he wanted me to leave the studio with a musical smile!" – Gary Katz

"Jeff Porcaro was an experience. You could not spend a day in the studio with him and his unquenchable smile and attitude that life was this fantastic opportunity to play the drums and not have it wear on you. I've met hundreds of musicians and celebrities in my life and he still stands out." – Jimmy Webb

"The thing that has to be noted about Jeff is there are a million great drummers in the world, but not only did he make it sound exactly like what you wanted—and even better—he made it feel like, 'Oh my God." There's never been anyone like Jeff since. I don't think there will ever be another Jeff Porcaro." – Randy Jackson

ABOUT THE INTERVIEWS

Unless otherwise noted, all the quotations in this book were sourced from interviews for this book conducted by the author. Regarding quotes from Jeff, except as noted in the text, all come from interviews conducted for *Modern Drummer* magazine.

Photos by Lissa Wales

APPENDIX

JEFF PORCARO DISCOGRAPHY

Provided by the website Jeff Porcaro Session Tracks
Maintained by Mary Oxborrow
View the full discography with future updates at http://www.frontiernet.net/~cybraria/

10cc / *Meanwhile* (Polydor, 1992) 10 + 3 tracks
Only drummer listed.
Note: Three songs from the *Meanwhile* sessions which didn't make it onto the album were released as B-sides of singles: "Man with a Mission" (B-side of "Women in Love") and "Don't" and "Lost in Love" (both B-sides of "Welcome to Paradise").

A

Ai To Lu Na No Motoni [TV soundtrack] (Alfa [Japan], 1992)
No track information

Airplay / *Airplay* (RCA, 1980) 7 tracks
"Stranded," "Cryin' All Night," "Nothin' You Can Do About It," "Should We Carry On," "Bix," "She Waits for Me," "After the Love has Gone"

Alessi Brothers / *Alessi* (A&M, 1977)
No track-specific credits; 1 of 4 drummers (also Frank Ravioli, Hal Blaine, John Guerin)

Alessi Brothers / *Long Time Friends* (Qwest, 1982) 1 track
"Still in Love"

Allan, Laura / *Laura Allan* (Elektra, 1978) 4 tracks
"Come as You Are," "Hole in my Bucket," "One Way Ticket," "Yes I Do"

Allen, Peter / *Bi-Coastal* (A&M, 1980) 3 tracks
"Hit in the Heart," "Pass this Time," "When this Love Affair is Over"

Allman, Gregg — see *Black Rain* [film soundtrack]

Alpert, Herb / *Keep Your Eyes On Me* (A&M, 1987) 2 tracks
"Cat Man Do," "Rocket to the Moon"

Alston, Gerald / *Open Invitation* (Motown, 1990) 4 tracks
"I'll Go Crazy," "Never Give Up," "Tell Me This Night Won't End," "Still in Love"

America / *View From the Ground* (Capitol, 1982)
No track-specific credits; 1 of 2 drummers (also Willie Leacox)

Anderson, Jon / ***In the City of Angels*** (Columbia, 1988) 3 tracks
"If It Wasn't for Love," "Is it Me," "Top of the World (The Glass Bead Game)"

Anka, Paul / *The Music Man* (United Artists, 1977)
1 of 2 drummers (also Ed Greene)

Anka, Paul / *Walk A Fine Line* (CBS, 1983) 3 tracks
"Darlin', Darlin'," "This is the First Time," "Golden Boy"

Anka, Paul / *Somebody Loves You* (Polydor [Ger], 1989) 6 tracks
"Somebody Loves You," "You and I," "A Steel Guitar and a Glass of Wine," "Can We," "The Lady Was," "Never Gonna Lose You"

Anri / *Circuit of Rainbow* (ForLife, 1989) 4 tracks
"Shoo-be Doo-be My Boy," "Who Knows My Loneliness?," "P.S. Kotoba ni Naranai," "Sentimental o Suteta Hito"

Anri / *16th Summer Breeze* (1994) 1 track
Disc 1, Track 14: "We Abandoned the Sentimental" (translation of Japanese)

Anri / *Opus 21* (For Life Records, 1995 [Japan]) 1 track
Track 6: "A Thousand Words are Inexhaustible" (translation of Japanese)

Armand, *Renee / In Time (Windsong*, 1978) 4 tracks
"Love on a Shoestring," "(We're) Dancin' in the Dark," "In Time," "The Bitter Taste of Wild Things"

Arthur [film soundtrack] (Warner, 1981) 7 tracks
"Arthur's Theme," "It's Only Love," "Touch (Instrumental)," "It's Only Love (Instrumental)," "Money (Instrumental)," "Moving Pictures (Instrumental)," "Arthur's Theme (Instrumental)"

Asakura, Miki / *Su Te Ki* (King [J], 1988) 3 tracks
"Find a New Way," "True Love," "Fall in Love"

Atkins, Chet / *Stay Tuned* (CBS, 1985) 2 tracks
"Please Stay Tuned," "The Boot and the Stone"

Austin, Patti / *The Real Me* (Qwest, 1988) 2 tracks
"Lazy Afternoon," "True Love"

Austin, Patti / *Love is Gonna Getcha* (GRP, 1990) 1 track
"The Girl Who Used to Be Me"
(Note: This track doesn't appear on the LP.)

Axton, Hoyt / *Fearless* (A&M, 1976) 2 tracks
"Lay Lady Lay," "Beyond These Walls"

Axton, Hoyt / *Road Songs* (A&M, 1977) 1 track
"Lay Lady Lay" (Previously appeared on Fearless, 1976)

B

B-52s / *Good Stuff* (A&M, 1992) 3 tracks
"Hot Pants Explosion," "Breezin'," "Bad Influence"

Bachman, Randy / *Survivo*r (Polydor, 1978) 8 tracks (entire album)

Bade, Lisa / *Suspicion* (A&M, 1982) 1 track
"Suspicion"

Ballard, Russ / *At the Third Stroke* (Epic, 1978) 6 tracks
"Dancer," "Helpless," "Cast the Spirit," "What Does it Take?," "I'm a Scorpio," "My Judgement Day"

Bateman, Justine & the Mystery — see *Satisfaction* [film soundtrack]

Batteau, David / *Happy in Hollywood* (A&M, 1976) 8 tracks
"Happy in Hollywood," "Festival of Fools," "Oh, My Little Darling," "Orphee," "Walk in Love," "Spaceship Earth," "You Need Love," "The Gates in Your Heart"

Beck, Robin / *Human Instinct* (DSB, 1992) 4 tracks
"Love Yourself," "Every Little Thing," "Bad on Love," "Changing with the Years"

Bee Gees / *Living Eyes* (RSO, 1981) 3 tracks
"Living Eyes," "Soldiers," "Cryin' Every Day"

Bel-Air / *Turquoise Blue* (1991) 1 track
"Salvia Flower "

Bell & James / *In Black and White* (A&M, 1981) 5 tracks
"Love Call My Name," "You've Got the Power," "Gimme the Gun," "Runnin' for Your Life," "Don't Take the Money"

Benoit, David / *Shadows* (GRP, 1991) 5 tracks
"Shadows," "Saudade," "Already There," "Castles," "Have You Forgotten"

Benoit, David / *Freedom At Midnight* (GRP, 1987) 5 tracks
"Freedom at Midnight," "Along the Milky Way," "The Man with the Panama Hat," "Passion Walk"

Benson, George / *The George Benson Collection* (Warner, 1981) 2 tracks
"Turn Your Love Around" (Linn drum machine), "Love all the Hurt Away"

Benson, George / *In Your Eyes* (Warner, 1983) 1 track
"Lady Love Me (One More Time)"

Berger, Michel / *Dreams in Stone* (Atlantic, 1982) 6 tracks
"JFK (Overture)," "American Island," "Walking through the Big Apple," "Apple Pie," "Rooftops," "Parade"

Berglund, Kristin / *Long Distance Love* (Talent Produksjon (Norway), 1979) No track-specific credits; 1 of 2 drummers (also Bruno Castellucci)

Berlin, Jeff / *Pump It* (Passport, 1986) 1 track
"All the Greats"

Big Blue Wrecking Crew: "We are the Champions/New York, New York" [single] (Elektra, 1981) 2 tracks

Bim / *Thistles* (Elektra, 1978) 7 tracks
"Tender Lullaby," "Right After My Heart," "Waitin' for You, Mama," "Shell of a Life," "Broke Down," "Woh, Me," "Thistles"

Bishop & Gwinn / *This Is Our Night* (Infinity, 1979) 5 tracks
"This is our Night," "Santa Monica Pier," "Livin' in Two Different Cities," "Ancient Egypt," "Delicate Harmony"

Black Rain [film soundtrack] (Virgin, 1989) 1 track
"I'll Be Holding On" (Gregg Allman)

Blades, Ruben / *Nothing but the Truth* (Elektra, 1988) 3 tracks

"I Can't Say," "The Miranda Syndrome," "In Salvador"

Blakeley, Peter / *Harry's Cafe De Wheels* (Capitol, 1989)
No track-specific credits; 1 of 5 drummers (also Jim Keltner, Russ Kunkel, John Robinson, Carlos Vega)

Blessing, The / *Prince of the Deep Water* (MCA, 1991) 3 tracks
"Highway 5," "Let's Make Love," "Birdhouse"

Blunstone, Colin / *Never Even Thought* (Rocket, 1978) 9 tracks (entire album)

Bodine, Rita Jean / *Sitting on Top of My World* (20th century, 1974) 8 tracks
"Pacified," "Sitting on Top of My World," "Wheels," "Frying Pan Song," "It Ain't Easy," "I was Mistaken," "Sweet Inspiration," "Knickerbocker Holiday"

Bolin, Tommy / *Teaser* (Atlantic, 1975) 4 tracks
"The Grind," "Homeward Strut," "Dreamer," "Teaser"

Bolton, Michael / *Time, Love & Tenderness* (Columbia, 1991) 1 track
"When a Man Loves a Woman"

Bolton, Michael / *Greatest Hits 1985-1995* (Columbia, 1995) 1 track
"When a Man Loves a Woman" (from Time, Love & Tenderness, 1991)

Boylan, Terence / *Terence Boylan* (Elektra, 1977) 2 tracks
"The War was Over," "Where are You Hiding?" (w/Boylan & Mickey McGee)

Brady, Paul / *Trick or Treat* (Fontana, 1991)
Only drummer listed, but Brady listed for drum programming

Branigan, Laura / *Laura Branigan* (Atlantic, 1990) 1 track
"Let Me In"

Brothers Johnson / *Winners* (A&M, 1981) 8 tracks
"Dancin' Free," "Teaser," "Caught Up," "In the Way," "I Want You," "Do it for Love," "Hot Mama," "Daydreamer Dream"

Brothers Johnson / *Blast! The Latest and Greatest* (A&M, 1982) 1 track
"I'm Giving You All My Love"

Browne, Jackson / *The Pretender* (Elektra, 1976) 4 tracks
"The Only Child," "Daddy's Tune," "Sleep's Dark and Silent Gate," "The Pretender"

Browne, Severin / *New Improved* (Motown, 1974)
No track-specific credits; 1 of 2 drummers (also Russ Kunkel)

Bugatti & Musker / *The Dukes* (Atlantic, 1982; re-issued Warner [Japan], 1999)
No track-specific credits; 1 of 2 drummers (also John Robinson)

C

Cadd, Brian / *Yesterdaydream* (Capitol, 1978)
No track-specific credits; 1 of 4 drummers (also Alvin Taylor, Doug Lavery, Richie Hayward)

Caldwell, Bobby / *Carry On* (Elektra, 1976; Polydor, 1982) 4 tracks
"Catwalk," "Jamaica," "Loving You," "Words"

Caldwell, Bobby / *August Moon* (Polydor, 1983) 4 tracks

"Fraulein," "Cover Girl," "Class of '69," "Once You Give In" Note: Drums and drum synthesizers

Camp, Steve / *One on One* (Sparrow, 1986) 9 tracks (entire album)

Carlos, Roberto / *Roberto Carlos* (1988) 4 tracks
"Todo Mundo é Alguém," "Como as Ondas do Mar," "Se o Amor se Vai," "Papo de Esquina"

Carlos, Roberto / *Roberto Carlos* (1990) 1 track
"Por Ela"

Carlton, Larry / *Larry Carlton* (Warner, 1978) 8 tracks (entire album)

Carlton, Larry / *Sleepwalk* (Warner, 1982) 5 tracks
"Blues Bird," "Song for Katie," "Frenchman's Flat," "Upper Kern," "10:00 P.M."

Carlton, Larry / *Friends* (Warner, 1983) 8 tracks (entire album)

Carlton, Larry / *Christmas at My House* (MCA, 1989) 3 tracks
"Silent Night/It Came Upon a Midnight Clear," "My Favorite Things/We Three Kings of Orient Are," "The Christmas Song"

Carmen, Eric / *Boats Against the Current* (Arista, 1977) 3 tracks
"Boats Against the Current," "Love is All that Matters," "She Did It"

Carmen, Eric / *Change of Heart* (Arista, 1978) 3 tracks
"Haven't We Come a Long Way," "End of the World," "Baby I Need Your Lovin'"

Carmen, Eric / *Eric Carmen* (Geffen, 1985) 1 track
"She Remembered"

Carter, Raymone / *Raymone Carter* (Reprise, 1991) 1 track
"I'll Always Be Around"

Carter, Valerie / *Just a Stone's Throw Away* (CBS, 1977) 8 tracks
"Ooh Child," "Ringing Doorbells in the Rain," "Face of Appalachia," "So, So, Happy," "A Stone's Throw Away," "Cowboy Angel," "City Lights," "Back to Blue Some More"

Carter, Valerie / *Wild Child* (Columbia, 1978) 10 tracks (entire album)

Cats / *Hard To Be Friends* (1975) ? tracks
No track-specific credits; 1 of 2 drummers (also John Raines)

Cavaliere, Felix / *Dreams in Motion* (Karambolage, 1994) 3 tracks
"Stay in Love," "Me for You," "Youngblood"

Cetera, Peter / *Solitude/Solitaire* (Warner, 1986)
Percussion only, no track-specific credits

Chamfort, Alain / *Rock 'n' Rose* (1977)
No track-specific credits; 1 of 3 drummers (also Mike Baird, Ed Greene)

Champlin, Bill / *Single* (Epic, 1978) 5 tracks
"What Good is Love," "We Both Tried," "Careless," "Elayne," "Keys to the Kingdom"

Champlin, Bill / *Runaway* (Elektra, 1981) 1 track
"Without You"

Chanson / *Chanson* (Ariola, 1978) 6 tracks
"Don't Hold Back," "I Can Tell," "I Love You More," "Why," "Did You Ever," "All the Time You Need"

Chanson / *Together We Stand* (1979)
No track-specific credits; 1 of 2 drummers (also Harvey Mason)

Char / *U.S.J.* (Seesaw, 1981) 6 tracks
"Give Me Some Time," "Street Information," "Cry Like a Baby," "Smokey," "You Can't Have Me," "Nice Changes"

Charles, Ray / *My World* (Warner, 1993) 2 tracks
"If I Could," "Still Crazy After All These Years"

Charts / *L'Ocean Sans Fond* (Klaxon [France], 1989) 1 track
"Terre"

Charts / *Notre Monde a Nous* (Klaxon [France], 1993) 5 tracks
"Comme un Magicien," "Insomnic," "Impazzire," "Aime Moi Encore," "Terre"

Chater, Kerry / *Part Time Love* (Warner, 1977) 10 tracks (entire album)

Cher / *Bittersweet White Light* (MCA, 1973) 9 tracks (entire album)

Cher / *Stars* (Warner, 1975)
No track-specific credits; 1 of 6 drummers (also Gary Mallaber, Hal Blaine, Harvey Mason, Jim Gordon, Jim Keltner)

Cher / *I'd Rather Believe in You* (Warner, 1976) 10 tracks (entire album)

Cher / *Prisoner* (Casablanca, 1979) 1 track
"Prisoner"

Cher / *Take Me Home* (Casablanca, 1979) 1 track
"Git Down (Guitar Groupie)"

Cher / *Love Hurts* (Geffen, 1990) 7 tracks
"Love Hurts," "Fires of Eden," "One Small Step," "Could've Been You," "When Love Calls Your Name," "Who You Gonna Believe," "The Shoop Shoop Song (It's in his Kiss)"

Chicago / *Chicago 17* (Full Moon/Warner Bros., 1984) 1 track
"Stay the Night"

Choir, Yves / *By Prescription Only* (New Musidisc, 1989) 6 tracks
"Mad about Town," "After the Rain," "DB," "Bianca," "By Prescription Only," "Morocco Junction"

Clapton, Eric / *Behind the Sun* (Warner, 1985) 2 tracks
"See What Love Can Do," "Forever Man"

Clark, Gene / *This Byrd has Flown* (1995) 1 track
"All I Want"

Clark, Terry / *Welcome* (Myrrh, 1978) 4 tracks
"Welcome," "Merry Go Round," "Red Cloud," "Living Loving Eyes"

Clarke, Stanley / *Modern Man* (Nemperor, 1978) 3 tracks

"He Lives On," "Slow Dance," "Modern Man"

Clover / *Sound City Sessions* (101 Distribution, 2008)
No track-specific credits; 1 of 2 drummers listed (also Michael Schreiner); previously unreleased sessions from 1975; "Child of the Streets," unknown others

Cocker, Joe / *I Can Stand a Little Rain* (A&M, 1983) 2 tracks
"I Can Stand a Little Rain," "Don't Forget Me"

Cocker, Joe / *Civilized Man* (Capitol, 1984) 4 tracks
"Civilized Man," "There Goes My Baby" (+ electric pencil guitar), "Come On In," "Tempted"

Cole, Jude / *A View from 3rd Street* (Reprise, 1990) 1 track
"Compared to Nothing"

Cole, Jude / *Start the Car* (Reprise, 1992) 2 tracks
"Open Road," "Tell the Truth"

Cole, Natalie / *Good to be Back* (EMI, 1989) 3 tracks
"Miss You Like Crazy," "Gonna Make You Mine," "Starting Over Again"

Coltrane, Chi / *Road to Tomorrow* (TK, 1977)
No track-specific credits; 1 of 3 drummers (also Jim Gordon, Michael Botts)

Conte, Luis / *Black Forest* (Denon, 1989) 3 tracks
"Do the Shrimp," "Working in the Coal Mine," "Black Forest"

Coolidge, Rita / *Heartbreak Radio* (A&M, 1981) 1 track
"Walk On In"

Crane, Stephan / *Kicks* (MCA, 1984) 2 tracks
"Joanne," "Kicks"

Crawford, Randy / *Secret Combination* (Warner, 1981) 10 tracks (entire album)

Crawford, Randy / *Nightline* (Warner [UK], 1983) 2 tracks
"Why," "Bottom Line"

Crawford, Randy / *Windsong* (Warner, 1982) 11 tracks (entire album)

Crosby, David / *Thousand Roads* (Atlantic, 1993) 2 tracks
"Through your Hand," "Helpless Heart"

Crosby, Stills & Nash / *Daylight Again* (Atlantic, 1982) 1 track
"Since I Met You"

Crosby, Stills & Nash / *Allies* (Atlantic, 1983) 2 tracks
"War Games," "Raise a Voice" (both tracks live)

Cross, Christopher / *Rendevous* (Polystar [Japan], 1991) 2 tracks
"Rendezvous," "Is There Something"

Cross, Christopher — see *Arthur* [film soundtrack]

Crowell, Rodney / Live is Messy (Columbia, 1992) 1 track
"It's Not for Me to Judge""

Cummings, Burton / *My Own Way to Rock* (Portrait, 1977) 8 tracks

1 of 4 drummers (also Ollie E. Brown, Rick Shlosser, Lenny Castro)
"Never Had a Lady Before," "Come On By" (with Ollie), "Try to Find Another Man," "Got to Find Another Way," "My Own Way to Rock," "Charlemagne" (with Ollie), "Framed" (with Lenny), "A Song for Him"

Cummings, Burton / *Dream of a Child* (Portrait, 1978; re-issued 2000) 3 tracks
"Hold On, I'm Comin'," "Guns, Guns, Guns," "Roll with the Punches" (all with Rick Schlosser)

Cummings, Burton / *Plus Signs* (Capitol, 1990) 10 tracks (entire album)

Curiosity Killed the Cat / *Getahead* (Phonogram, 1989) 3 tracks
"Cascade," "Trees Don't Grow on Money," "Who Are You"

D

Dal Bello, Lisa / *Lisa Dal Bello* (MCA, 1977) 9 tracks
"Look at Me (Millions of People)," "(Don't Want to) Stand in Your Way," "My Mind's Made Up," "Snow White," "Touch Me," "Talk it Over (Even Though My Body's Cold)," "Stay with Me," "Day Dream," "Milk & Honey"

Danny & Joyce / *Ma La Lady* (Jasmine, 1975)
No track-specific credits; 1 of 4 drummers (also David Kemper, David Paich, Jim Varley)

Daugherty, Jack / *Jack Daugherty and the Class of Nineteen Hundred and Seventy One* (A&M, 1971) 3 tracks (?)
No track-specific credits; 1 of 4 drummers (also Jim Keltner, Hal Blaine, Paul Humphrey). It is probable Jeff is double-drumming with Jim Keltner on "Getting Up," "Feel so Good," and "Number Nine."

Deardorff & Joseph / *Deardorff & Joseph* (Arista, 1976) ? tracks
No specific track credits; 1 of 5 drummers (also David Kemper, David Paich, John Guerin, Ron Tutt)

Dee, Kiki / *Stay with Me* (Rocket, 1979)
No track-specific credits; 1 of 2 drummers (also Jim Keltner)

Denander, Tommy / *Less Is More, Part One* (Local Dealer, 1995) 1 track
"5492"

Denander, Tommy / *Limited Access* (Noble House, 1997) 2 tracks
"5492," "Remember My Conscience"
"5492" appeared previously on Less Is More, Part One (1995)

DeVille, Willy / *Miracle* (A&M, 1987) 2 tracks
"Could You Would You," "Miracle"

Dick Tracy [film soundtrack] — see Madonna / I'm Breathless

Dion, Celine / *Unison* (Epic, 1990) 1 track
"Have a Heart"

Dire Straits / *On Every Street* (Warner, 1991) 8 tracks

"Fade to Black," "When it Comes to You," "On Every Street," "How Long," My Parties," "Ticket to Heaven," "Iron Hand," You and Your Friend."

Doheny, Ned / *Prone* (Columbia, 1979) 2 tracks

"Guess Who's Looking for Love Again," "The Devil in You"

Donovan / *Lady of the Stars* (Allegiance, 1984) 1 track
"I Love You Baby"

Doonesbury — see Thudpucker, Jimmy

Dore, Charlie / *Listen* (Chrysalis, 1981) 10 tracks (entire album)

Dr. John / *In a Sentimental Mood* (Warner, 1989) 4 tracks
"My Buddy," "In a Sentimental Mood," "Don't Let the Sun Catch You Cryin'," "More Than You Know"

Dudek, Les / *Les Dudek* (CBS, 1976) 8 tracks
"City Magic," "Sad Clown, Don't Stop Now," "Each Morning," "It Can Do," "Take the Time," "Cruisin' Groove," "What a Sacrifice"

Dudek, Les / *Say No More* (CBS, 1977) 6 tracks
"Jailabamboozle," "Lady You're Nasty," "One to Beam Up," "Avatar," "Old Judge Jones," "What's it Gonna Be"

Dudek, Les / *Ghost Town Parade* (CBS, 1978) 2 tracks
Both with Jim Keltner: "Bound to be a Change," "Friend of Mine"

Dudek, Les / *Deeper Shades of Blue* (Geosynchronous, 1994) 9 tracks (entire album)

Dudek, Les / *Freestyle* (E Flat Productions, 2003) 2 tracks
"Hot Fun in Dixieland," "Wild Hearted Weekend"

Duncan, Bryan / *Anonymous Confessions Of A Lunatic Friend* (Myrrh, 1990) 11 tracks (entire album)

Dune [film soundtrack] (Polydor, 1984)
Score composed by Toto; mostly performed by Vienna Symphony Orchestra; 1997 reissue includes previously unreleased tracks

E

Earth, Wind & Fire / *Touch The World* (Sony, 1987) 2 tracks
"You and I," "Every Now and Then"

Edelman, Randy / *If Love Is Rea*l (Arista, 1977) 9 tracks (entire album)

Elias, Jonathan / *Requiem For The Americas* (Enigma, 1990) 1 track
"Within the Lost World"

Elliman, Yvonne / *Yvonne* (RSO, 1979) 3 tracks
"Love Pains," "Greenlight," "Rock Me Slowly"

Elliot, Brian / *Brian Elliot* (Warner, 1978)
No track-specific credits; 1 of 4 drummers (also Mike Baird, James Gadson, Gary Ferguson)

England Dan & John Ford Coley / *I Hear the Music* (A&M, 1977)
No track-specific credits; 1 of 3 drummers (also Jim Gordon and Ronnie Tutt)

England Dan & John Ford Coley / *Dr. Heckle and Mr. Jive* (Big Tree, 1979) 2 tracks
"Hollywood Heckle & Jive," "Broken Hearted Me"

Evans, Linda / *You Control Me* (Ariola, 1979) 6 tracks
No track-specific credits; only drummer listed; 1 of 3 on percussion (also David Williams and James Jamerson, Jr)

Eye to Eye / *Eye to Eye* (Warner, 1982) 6 tracks
"Hunger Pains," "Life in Motion," "Nice Girls," "Progress Ahead," "Physical Attraction," "Time Flys"

F

Fagen, Donald / *The Nightfly* (Warner, 1982) 5 tracks
"I.G.Y.," "Green Flower Street," "Ruby Baby," "The Nightfly," "The Goodbye Look"

Farina, Sandy / *All Alone In the Night* (MCA, 1980)
No track-specific credits; 1 of 3 drummers (also Ed Greene, Rich Slauser)

Farrell, Joe / *Night Dancing* (1978) 1 track
"Night Dancing"

Fields, Brandon / *Other Places* (Nova, 1990) 3 tracks
"Undercover," "Gina," "Know How"

Fifth Dimension / *Earthbound* (ABC, 1975) 1 track
"Moonlight Mile"

Finnigan, Mike / *Black and White* (CBS, 1978) 8 tracks
"How Wrong Can You Be," "The Words," "Can't Keep a Secret" "I Could Never Leave You," "Sailfish," "Expressway to Your Heart," "Love Might Keep Us Forever," "Let Me Love You"

Flower / *Flower* (United Artists, 1977)
No track-specific credits; 1 of 3 drummers (also David Wolfert, Ed Greene)

Flyer / *Send a Little Love My Way* (Infinity Records, 1979) 1 track
"Send a Little Love My Way"

Fogelberg, Dan / *Windows and Walls* (Epic, 1984) 1 track
"Gone Too Far"

Fools Gold / *Mr. Lucky* (CBS, 1977) 9 tracks (entire album)
No track-specific credits; only drummer listed; also percussion

For the Boys [film soundtrack] (Atlantic, 1991) 1 track
"Every Road Leads Back to You" (Bette Midler)

Ford, Dwayne / *Needless Freaking* (Epic, 1982) 4 tracks
"Lovin' and Losin' You," "Stranger in Paradise," "The Hurricane," "Midnight Ride"

Ford, Robben / *Talk to Your Daughter* (Warner, 1988) 1 track
"I Got Over It"

Four Tops / *Tonight* (Casablanca, 1981) 9 tracks (entire album)

Fra Lippo Lippi / *Light And Shade* (Virgin, 1987) 3 tracks
"Home," "Light and Shade," "Crazy Wisdom"

Frampton, Peter / *Breaking all the Rules* (A&M, 1981) 9 tracks (entire album)

Franke and the Knockouts / *Makin' the Point* (MCA, 1984) 1 track
"Come Rain or Shine"

Franklin, Aretha / *Aretha* (Columbia, 1980) 4 tracks
"What a Fool Believes," "Come to Me," "Can't Turn You Loose," "Love Me Forever"

Franklin, Aretha / *Love all the Hurt Away* (Arista, 1981) 10 tracks (entire album)

Franklin, Rodney / *In the Center* (Columbia, 1978) 5 tracks
"Spanish Flight," "I Like the Music Make it Hot," "On the Path," "Sunrise," "Life Moves On"

Franklin, Rodney / *Rodney Franklin* (CBS, 1980) 3 tracks
"Life Moves On," "I Like the Music Make it Hot," "On the Path"
Note: These tracks previous appeared on *In the Center* (1978)

Freneticas / *Caia Na Gandaia* (1978) 1 track
"Dancin' Days"

Friendly Enemies / *Round One* (Prodigal, 1978) 1 track
"Dark Eyes"

Fromholz, Steven / *A Rumour in My Time* (Capitol, 1976) 2 tracks
"She's a Lady," "I'd Have to Be Crazy"

G

Gable, Bill / *There Were Signs* (BMG, 1989) 2 tracks
"Go Ahead and Run" (hi-hat, surdo) "High Trapeze" (drums and percussion)

Gardestad, Ted / *Blue Virgin Isles* (Polar(Sweden) 1978)
1 of 2 drummers on 10 of 12 tracks (also Jim Keltner); 1 of several on percussion

Gatlin, Larry and the Gatlin Brothers / *Smile* (CBS, 1985) 7 tracks
"One on One," "Say," "I Saved Your Place," "Can't Stay Away from Her Fire," "Get Me into This Love, Lord," "I'd Throw It All Away," "Indian Summer"

George, Lowell / *Thanks I'll Eat It Here* (Warner, 1979)
No track-specific credits; one of several drummers

Getz, Stan / *Apasionado* (A&M, 1990) 8 tracks (entire album)

Gianco, Ricky / *E' Rock'n'Roll* (Fonit Cetra [Italy], 1990) 13 tracks (entire album)

Gilmour, David / *About Face* (CBS, 1984) 10 tracks (entire album)

Give My Regards to Broad Street [film soundtrack] (Capitol, 1984) 1 track
"Silly Love Songs" (Paul McCartney), "Silly Love Songs (Reprise)" Note: *Jeff (along with Steve Lukather) also appeared in the film with the band that played this song.*

Glengarry Glen Ross [film soundtrack] (Elektra, 1992) 6 tracks
"Main Title," "You Met My Wife," "The Plot," "In the Car," "Don't Sell to Doctors," "The Nyborgs"

Go West / *Indian Summer* (EMI, 1992) 2 tracks
"Faithful" (cymbals kit), "The Sun and the Moon"

Gold, Andrew / *All This and Heaven Too* (Asylum, 1978) 3 tracks
"Always for You," "Thank You for Being a Friend," "I'm On My Way"

Goodrum, Randy / *Fool's Paradise* (Polydor, 1982) 10 tracks (entire album)

Goodrum, Randy / *An Exhibition* (Polydor, 1992) 11 tracks (entire album)

Grand Canyon [film soundtrack] (RCA, 1992)
No track-specific credits; on percussion only

Green, Kathe / *Kathe Green* (Prodigal, 1976)
No track-specific credits; 1 of 2 drummers (also Kenny "Spider" Rice)

Greg Mathieson Project / *Baked Potato Super Live!* (CBS/Sony [Japan], 1982; re-issued Cool Sounds [Japan], 1989) all tracks
"Bomp Me," "Thank You," "First Time Around," "Goe," "I Don't Know," "I'm Home," "The Spud Shuffle"
Note: A different version of "Bomp Me" appeared on the *Zapped* film soundtrack.

Grimaldi-Zeiher / *Grimaldi/Zeiher* (1978) 3 tracks
"La Star Des Couloirs," "Conversations," "Et Je Recommence"

Grimaldi-Zeiher / *Recidive* (RCA, 1980; re-issued Culture Press, 1998) 7 tracks
"Sidonie," "Derniers Moments," "Cache-Toi," "Debout en Haut du Toit," "Recidive," "Petit Melo Dans la Tete," "La Califusa"

Grimaldi, Bernard / ***Toute Ressemblance Avec Des Personnes Ayant*** (Antenna, 1991) 4 tracks
"La Star Des Couloirs," "Melo Dans La Tęte," "Sidonie," "Cité Des Anges"

Gross, Henry / *What's in a Name* (Capitol, 1981) 1 track
"Why Go Falling in Love"

Guitar Workshop / *Guitar Workshop in L.A.* (JVC, 1988) 4 tracks
"Take it All," "Donna," "Bawls," "Bull Funk"

Guitar Workshop / *Tribute to Otis Redding* (JVC, 1989) 2 tracks
"I Can't Turn You Loose," "A Tribute to a King"

Gurvitz, Adrian / *Sweet Vendetta* (Jet, 1979) 4 tracks
"The Wonder of it All," "The Way I Feel," "Free Ride," "One More Time"

H

Hall and Oates / *Beauty on a Back Street* (RCA, 1977) 8 tracks (entire album) Also on electronic drums

Hall, Lani / *Blush* (A&M, 1980) 1 track
"Wish I Would've Stayed"

Hamlisch, Marvin / "Pachelbel Canon In D" (Planet, 1980)
(B-side of 7"vinyl release of "Theme from *Ordinary People*")

Hamada, Mari / *In the Precious Age* (Victor, 1987) 2 tracks
"999," "My Trial"

Hamilton, Dirk / *You Can Sing on the Left or Bark on the Right* (ABC, 1976) 9 tracks (entire album)

Hamilton, Dirk / *Alias I* (ABC, 1977) 1 track
"In the Eyes of the Night"

Hammond, Albert / *Your World and My World* (CBS, 1980) 3 tracks

"When I'm Gone," "Experience," "Take Me Sailing"

Hancock, Herbie / ***Lite Me Up*** (CBS, 1982) 1 track
"Paradise"

Harris, Hugh / *Words for Our Years* (Capitol, 1990) 2 tracks
"Love Kicks," "Rhythm of Life"
Note: Credit on first track reads Jeff "Drums is drums" Porcaro

Hathaway, Lalah / *Lalah Hathaway* (Virgin, 1990) 1 track
"Somethin'"

Hawkins, George Jr. / *Every Dog Has It's Day* (1996) 1 track
"Every Dog" [sample]

Henderson, Finis / *Finis* (Motown, 1983)
No track-specific credits; 1 of 3 drummers (also Carlos Vega, J.R. Robinson)

Henley, Don / *I Can't Stand Still* (Elektra, 1982) 4 tracks
"You Better Hang Up" (with Don Henley), "Long Way Home," "Talking to the Moon," "Dirty Laundry"

Henley, Don / *The End of the Innocence* (Geffen, 1989) 1 track
"New York Minute"

Henley, Don / *Actual Miles: Henley's Greatest Hits* (Geffen, 1995) 2 tracks
"Dirty Laundry," "New York Minute"

Hester, Benny / *Perfect* (Frontline, 1989) 10 tracks (entire album)

Hewett, Howard / *Howard Hewett* (Elektra, 1990) 1 track
"If I Could Only Have That Day Back"

Hill, Warren / *Devotion* (RCA, 1993) 1 track
"Another Goodbye"

Hodges, James & Smith / *What Have You Done for Love* (London, 1978)
1 of multiple drummers

Hodgson, Roger / *Hai-Hai* (A&M, 1987) 5 tracks
"My Magazine," "London," "You Make Me Love You," "Who's Afraid?," "House on the Corner"

Holland, Amy / *On Your Every Word* (Capitol, 1981) 3 tracks
"Anytime You Want Me," "I'll never give up," "Rollin' By"

Horn, Jim / *Work It Out* (Warner, 1990) 2 tracks
"My Reggae Love," "Rio Sunrise"

Howard, James Newton / *James Newton Howard & Friends* (Sheffield Lab, 1984) 8 tracks
"Caesar," "Gone Buttlefishin'," "She," "L'Daddy," "Tandoori," "E-Minor Shuffle," "Slippin' Away II," "Amuseum"

Hudson Hawk [film soundtrack] (Varese Saraband, 1992) 1 track
"*Hudson Hawk* Theme (Instrumental)"

Hughes, Bill / *Dream Master* (Epic, 1979) 4 tracks
"Waiting for You to Fly," "Gypsy Lady," "Only Your Heart Can Say," "Dream Master"

Humperdink, Engelbert / *Don't You Love Me Anymore* (Columbia, 1981) 7 tracks
"Don't You Love Me Anymore?," "Stay Away," "Say Goodnight," "Maybe This Time," "Baby Me Baby," "Heart Don't Fail Me Now," "Till I Get It Right"

Hungate, David / *Souvenir* (CBS, 1990; re-issued Clubhouse, 1994) 7 tracks
"Lament," "Souvenir," "Dreamland," "Only a Heart Can Know," "Third Stone from the Sun," "A Perfect Love," "The Leap"

Hurley, Arthur & Gottlieb / *Sunlight Shinin'* (A&M) 1 of 3 drummers (also Jim Keltner, John Raines)

Ian, Janis / *Restless Eyes* (Columbia, 1981) 1 track
"Passion Play"

Iglesias, Julio / *Starry Night* (Columbia, 1990)
No track-specific credits; 1 of 2 drummers (also Carlos Vega)

Iijima, Mari / *My Heart in Red* (Alfa Moon, 1989) 4 tracks
"Still," "Send Love to Me," "Boyfriend," "Believe in Love"

Imperials / *Stand by the Power* (Day Spring, 1982)
No track-specific credits; 1 of 2 drummers (also Carlos Vega)

Indigo / *Indigo* (Warner, 1977) 10 tracks (entire album)

Ingram, James / *It's Real* (Warner, 1989) 1 track
"Love 1 Day at a Time"

I Ought to be in Pictures [film soundtrack] (Warner, 1982) 1 track
"One Hello" (Randy Crawford)

J

Jackson, La Toya / *La Toya Jackson* (RCA, 1980) 1 track
"Night Time Lover"

Jackson, Michael / *Thriller* (Epic, 1982) 4 tracks
"The Girl is Mine," "Beat It," "Human Nature," "The Lady in My Life"

Jackson, Michael / *Dangerous* (Epic, 1991) 1 track
"Heal the World"

Jackson, Michael / *Thriller: 25th Anniversary Edition* (Sony, 2008) 1 track
"For All Time" (unreleased track from the original *Thriller* sessions)

Jacksons / *Victory* (Epic, 1984) 2 tracks
"Torture," "Wait"

Jacksons / *2300 Jackson Street* (1989) 1 track
"Midnight Rendezvous"

James, Etta / *Deep In the Night* (Warner, 1978) 10 tracks (entire album)

Jans, Tom / *Eyes of an Only Child* (Columbia, 1975)
No tracks specific credits; 1 of 3 drummers (also Jim Keltner, Harvey Mason)

Jans, Tom / *Champion* (Canyon, 1982) 2 tracks
"Chambers of the Heart," "Visions"

Jarreau, Al / *Breakin' Away* (Warner, 1981) 1 track
"Breakin' Away"

Jarreau, Al / *Jarreau* (Warner, 1983) 3 tracks
"Mornin'," "Step by Step," "Black and Blues"

Jason, Lisa / *Envision* (2000)
1 of 4 drummers (also Carlos Vega, Joe Pet, John Morelli)

Jelly / *A True Story* (Asylum, 1977) 1 track
"Susan"

John, Elton / *Jump Up* (Geffen, 1982) 10 tracks (entire album)

Jones, Rickie Lee / *Rickie Lee Jones* (Warner, 1979)
1 of 3 drummers (also Steve Gadd, Andy Newmark)

Jones, Rickie Lee / *Magazine* (Warner, 1984) 2 tracks
"It Must Be Love," "Magazine"'

Jordan, Marc / *Mannequin* (Warner, 1978) 2 tracks
"Marina del Ray," "Survival"

Jordan, Marc / *Blue Desert* (Warner, 1979) 3 tracks
"I'm a Camera," "From Nowhere to This Town," "Release Yourself"

K

Kante, Mory / *Touma* (Mercury, 1990) 3 tracks
"Kroughegne," "Mankene," "Faden"

Kapono, Henry / *Same World* (Browntown Records,1991) 4 tracks
"Insy'a" (percussion), "All Because I Love You," "Papaya Blues," "The Hero"

Karizma / *Dreams Come True* (Vap, 1987) 1 track
"Blues for Ronnie" (with Carlos Vega)

Katsuragi, Yuki / *L.A. Spirits* (Radio C, 1982) 9 tracks (entire album)

Kawai, Naoko / *Daydream Coast* (Columbia, 1984) 5 tracks
"If You Want Me," "Second Nature," "Live Inside Your Love," "I Love It," "As Long as We're Dreaming"

Kawauchi, Junichi / *Juice* (Fun House, 1992) 9 tracks
"Kimi no ude ni Dakaretai," "Save Our Love," "Virgin Smile no Kimi," "White Venus," "You're the Only One," "Rainy Weekend," "Studio-A no Yuujin," "Todokanu Omoi (Lovesick Blues)," "Murderess"

Kazu Matsui Project / *Time No Longer* (RVC, 1981) 4 tracks
"Overture (Rainy Moon)," "Sunset and the Minstrel," "Voice from the Dark," "Bonfire (Centerdance)"

Keane Brothers / *Keane Brothers* (20th Century, 1977)
No track-specific credits; 1 of 5 drummers (also Ed Greene, Harvey Mason, John Keane, Nigel Olsson)

Kennedy, Ray / *Ray Kennedy* (Columbia, 1980) ? tracks

No track-specific credits; 1 of 3 drummers (also Rick Shlosser, Mike Baird)

Kershaw, Nik / *The Works* (MCA, 1989) 1 track
"Walkabout"

King, Marva / *Feels Right* (Planet, 1981) 2 tracks
"Memories," "Feeling Wonderful Feelings"

Kipner, Steve / *Knock the Walls Down* (Elektra, 1980) 9 tracks
"The Beginning," "Knock the Walls Down," "Lovemaker," "School of Broken Hearts," "War Games," "Love is Its Own Reward," "Cryin' Out for Love," "Guilty," "The Ending"

Kleinow, "Sneaky Pete" / *The Legend and the Legacy* (Shiloh, 1994) 2 tracks
"Louisiana," "Silverbird"

Knighton, Reggie / *Reggie Knighton* (Columbia, 1977)
No track-specific credits; 1 of 3 drummers (also Curly Smith, Richie Hayward)

Kraft, Robert / *Retro Active* (RCA, 1983) 4 tracks
"Single, Solo," "Just Another Notch on the Bedpost," "Heartless," "On the West Side"

Kunkel, Leah / *I Run With Trouble* (CBS, 1980) 2 tracks
"Let's Begin," "Never Gonna Lose My Dream of Love Again"

Kurozumi, Kengo / *Pillow Talk* (Sony, 1989) 3 tracks
"Kanojyo wa Warukunai," "Pillow Talk," "You and Me"

L

L.A. Workshop with New Yorker / *Norwegian Wood II* (Denon, 1989) 5 tracks
" Sgt. Pepper's Lonely Hearts Club Band," "Eleanor Rigby," "Norwegian Wood (This Bird has Flown)," "This Boy," "Roll Over Beethoven"

LaBelle, Patti / *Be Yourself* (MCA, 1989) 1 track
"Need a Little Faith"

LaBounty, Bill / *This Night Won't Last Forever* (Warner, 1978) 3 tracks
"A Tear Can Tell," "Crazy," "I Hope You'll Be Very Unhappy Without Me"

LaBounty, Bill / *Bill LaBounty* (Warner, 1982) 4 tracks
"Dream On," "Comin' Back," "Look Who's Lonely Now," "Nobody's Fool"

LaBounty, Bill / *Time Starts Now: The Definitive Anthology 75/11* (Rhino France, 2011, box set, import) 8 tracks
"She's So Popular" (previously unreleased track) and all tracks on the two albums listed above

Lake, Greg / *Greg Lake* (Chrysalis, 1981)
No track-specific credits; 1 of 4 drummers (also Jode Leigh, Michael Giles, Ted McKenna)

Lasley, David / *Soldiers on the Moon* (Agenda, 1990) 9 tracks
"It's Too Late," "Soldiers on the Moon," "Audrey," "You Bring Me Joy," "Give My Heart Back to Me," "Without the One You Love," "Roslyn," "Since I Fell for You," "God Bless the Child"

Liaison / *Liaison* (Frontline, 1989) 9 tracks
"When the Kingdom Comes Down," "You are His Main Concern," "Go and Sin No More,"

"Man with a Mission," "The Way, the Truth, and Life," "Kick it Down," "The Light is On," "He Lives," "Give Me One Day at a Time"

Lofgren, Nils (& Grin) / *Night Fades Away* (MCA, 1981) 2 tracks
"Sailor Boy," "Anytime at All"

Loggins, Kenny — see Various Artists / *In Harmony 2*

Los Lobotomys / *Los Lobotomys* (Maxus, 1992; originally Creatchy, 1989) 7 tracks
"Oozer," "Purple Haze (truncated)," "Big Bone," "Jorainbo," "Lobotomy Stew," "Little Wing," "All Blues"

Love and Money / *Strange Kind of Love* (Polygram, 1988) 11 tracks (entire album)

Lukather, Steve / *Lukather* (CBS, 1989) 2 tracks
"Drive a Crooked Road," "Steppin' on Top of Your World"

Lynn, Cheryl / *Start Over* (Columbia, 1987) 1 track
"Don't Run Away"

Lyons & Clark / *Prisms* (Shelter, 1976) 3 tracks
"Keepin' the Heat Down," "Sweet Misery," "Open the Door"

M

MacGregor, Mary / *...In Your Eyes* (Ariola, 1978) 3 tracks
"Memories," "Satisfied," "Hold Tight"

Madonna / *Like A Prayer* (Sire, 1989) 1 track
"Cherish"

Madonna / *I'm Breathless* (Sire, 1990) 4 tracks
(On cover: Music from and inspired by the film *Dick Tracy)* "He's a Man," "Hanky Panky," "Cry Baby," "Something to Remember"

Magnusson, Jacob / *Jack Magnet* (1981) 5 tracks
"Meet Me After Midnight," "Movies," "From Now On," "Shell Shock," "Lifesaver"

Manchester, Melissa / *Hey Ricky* (Arista, 1982) 7 tracks
"You Should Hear How She Talks About You," "Slowly," "Hey Ricky (You're a Low Down Heel)," "I'll Always Love You," "Race to the End," "Come in from the Rain," "Looking for the Perfect Ahh"

Mancini, Chris / *No Strings* (Atlantic, 1983) 2 tracks
"(Here Comes That) Hurt Again," "Lovers in Love"

Mangione, Gap / *Suite Lady* (A&M, 1978) 5 tracks
"Mellow Out!," "I Don't Know," "You Can't Cry for Help," "Sister Jo/Time of the Season," "King Snake"

Mangione, Gap / *Ardis* (Josh Music, 2002) 2 tracks
"I Don't Know," "Time of the Season"

Manhattan Transfer / *Pastiche* (Atlantic, 1978) 2 tracks
"Who, What, Where, When, Why," "Pieces of Dreams"

Manhattan Transfer / *Extensions* (Atlantic, 1979) 2 tracks

"Birdland" (with Ralph Humphrey), "Twilight Tone" (also bongos & anvil)

Manhattan Transfer / *Bodies and Souls* (Atlantic, 1983) 2 tracks
"This Independence," "American Pop"

Manhattan Transfer / *The Offbeat of Avenues* (Columbia, 1991) 1 track
"Confide in Me"

Manilow, Barry / *Showstoppers* (1991)
1 of several on percussion

Marc Tanner Band / *No Escape* (Elektra, 1979) 2 tracks
"Getaway," "Lost at Love"

Mardones, Benny / *Benny Mardones* (Curb, 1989) 5 tracks
"I Never Really Loved You at All," "For a Little Ride," "How Could You Love Me," "Never Far Away," "Run to You"

Marlo, Clair / *Let It Go* (Sheffield Lab, 1989) 6 tracks
"Til They Take My Heart Away," "Lonely Nights," "Let it Go," "All for the Feeling," "I Believe (When I Fall in Love it will be Forever)," "Where You Are"

Marx, Richard / *Rush Street* (Capitol, 1991) 4 tracks
"Hand in Your Pocket," "Calling You," "Superstar," "Chains Around My Heart"

Marx, Richard / *Paid Vacation* (Capitol, 1994) 1 track
"One Man"

Mason, Dave / *Mariposa De Oro* (CBS, 1978) 2 tracks
"Will You Still Love Me Tomorrow," "Bird on the Wind"

Mathieson, Greg — see Greg Mathieson Project

Mathis, Johnny / *The Island* (recorded 1989; released Real Gone Music 2020) 10 tracks (entire album)

Matsuda, Hiroyuki / *Two of Us* (Tokuma, 1992) 3 tracks
"Moving Night," "Stop Your Crying," "Surely Night Will Come" (translated from Japanese)

Matsui, Kazu — see Kazu Matsui Project

Mattogrosso, Ney / *Feitico* (1978) 1 track
"Nao Existe Pecado au sul do Equador"

Mayall, John / *Bottom Line* (DJM, 1979) 2 tracks
"Celebration," "Come with Me"

McCartney, Paul — see *Give My Regards to Broad Street* [film soundtrack]

McCluskey, David / *A Long Time Coming* (GRT, 1978) 3 tracks
"A Long Time Coming," "Let Me Be Alone," "One More Try"

McDonald, County Joe / *Rock and Roll Music from the Planet Earth* (Fantasy, 1978) 10 tracks (entire album)
Note: With Chilli Charles on one track

McDonald, Country Joe / *Child's Play* (Rag Baby, 1983) 1 track

"Power Plant Blues"

McDonald, Michael / *If That's What It Takes* (Warner, 1982) 3 tracks
"I Keep Forgettin'," "That's Why," "No Such Luck"

McDonald, Michael / *No Lookin' Back* (Warner, 1985) 9 tracks (entire album)

McDonald, Michael / *Take It to Heart* (Reprise, 1990) 7 tracks
"Love Can Break Your Heart," "Lonely Talk," "Searchin' for Understanding," "Homeboy," "No Amount of Reason," "One Step Away" (programmed), "You Show Me"

Medeiros, Glenn / *Not Me* (MCA, 1988) 2 tracks
"Someday Love," "Fallin'"

Meissner, Stan / *Dangerous Games* (Polygram [CA], 1984) 1 track
"You Make It All So Easy"

Melanie / *Photograph* (Atlantic, 1979)
No track-specific credits; 1 of 3 drummers (also Jim Gordon, John Guerin)

Melanie / *Seventh Wave* (Neighbourhood [UK], 1983) ? tracks
No track-specific credits; 1 of 5 drummers (also Jim Gordon, Liberty DeVitto, John Guerin & Dennis Bryan)

Mendes, Sergio / *Brasil 86* (A&M, 1986) 5 tracks
"Daylight," "Take This Love," "The River (O Rio)," "Flower of Bahia (Flor da Bahia)," "No Place to Hide"

Mendes, Sergio / *Arara* (A&M, 1989) 1 track
"Some Morning"

Mendes, Sergio / *Brasileiro* (Elektra, 1992) 5 tracks
"Indiado," "Lua Soberana," "Senhoras do Amazonas" (percussion), "Kalimba," "Barabare"

Messina, Jim / *Messina* (Warner, 1981) 9 tracks (entire album)

Meyers, Bill / *The Color of the Truth* (Agenda, 1990) 4 tracks
"I'm Still Standing," "Perfect Crime," "Just Say the Word," "Say What You Mean"

Midler, Bette — see *For the Boys* [film soundtrack]

Miguel, Luis / *Busca una Mujer* (WEA, 1989) 5 tracks
"Esa Nina," "Separados," "Por Favor Senora," "Pupilas de Gato," "Soy un Perderdor"

Misato / *Flowerbed* (Epic, 1989) 1 track
Track #7

Mitre, Fahed / *Toda La Verdad* (Sonosur, 1990) 4 tracks
"Toda la Verdad," "Jennifer," "Si no Estas," "Un Juego"

Mizukoshi, Keiko / *I'm Fine* (Tourus, 1982) 10 tracks (entire album)

Moore, Patsy / *Regarding the Human Condition* (Warner, 1993) 6 tracks
"These Loving Eyes," "A City on a Hill," "Lies (That I Have Known)," "Shooting the Breeze," "With Regard," "The Pilgrim Song"

Moore, Sally / *Sally Moore* (Curb, 1990) 3 tracks

"My Heart has a Mind of Its Own," "What are You Waiting For," "Love is a Step Away"

Moore, Tim / *White Shadows* (Asylum, 1977) 8 tracks
"In the Middle," "Love Overnight," "It's Your Life," "Dolorosa," "I Got Lost Tonight," "The Devil Inside My Heart," "Little Bo's Peep Show," "To Cry for Love"

Morgan, Jaye P. / *Jaye P. Morgan* (Candor,1976) 4 tracks
"Keepin' it to Myself," "Here is Where Your Love Belongs," "It's Been So Long," "Let's Get Together"

Moyet, Alison / *Raindancing* (Epic, 1986) 4 tracks
"Weak in the Presence of Beauty," "You Got Me Wrong," "Without You," "Is this Love?"

Murph the Surf [film soundtrack] (Motown, 1975)
No track-specific credits; percussion only

N

N.S.P. / *2-nen-me No Tobira* (Canyon, 1976) 5 tracks
"Haru wo Mitsuketa," "Rizumu mo Yoroshiku," "Kimi wo Yuuwaku," "Soup in the Morning," "Oshitaoshitai"

Nakajima, Fumiaki / *Girl Like You* (Hoshizora, 1992) 2 tracks
Tracks 3 and 8 (titles in Japanese)

Nakamura, Masatoshi / *Across The Universe* (Columbia, 1988) 8 tracks
Tracks 2,4,5,6,7,8,9,10 (titles in Japanese)

Neville, Ivan / *If My Ancestors Could See Me Now* (Polygram, 1988) 9 tracks
"Sun," "Primitive Man" (percussion), "Not Just Another Girl," "Falling Out of Love," "Out in the Streets," "Never Should Have Told Me," "Up to You," "Another Day's Gone By," "After All That Time"

Newman, Randy / *Trouble in Paradise* (Warner, 1983) 10 tracks
"I Love L.A.," "Christmas in Cape Town," "The Blues," "Mikey's," "My Life is Good," "Miami," "Take Me Back," "There's a Party at My House," "I'm Different," "Song for the Dead"

Newman, Randy / *Land of Dreams* (Reprise, 1988) 4 tracks
For these 4 tracks both Jeff and John Robinson are listed: "Four Eyes," "Something Special," "Red Bandana," "I Want You to Hurt Like I Do"

NewSong / *Living Proof* (DaySpring/Word, 1991)
No track-specific credits; only drummer listed, but others on drum programming. Jeff also credited for "miscellaneous percussion and extraneous noise"

Newton, Juice / *Juice Newton & Silver Spur* (RCA, 1975) 1 track
"Catwillow River"

Newton, Juice / *Well Kept Secret* (Capitol, 1978) 2 tracks
Tracks unidentified

Newton-John, Olivia / *Making a Good Thing Better* (EMI, 1977) 10 tracks
"Making a Good Thing Better," "Slow Dancing," "Ring of Fire," "Coolin' Down," "Sad Songs," "You Won't See Me Cry," "So Easy to Begin," "I Think I'll Say Goodbye," "Don't Ask a Friend," "If Love is Real"

Nougaro / *Pacifique* (1989) 2 tracks

"Pacifique," "Kine"

Nunn, Terri — see *Sing* [film soundtrack]

O

Oda, Kazumasa / *K. Oda* (Fun House, 1986) 8 tracks
Note: May be same as album titled *Oh Yeah!*; titles translated from Japanese "Let Me Listen to the Love," "Two of Us in Winter," "Stay the Sadness," "1985," "Nights Fade Away," "Believe Me," "See You in the Sea Tomorrow," "This Sky is Too High"

O'Day, Alan / *Appetizers* (Pacific, 1977) 10 tracks
"Soldier of Fortune," "Satisfied," "Started Out Dancing, Ended Up Making Love," "Gifts," "Slot Machine," "Undercover Angel," "Do Me Wrong But Do Me," "Catch My Breath," "Angie Baby," "Caress Me Pretty Music"

O'Day, Alan / *Oh Johnny* (Pacific, 1979)
No track-specific credits; 1 of 2 drummers (also Mike Baird)

Off Course / *As Close As Possible* (Fun House, 1987) 1 track
"Love Everlasting"

Off Limits [film soundtrack] (Varese, 1988)
No track-specific credits; 1 of 4 on percussion (also Joe Porcaro, Emil Richards, Michael Fisher)

O'Kane, John / *Solid* (Charisma, 1991) 4 tracks
"Second Time Around," "Move Away," "Solid Ground," "Love Cars"

Okumoto, Ryo / *Makin' Rock* (SeeSaw, 1980) 7 tracks
"Keep on Rockin'," "Crystal Highway," "Solid Gold," "L.A. Express," "Freedom," "Original View," "Mystery White"

Omura, Kenji / *Kenji Shock* (Alfa, 1978) 6 tracks
"Left-Handed Woman," "Better Make it Through Today," "Yumedono," "Shock," "Boston Flight," "The Mase"

Orbison, Roy / *King of Hearts* (Virgin, 1992) 1 track
"We'll Take the Night"

Originals / *Communique* (Soul, 1976)
No track-specific credits; 1 of 2 drummers (also Alvin Taylor)

Originals / *Down To Love Town* (Soul, 1977) 1 track
"Down to Love Town" (with Alvin Taylor)

Or-N-More / *Or-N-More* (EMI, 1991) 4 tracks
"Only 2 Hearts," "Half a Heart," "Sail On," "I Need Someone to Talk To"

Ozaki, Ami / *Hot Baby* (Canyon, 1981) 8 tracks
"Love is Easy," "Karada ni Nokoru Wine," "Cats Eye," "Kagirinai Nikushimi no Hate Ni," "Angela," "Prism," "Wanderer in Love," "Serenade"

P

Pacific Winds / *Pacific Coast Highway* (Interface[Japan], 1989)
No track-specific credits; 1 of 2 drummers (also Mike Baird)

Pack, David / *Anywhere You Go* (Warner, 1985) 1 track
"Prove Me Wrong"

Pages / *Pages* (EMI, 1981) 3 tracks
"You Need a Hero," "Come on Home," "Automatic"

Palmer, Robert / *Some People Can Do What They Want* (Island, 1976)
No track-specific credits; 1 of 3 drummers (also Richie Hayward, Spider Webb)

Parker, Ray Jr. / *After Dark* (Geffen, 1987)
No track-specific credits; 1 of 3 drummers (also Carlos Vega, Ollie E. Brown)

Parr, John / *Running the Endless Mile* (Atlantic, 1986) 1 track
"Don't Leave Your Mark on Me"

Parton, Dolly / *Dolly, Dolly, Dolly* (RCA, 1980) 10 tracks (entire album)

Patti, Sandi / *Another Time...Another Place* (Word/Epic, 1990) 10 tracks
"Unto Us (Isaiah 9)," "Another Time, Another Place," "I Will Rejoice," "Unexpected Friends," "I'll Give You Peace," "For All the World," "Rejoice," "Willing to Wait," "I Lift my Hands," "O Calvary's Lamb"

Patti, Sandi / *Find It On The Wings* (1994) 1 track
"Imagine (How God can Sing)" (percussion)

Patton, Robbie / *Do You Wanna Tonight* (1979)
No track-specific credits; 1 of 2 drummers (also Ed Greene)

Peck, Danny / *Heart and Soul* (Arista, 1977) 4 tracks
"Halo of Fire," "Looking so Hard," "Brother of Mine," "Where is my Heart"

Perry, Phil / *The Heart of the Man* (Manhattan, 1991) 1 track
"Good-Bye"

Phillips, Shawn / *Transcendence* (RCA, 1978) 1 track
"Lady in Velvet"

Pink Floyd / *The Wall* (Columbia, 1979) 1 track
"Mother"

Poco / *Legacy* (RCA, 1989)
No track-specific credits; 1 of 3 drummers (also George Grantham [Poco] and Gary Mallaber)

Pointer Sisters / *Energy* (Planet, 1978) 7 tracks
"Lay It on the Line," "Hypnotized," "As I Come of Age," "Come and Get Your Love," "Happiness," "Echoes of Love," "Everybody is a Star"

Pointer, June / *June Pointer* (Columbia, 1989) 3 tracks
"Why Can't We be Together," "Put Your Dreams Where Your Heart Is," "Love Calling"

Preston, Billy / *The Way I Am* (Motown, 1981)
No track-specific credits; 1 of 4 drummers (also Rick Shlosser, James Gadson, Ollie E. Brown)

R

Radioactive / *Ceremony of Innocence* (Marquee/Avalon [Japan], 2001) 8 tracks

"Story of Love," "Crimes of Passion," "Waiting for a Miracle," "Ceremony of Innocence," "Liquid," "A Case of Right or Wrong," "Silent Cries," "When You're in Love," "Remember My Conscience" (bonus track on Japanese release, hidden track on European release)

Radioactive / *Taken* (MTM-Music, 2005) 1 track
"Stronger than Yesterday"

Raitt, Bonnie / *Home Plate* (Warner, 1975)
No track-specific credits; 1 of 2 on percussion (also Joe Porcaro)

Raitt, Bonnie / *Luck of the Draw* (Capitol, 1991) 1 track
"Luck of the Draw"

Randall, Elliott / *Randall's New York* (Kirshner, 1977) 4 tracks
"Just a Thought" (with Allan Schwartzberg)," "It's Gonna be Great," "I Give Up," "When You got the Music (Part 3)"

Reddy, Helen / *Music, Music* (Capitol, 1976) 2 tracks
"Music, Music," "Music is my Life"

Reddy, Helen / *Ear Candy* (Capitol, 1977)
No track-specific credits; 1 of several drummers

Remler, Emily / *This is Me* (Justice, 1990) 2 tracks
"Deep in a Trance," "Love Colors"

Rene & Angela / *Rise* (Capitol, 1983)
No track-specific credits; 1 of 4 drummers (also Andre Fischer, John Robinson, Ollie Brown)

Richie, Lionel / *Can't Slow Down* (Motown, 1983) 1 track
"Running with the Night"

Richie, Lionel / *Louder than Words* (Motown, 1996) 1 track
"Climbing"

Ritenour, Lee / *Captain Fingers* (Epic, 1977) 2 tracks
"Isn't She Lovely," "Space Glide"

Ritenour, Lee / *Rit* (Elektra, 1981) 2 tracks
"Mr. Briefcase," "Good Question"

Ritenour, Lee / *Rit 2* (Elektra, 1982) 1 track
"Voices"

Rivera, Danny / *Danny* (1983)
1 of 2 drummers (also Mike Baird)

Roberts, Bruce / *Bruce Roberts* (Elektra, 1977)
No track-specific credits; 1 of 2 drummers (also Grady Tate)

Roberts, David / *All Dressed Up* (Elektra, 1982) 10 tracks (entire album)

Rogers, D.J. / *Love, Music and Life* (RCA, 1977) 10 tracks (entire album)

Rogers, D.J. / *On the Road Again* (RCA, 1976)
No track-specific credits; 1 of 4 drummers (also Harvey Mason, Paul Mabrey, Rick Calhoun)

Ross, Diana / *Baby It's Me* (Motown, 1977) 5 tracks
"Gettin' Ready for Love," "You Got It," "Baby it's Me," "Your Love is So Good for Me," "Top of the World"

Ross, Diana / *Ross* (RCA, 1983) 5 tracks
"That's How You Start Over," "Love will Make it Right," "You Do It," "Pieces of Ice," "Let's Go Up" (Drums and drum synthesizer)

Russell, Brenda / *Love Life* (A&M, 1981) 8 tracks
"Love Life," "Rainbow," "Something I Like to Do," "Lucky," "Sensitive Man," "Deep Dark and Mysterious," "If You Love," "Thank You"

Russell, Brenda / *Two Eyes* (Warner, 1983) 1 track
"Hello People" (tambourine)

Russell, Brenda / *Kiss Me with the Wind* (A&M, 1990) 2 tracks
"Justice in Truth," "On Your Side"

S

Sager, Carol Bayer / *Too* (Elektra, 1978) 1 track
"I Don't Wanna Dance No More"

Sager, Carol Bayer / *Sometimes Late at Night* (Epic, 1981) 6 tracks
"I Won't Break," "Tell Her," "You and Me (We Wanted it All)," "Wild Again," "Easy to Love Again," "Stronger than Before"

Sanford & Townsend / *Duo-Glide* (Warner, 1977) 9 tracks
"Paradise," "Ain't it So, Love," "Livin's Easy," "Starbrite," "Voodoo," "Mississippi Sunshine," "Eights and Aces," "Sometimes When the Wind Blows," "Eye of my Storm (Oh Woman)" 1 of 2 drummers (also Mike Baird)

Satisfaction [film soundtrack] (AJK, 1988) 1 track
"(I Can't Get No) Satisfaction" [version 2] (Justine Bateman & the Mystery)

Saunders, Fernando / *Cashmere Dreams* (Grudge, 1989) 2 tracks
"Love is Blind," "Let's Talk About It"

Sayer, Leo / *Endless Flight* (Chrysalis, 1976) 3 tracks
"When I Need You," "No Business like Love Business," "Magdalena"

Sayer, Leo / *Thunder in my Heart* (Warner, 1977) 6 tracks
"Thunder in my Heart," "Easy to Love," "I Want You Back," "World Keeps on Turning," "There isn't Anything," "Everything I've Got" (Drums and drum synthesizer)

Sayer, Leo / *Leo Sayer* (Warner, 1978) 6 tracks
"Stormy Weather," "Dancing the Night Away," "La Booga Rooga," "Running to my Freedom," "Frankie Lee," "Don't Look Away"

Sayer, Leo / *World Radio* (Warner, 1982) 10 tracks (entire album)

Scaggs, Boz / *Silk Degrees* (CBS, 1976) 10 tracks (entire album)

Scaggs, Boz / *Down Two Then Left* (CBS, 1977) 10 tracks (entire album)
Drums and drum synthesizer

Scaggs, Boz / *Middle Man* (CBS, 1980) 6 tracks
"Jojo," "Simone," "You Can Have Me Anytime," "Middle Man," "Angel You," "You Got

Some Imagination"

Scaggs, Boz / *Hits!* (Columbia/Legacy, 1980) 7 tracks
"Lowdown," "Miss Sun" (not previously released on an album), "Lido Shuffle," "We're All Alone," "Look What You've Done to Me" (not previously released on an album), "Jojo," "You Can Have Me Anytime"

Scaggs, Boz / *Other Roads* (CBS, 1988) 6 tracks
"What's Number One," "Right out of my Head," "I Don't Hear You," "Mental Shakedown," "Crimes of Passion," "Cool Running," "The Night of Van Gogh"

Scaggs, Boz — see also *Two of a Kind* [film soundtrack]

Schaffer, Janne / *Earmeal* (CBS, 1978) 9 tracks (entire album)

Schascle / *Haunted by Real Life* (Reprise, 1991) 4 tracks
"Restless Sun," "Haunted by Real Life," "Freedom," "Hold Me"

Schmit, Timothy B. / *Playin' It Cool* (Asylum 1984) 3 tracks
"Wrong Number," "Take a Good Look Around You," "Tell Me What You Dream"

Schmit, Timothy B. / *Tell Me the Truth* (MCA, 1990) 1 track
"Something Sad"

Scialfa, Patti / *Rumble Doll* (Columbia, 1993) 2 tracks
"Come Tomorrow," "Talk to Me like the Rain"

Scott, Marilyn: "God Only Knows"/"Lay Back Daddy" (single) (Big Tree, 1977) 2 tracks

Scott, Tom / *Street Beat* (Columbia, 1979) 6 tracks
"Street Beat," "Greed," "Come Closer, Baby," "Heading Home," "Give Me Your Love," "The Shakedown"

Seals & Crofts / *Diamond Girl* (Warner, 1973) 10 tracks
No track-specific credits; 1 of 4 drummers (also Jim Gordon, John Guerin, Harvey Mason, Sr.)

Seals & Crofts / *Unborn Child* (Warner, 1974) 12 tracks (entire album)

Seals & Crofts / *I'll Play for You* (Warner, 1975) 1 track
"Golden Rainbow"

Seals & Crofts / *Get Closer* (Warner, 1976)
No track-specific credits; 1 of 2 drummers (also Ed Greene)

Sebastian, John / *Welcome Back* (Reprise, 1976) 10 tracks (entire album)

Sgt. Pepper's Lonely Hearts Club Band [film soundtrack] (RSO, 1979)
No track-specific credits; 1 of 3 drummers (also Bernard Purdie, David Dowell)

Sharp, Randy / *First in Line* (Nautilus, 1976) 9 tracks (entire album)

Shepard, Vonda / *Vonda Shepard* (Reprise, 1989) 2 tracks
"Hold Out," "Baby Don't You Break my Heart Slow"

Shepard, Vonda / *The Radical Light* (Reprise, 1992) 3 tracks
"Searchin' My Soul," "100 Tears Away," "Wake Up the House"

Shiratori, Emiko / *Hello* (King, 1991) 2 tracks
"Close Your Eyes," "Hello"

Shot in the Dark / *Shot in the Dark* (RSO, 1981)
No track-specific credits; 1 of 3 drummers (also Harry Stinson, Russ Kunkel)

Silveira, Ricardo / *Small World* (Verve, 1992) 2 tracks
"Small World," "Haven't We Met"

Simon, Carly — see *The Spy Who Loved Me* [film soundtrack]

Simon, Paul / *Hearts and Bones* (Warner, 1983) 1 track
"Train in the Distance"

Simon, Paul / *Negotiations and Love Songs 1971-1986* (Warner, 1988) 1 track
"Train in the Distance" (from *Hearts and Bones*, 1983)

Sinclair, Stephen / *A+* (U.A., 1977)
No track-specific credits; 1 of 2 drummers (also Ed Greene)

Sing [film soundtrack] (Columbia, 1989) 1 track
"Romance (Love Theme)" (Paul Carrack and Terri Nunn)

Sing Like Talking / *Reunion* (Fun House, 1992) 1 track
"Stay Gold (Live)"

Snow, Tom / *Taking it All in Stride* (Capitol, 1975) 1 track
"Everybody Lives Everybody Dies"

Snow, Tom / *Tom Snow (*Capitol, 1976) 6 tracks
"Hurry Boy," "Doin' it All Again," "Rosanna," "Rock & Roll Widow," "Shoestring Destiny," "I'm Only Passin' Through"

Snow, Tom / *Hungry Nights* (Arista, 1982) 2 tracks
"Straight for the Heart," "Don't Call it Love"

Sonny & Cher / *Mama was a Rock 'n' Roll Singer* (MCA, 1973) 10 tracks (entire album)

Sonny & Cher / *Live In Las Vegas, Vol. 2* (MCA, 1974) 12 tracks (entire album)

Sorrenti, Alan / *Angeli di Strada* (1982) 1 track
"Angeli de Strada (Maybe I Love You)"

Spence, Judson / *Judson Spence* (Atlantic, 1988) 3 tracks
"Attitude," "Dance with Me," "Take Your Time" (bonus track on CD)

Springsteen, Bruce / *Human Touch* (Columbia, 1992) 12 tracks
All tracks except "With Every Wish" (Kurt Wortman) and "Pony Boy" (no drums)

Springsteen, Bruce / *Tracks* (4 CD set) (Columbia, 1998) 5 tracks
"Leavin' Train," "Sad Eyes," "My Lover Man," "When the Lights Go Out," "Trouble in Paradise"

Springsteen, Bruce / *18 Tracks* (Columbia, 1999) 2 tracks
"Sad Eyes," "Trouble River"

Spy Who Loved Me, The [film soundtrack] (EMI, 1977) 1 track

"Nobody Does it Better" (Carly Simon)

Steely Dan / *Pretzel Logic* (MCA, 1974) 2 tracks
"Night by Night," "Parker's Band"

Steely Dan / *Katy Lied* (MCA, 1975) 9 tracks
"Black Friday," "Bad Sneakers," "Rose Darling," "Daddy Don't Live in that New York City No More," "Doctor Wu," "Everyone's Gone to the Movies," "Your Gold Teeth II," "Chain Lightning," "Throw Back the Little Ones"

Steely Dan / *Gaucho (*MCA, 1980) 1 track
"Gaucho"

Steely Dan / *Gold* (Expanded version) (MCA, 1991) 3 tracks
"Chain Lightning," "FM," "Bodhisattva (Live)" (with Jim Hodder)

Steinberg, Dianne / *Universal Child* (ABC, 1977) 1 track
"Amazing"

Stewart, Al / *Time Passages* (Arista, 1978) 1 track
"Valentina Way"

Stewart, Al / *24 Carrots* (Arista, 1980)
No track-specific credits; 1 of 5 drummers (also Russell Kunkel, Mark Sanders, Steve Chapman, Beau Segal)

Stewart, Rod / *Vagabond Heart* (Warner, 1991) 1 track
"The Motown Song"

Stigers, Curtis / *Curtis Stigers* (Arista, 1991) 4 tracks
"Sleeping with the Lights On," "The Man You're Gonna Fall in Love With," "I Keep Telling Myself," "The Last Time I Said Goodbye"

The Strand / *The Strand* (Island, 1980) 2 tracks
"Can't Look Back" (drums), "Just a Little More Time" (percussion), also produced all 10 tracks

Streisand, Barbra / *Streisand Superman (*CBS, 1977)
No track-specific credits; 1 of 3 drummers (also Harvey Mason, Ed Greene)

Streisand, Barbra / *Songbird* (CBS, 1978) 4 tracks
"Love Breakdown," "Honey Can I Put on Your Clothes," "Songbird," "One More Night"

Streisand, Barbra / *Wet* (CBS, 1979) 2 tracks
"Come Rain or Come Shine," "Kiss Me in the Rain"

Streisand, Barbra / *Til I Loved You* (Columbia, 1988) 1 track
"Some Good Things Never Last"

Summer, Donna / *Donna Summer* (Casablanca, 1982) 1 track
"Protection"

Suzuki, Yoshiyuki / *L.A. Lullaby* (Teichiku, 1981) 9 tracks (entire album)

Syreeta / *The Spell* (Tamla, 1983) 3 tracks
"Freddie Um Ready," "Once Love Touches Your Life," "Fall Apart"

T

Taff, Russ / *Walls of Glass* (Myrrh, 1983) 4 tracks
"Walls of Glass," "Jeremiah," "Inside Look," "Just Believe"

Taff, Russ / *Russ Taff* (Word, 1987) 1 track
"I Still Believe" (hi-hat only)

Tagg, Eric / *Smilin' Memories* (EMI, 1975) 10 tracks
"Tell-Tale Eyes," "Love to Love You," "Castle of Loneliness," "Steamboat," "Sandman (Bring me a Dream)," "The Only Thing You Said," "A Fantasy," "After All," "Never had the Feelin'," "Hang On"

Takanaka, Masayoshi / *Brasilian Skies* (Kitty, 1978)
No track-specific credits; 1 of 4 drummers (also James Gadson, Shi-Shan Inoe, Wilson Das Neves)

Takeuchi, Mariya / *Miss M* (RCA, 1980) 5 tracks
"Sweetest Music," "Every Night," "Morning Glory," "Secret Love," "Heart to Heart"

Tanner, Marc — see Marc Tanner Band

Taupin, Bernie / *He Who Rides the Tiger* (Asylum, 1980)
No track-specific credits; 1 of 2 drummers (also Carlos Vega)

Taylor, James "J.T." / *Master of the Game* (MCA, 1989) 1 track
"Master of the Game" (Note: only track featuring a live drummer)

Taylor, Livingston / *Man's Best Friend* (Epic, 1980) 1 track
"Sunshine Girl"

Temptations / *Surface Thrills* (Motown, 1983) 2 tracks
"One Man Woman," "Made in America"

Temptations / *Milestone* (1991) 1 track
"Get Ready" (tambourine, drums (overdub))

Thomas, Mickey / *As Long as You Love Me* (RCA, 1976) 5 tracks
"The Street Only Knew Your Name," "Take Me to Your Lover," "Can You Fool," "Somebody to Love," "Dance it Off"

Three Dog Night / *American Pastime* (ABC, 1976)
1 of 3 drummers (also Micky McMeel, Ed Greene)

Thudpucker, Jimmy / *Doonesbury's Jimmy Thudpucker and the Walden West Rhythm Section Greatest Hits* (Windsong, 1977)
No track-specific credits; 1 of 2 drummers (also Mike Baird)

Thudpucker, Jimmy / *Jimmy Thudpucker's Greatest Hits* (Windsong, 1977)
No track-specific credits; 1 of 2 drummers (also Mike Baird)

Torrance, Richard / *Bareback* (Capitol, 1977) 5 tracks
"Moonlight Trippin'," "Stay Young," "Lovin' Good," "Tender Memory," "Circle of Confusion"

Toto / *Toto* (Columbia, 1978) 10 tracks

Toto / *Hydra* (Columbia, 1979) 8 tracks

Toto / *Turn Back* (Columbia, 1980) 8 tracks

Toto / *Toto IV* (Columbia, 1982) 10 tracks

Toto / *Isolation* (Columbia, 1984) 10 tracks

Toto / *Fahrenheit* (Columbia, 1986) 10 tracks
(Steve Jordan plays drums on "Lea," Jeff is on percussion)

Toto / *The Seventh One* (Columbia, 1988) 11 tracks

Toto / *Past to Present, 1977-1990* 13 tracks
Includes four previously unreleased tracks: "Love has the Power," "Out of Love," "Can You Hear What I'm Saying," "Animal"

Toto / *Kingdom of Desire* (Relativity, 1992) 12 tracks

Toto / *XX* (1977-1997) (Columbia, 1998) 10 tracks
"Goin' Home," "Tale of a Man," "Last Night," "In a Word," "Modern Eyes," "Right Part of Me," "Mrs. Johnson," "Miss Sun," "Love is a Man's World," "On the Run (Live)"

Toto — see also *Dune* [film soundtrack]

Toussaint, Allen / *Motion* (Warner, 1978) 10 tracks (entire album)

Triplets / *Thicker than Water* (Mercury, 1990) 6 tracks
"Dancing in the Shadows," "Light a Candle," "So Hard," "Spanish Surrender," "Where Were You When I Needed You," "Reminds Me of You"

Triumvirat / *Russian Roulette* (Harvest, 1980) 11 tracks (entire album)

Turrentine, Stanley / *Betcha* (Elektra, 1979) 4 tracks
"Betcha," "Take Me Home," "Hamlet," "Long Time Gone"

Tutone, Tommy / *National Emotion* (Columbia, 1983) 1 track
"National Emotion"

Twenty Mondays / *The Twist Inside* (Spindletop, 1986) 4 tracks
"God's Song," "Cracks in the Wall," "The Twist Inside," "Little Girl"

Two of a Kind [film soundtrack] (MCA, 1983) 1 track
"The Perfect One" (Boz Scaggs)

V

Various Artists / *12th Annual Battle of The Bands Hollywood Bowl 1971* (Custom Fidelity, 1971)
Jeff was invited to play with the production band after his group performed in this event. Unknown if he appears on any tracks included in this 2-record set.

Various Artists / *In Harmony 2* (Columbia, 1981) 1 track
"Some Kitties Don't Care" (Kenny Loggins)

Various Artists / "Hands Across America" [single] (EMI, 1986) 1 track

Various Artists / *Last Temptation of Elvis* (Mayking, 1990) 1 track
"Viva Las Vegas" (Bruce Springsteen cover done for this charity album)

Vaughan, Sarah / *Songs of the Beatles* (Atlantic, 1981; re-issued on CD) 12 tracks
"Get Back," "And I Love Her," "Eleanor Rigby," "Fool on the Hill," "You Never Give Me

Your Money," "Come Together," "I Want You (She's so Heavy)," "Blackbird," "Something," "Here There and Everywhere," "The Long and Winding Road," "Hey Jude"

Voudouris, Roger / *On the Heels of Love* (Boardwalk, 1981) 8 tracks (entire album)

W

Walsh, Brock / *Dateline: Tokyo* (Warner, 1983)
No track-specific credits; 1 of 3 drummers (also Beau Segal, Mike Botts)

Walsh, Joe / *The Confessor* (Warner, 1985)
No track-specific credits; 1 of 5 drummers (also Denny Carmassi, Jim Keltner, Chet McCracken, Rick Marotta)

Wandelmer, Emile / *Lover Cafe* (WEA, 1990) 6 tracks
"Lovers Cafe," "Nora," "Charlie," "Vends Pas Ton Blues," "Dame," "Seul"

Ware, Leon / *Leon Ware* (Elektra, 1982) 6 tracks
"Slippin' Away," "Lost in Love with You," "Shelter," "Can I Touch You There," "Miracles," "Where are They Now"

Warwick, Dionne / *Friends In Love* (Arista, 1982) 1 track
"What is This"

Warwick, Dionne / *Friends* (Arista, 1985) 2 tracks
"Whisper in the Dark," "Remember Your Heart"

Watanabe, Misato / *Flower Bed* (Sony, 1989) 1 track
"Pineapple Romance"

Watanabe, Misato / *Hello Lovers* (Sony, 1992) 2 tracks
"Lovin' You," Japanese title

Watanabe, Sadao / *Front Seat* (Warner, 1989) 4 tracks
"Only in My Mind," "Miles Apart," "Any Other Fool," "Takin' Time"

The Waters / *Waters* (Warner, 1977) 7 tracks
"I Just Wanna Be the One (In Your Life)," "What am I Doing Wrong," "If There's a Way," "Could it be the Magic," "Party, Party," "We Can Change It," "Peace at Last"

Waters, Roger / *Amused To Death* (Columbia, 1992) 1 track
"It's a Miracle"

Waybill, Fee / *Read My Lips* (Capitol, 1984) 1 track
"Caribbean Sunsets"

Weaver, Patty / *Patty Weaver* (Warner, 1982)
No track-specific credits; 1 of 2 drummers (also Mike Baird)

Webb, Jimmy / *Angel Heart* (Columbia, 1982) 10 tracks (entire album)

Webb, Susan / *Bye Bye Pretty Baby* (Anchor, 1975)
No track-specific credits; also Jim Keltner, and others?

Weisberg, Tim / *Outrageous Temptations* (Cypress, 1989) 3 tracks
"Outrageous Temptations," "Promise Me," "Margarita"

White Horse / *White Horse* (Capitol, 1977) 5 tracks

"It Doesn't Take Much," "Lost and in Trouble," "Can't Stop Loving You (Though I Try)," "Everloving Arms," "Take Me Back"

Williams, David / *Take the Ball and Run* (O.F., 1983) 3 tracks
"When Your Dreams Come True," "I Don't Want to Say Goodbye," "She's That Lady"

Williams, David / *Somethin' Special* (1991) 1 track
"Tell the World"

Williams, Deniece / *When Love Comes Calling* (CBS, 1979) 5 tracks
"When Love Comes Calling," "Why Can't We Fall in Love?," "God Knows," "I Found Love," "Turn Around"

Williams, Jerry [Lynn] / *Gone* (Warner, 1979) 5 tracks
"Gone," "Easy on Yourself," "Talk to Me," "Song for my Father," "Getting Stronger"

Williams, Joseph / *I Am Alive* (Kitty (J), 1996) 1 track
"I am Alive"

Williams, Paul / *Classics* (1977) 2 tracks
"Evergreen (Love Theme from A Star is Born)," "With One More Look at You"

Wood, Lauren / *Lauren Wood* (Warner, 1979)
No track-specific credits; 1 of 5 drummers (also Alvin Taylor, Jim Keltner, Mike Baird, Rick Shlosser)

Woods, Ren / *Out of the Woods* (1979)
No track-specific credits; 1 of 3 drummers (also Ed Greene, James Gadson)

Wright, Gary / *Headin' Home* (Warner, 1979) 1 track
"Moonbeams"

Y

Yamamoto, Tatsuhiko / *Next* (Alfa, 1990) 6 tracks
"Swinging in the Rain," "Phoenix Islands," "Rain and Pain," "Heroine with No Name," 2 Japanese titles

Yazawa, Eikichi / *P.M. 9* (Warner, 1982)
No track-specific credits; 1 of 3 drummers (also Gary Ferguson, Rick Shlosser)

Yazawa, Eikichi / *I am a Model* (Warner, 1983) 9 tracks (entire album)

Young, Paul / *The Crossing* (Columbia, 1993) 6 tracks
"Hope in a Hopeless World," "Won't Look Back," "Only Game in Town," "Love Has No Pride," "Half a Step Away," "Follow On"

Z

Zevon, Warren / *Excitable Boy* (Asylum, 1978) 1 track
"Night Time in the Switching Yard"

Zevon, Warren / *The Envoy* (Asylum, 1982) 5 tracks
"The Envoy," "The Overdraft," "The Hula Hula Boys" (+ Tahitian log drums, pule sticks), "Let Nothing Come Between You," "Looking for the Next Best Thing"

Zevon, Warren / *Mr. Bad Example* (Giant, 1991) 8 tracks
All tracks except "Things to Do in Denver When You're Dead" and "Mr. Bad Example" (Jim Keltner)

INTERVIEW WITH PAUL "JAMO" JAMIESON: GEAR AND MORE

What were the main snare drums Jeff used?
His two main snare drums were customized by me. One was a 1950 Gretsch 6-1/2 x 14 and the other was a Slingerland Radio King from the 1930s. The blonde Gretsch was his go-to drum. He had three or four others for different sounds (just in case). He was hired for his sound as well as his playing.

What kind of cymbals did Jeff use?
He had Paiste 14" 602 hi-hats and a 20" Paiste 602 ride. He'd use two to four crashes, depending on his mood, which were Paiste and Zildjian. He usually used the same cymbals most of the time.

Do you remember what he used for any of the Toto sessions?
For "Hold the Line" he used my 1970 Ludwig blonde drum set: 26" bass drum, 13" and 14" toms and 16" and 18" floor toms. For "Rosanna" and "Africa," Jeff used his black Yamaha prototype (no serial numbers). It was a 22" bass drum with 10", 12" and 13" rack toms and a 16" floor tom. I own these drums today, as he traded them with me in 1984.

(*Note: As explained in the text, "Africa" was a drum loop Jeff played over.*)

Do you remember what Jeff used for Michael Jackson's "Beat It"?
For "Beat It," Jeff used a Ludwig 16" x 22" bass drum; 10", 12" and 13" rack toms and a 16" floor tom from a custom sunburst Gretsch kit that I did for him during the Boz Scaggs days in 1977/78. He used Gretsch in the studio after using my drums in 1978 (for Toto's first album). On tour he used whoever he was endorsed by: Ludwig and then Pearl.

What about his drumheads?
Jeff liked Remo Coated Ambassadors in the studio. He once told me, "If I could I'd buy them like this..." It was a head that was used and broken-in but not pitted. On the road he used Remo Clear Ambassadors and a Remo coated head on the snare drum. In the studio, I changed them when needed. On the road, I changed the snare and rack toms daily and the kick and floor tom every other day.

Did Jeff's tuning vary from the studio to the road?
Live tuning was more wide open. He liked the drums with more ring to them.

Did Jeff use a click for live playing?
We had a small Yamaha RX drum machine. It had a cowbell sound he used to set to the tempo. Sometimes (not very often) he would ask me to start it. He'd listen for five seconds and have me turn it off. He never used it during the song.

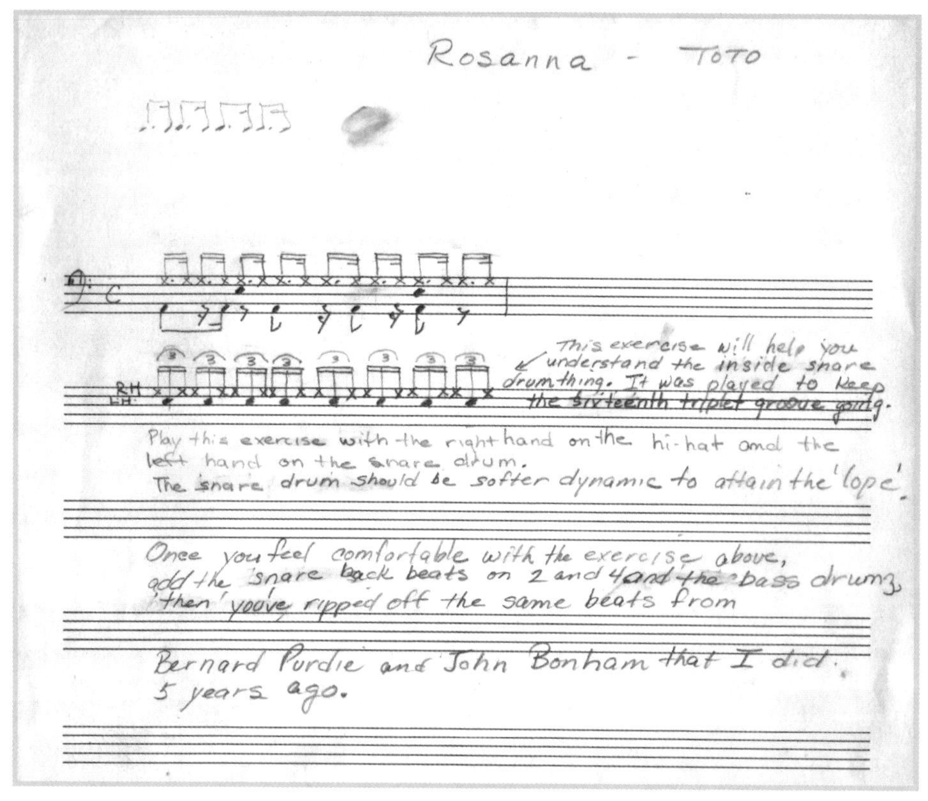

"Rosanna" handwritten chart by Jeff.

(Courtesy of Rick Van Horn)

INDEX